C000070110

Gentle rain on tender grass

Gentle rain

on

tender grass

Daily Readings from the Pentateuch

Sharon James

EVANGELICAL PRESS

EVANGELICAL PRESS
Faverdale North, Darlington, DL3 0PH, England

e-mail: sales@evangelicalpress.org

Evangelical Press USA
P. O. Box 825, Webster, New York 14580, USA

e-mail: usa.sales@evangelicalpress.org

web: http://www.evangelicalpress.org

First published 2006

British Library Cataloguing in Publication Data available

ISBN-13 978-0-85234-630-3   ISBN 0-85234-630-1

Printed and bound in Great Britain by Creative Print & Design Wales,
Ebbw Vale

Introduction

When Moses came to bid farewell to the people of Israel, he summarized God's message to them in a song, opening with the words:

May my teaching drop as the rain,
my speech distil as the dew,
like gentle rain upon the tender grass

(Deut. 32:2-3).

Grass needs regular rainfall, not just the occasional torrent. And so it is with us. Saying, 'I don't have time to study the Bible each day,' is saying, 'I don't want to listen to the voice of God.' When we hear the Word preached it can be like a torrent, drenching our spiritual lives. But 'gentle rain on tender grass' is steady, non-dramatic and refreshing. It is a lovely picture of continual, persevering study of the Word of God. There is no substitute for exposing ourselves daily to God's own infallible, authoritative Word.

These studies in the first five books of the Bible are designed for daily devotions. The most important thing is to read the Bible passage first, before reading the accompanying devotion. It is helpful then, if possible, to take time to look up the other texts referred to. A basic principle of interpretation is to 'let Scripture interpret Scripture'. The first five books of the Bible are foundational to understanding the story of salvation as taught in the rest of the Bible. They are only fully appreciated as the light of the gospel shines onto them; hence the many New Testament cross references.

The first five books form about one sixth of the length of the Bible. I have divided the material so that it can be covered in 123 days. The main themes are emphasized, and not every chapter is included. The most natural way to read the narrative portions is fairly quickly and in longer sections, whereas some passages, such as the Ten Commandments, demand verse-by-verse treatment. You may want to spend more than one day on some of the longer readings.

David testified: 'O LORD, in the morning you hear my voice; in the morning I prepare a sacrifice for you and watch' (Ps. 5:3). The best way to start the day is by reading God's Word, and then committing the day to him. It is even better if, after reading a section of God's Word, we can focus on one verse of Scripture sufficiently to take that truth into the day with us. In our hurried lives, meditation is something of a lost art. But at the end of each daily study there is a 'text for the day'. I have found it enormously helpful to take a verse with me into each day, and then bring my mind back to that verse during the day.

It is also helpful if our prayers arise naturally out of our reading of the Word. Each day I have suggested just one prayer, focused on the study. To focus private prayers there are various helps available, and I would especially commend *The Valley of Vision* (Banner of Truth), and *Operation World* (Paternoster/ WEC International). For some days I have provided a hymn or psalm as a 'springboard' for prayer and praise.

Unless otherwise indicated, I have used and quoted from the ESV.

May my teaching drop as the rain,
my speech distil as the dew,
like gentle rain upon the tender
grass,
and like showers upon the herb.
For I will proclaim the name of the
LORD;
ascribe greatness to our God!
(Deut. 32:2-3).

'In the beginning, God created the heavens and the earth'

The first sentence in the Bible is the foundation of our existence. God, the source of all life, created the whole universe. As we look at creation, we marvel at its immense variety, beauty, detail, power, order and mystery. It bears witness to an infinitely intelligent and glorious designer. Only those who are morally blind deny this: 'The fool says in his heart, "There is no God"' (Ps. 14:1).

> *But ask the beasts, and they will teach you;*
> *the birds of the heavens, and they will tell you;*
> *or the bushes of the earth, and they will teach you;*
> *and the fish of the sea will declare to you.*
> *Who among all these does not know*
> *that the hand of the LORD has done this?*
> *In his hand is the life of every living thing*
>
> (Job 12:7-10).

Genesis 1 speaks of *Elohim* the mighty God, and a God in whom there is a plurality of persons. The New Testament proclaims that Jesus Christ, God the Son, was the agent of creation. The writer to the Hebrews takes the following quotation about 'the LORD' (*Yahweh* or *Jehovah*) and applies it directly to Christ:

> *Of old you laid the foundation of the earth,*
> *and the heavens are the work of your hands.*
> *They will perish, but you remain;*
> *they will all wear out like a garment.*
> *You will change them like a robe, and they will pass away,*
> *but you are the same, and your years have no end*
>
> (Ps. 102:25-27).

> *But of the Son he says ...*
> *'You, Lord, laid the foundation of the earth in the beginning,*
> *and the heavens are the work of your hands;*
> *they will perish, but you remain;*

they will all wear out like a garment,
like a robe you will roll them up,
    like a garment they will be changed.
But you are the same,
    and your years will have no end'

(Heb. 1:8,10-12).

Paul speaks of Christ as the one through whom and for whom all things were made, and the one who sustains all things. He not only created the physical universe, but all spiritual powers and authorities:

He is the image of the invisible God, the firstborn of all creation. For by him all things were created, in heaven and on earth, visible and invisible, whether thrones or dominions or rulers or authorities — all things were created through him and for him. And he is before all things, and in him all things hold together (Col. 1:16-17).

In Genesis 1 we glimpse the mysterious activity of the Holy Spirit (1:2). The psalmist expands on this: 'When you send forth your Spirit they are created, and you renew the face of the ground' (Ps. 104:30).

The creation demands that we honour the triune God as our Creator, and give him praise (Rom. 1:19-21). Failing to worship our Creator is the sin of sins. The gospel summons us back from the dead end of worshipping created things (idols) to 'worship him who made heaven and earth, the sea and the springs of water' (Rev. 14:7).

Prayer: Triune God, forgive me for my failure to praise you as my Creator and my Lord. May the glory of your creation draw out my worship today.

Text for the day: *All things were created through him and for him* (Col. 1:16).

'In the image of God he created him'

It is part of being human to want assurance of meaning and significance. Why am I here? What is the point of my life? In a modern scientific age, we have been told that we are 'free' from being accountable to a creator. But that 'freedom' has resulted in the despair of meaninglessness.

This passage tells us that we are not an evolutionary accident. We have been created by God. Thus every single human life is to be respected. That is why wherever Christianity has spread there has been an improvement in the status of women. The places in the world today where there is most oppression of women are places where there has been least exposure to the gospel. Historically, the major advances in terms of concern for the poor and oppressed and underprivileged have been driven forward by Christians. William Wilberforce was convinced that slaves also were made in the image of God: therefore the slave trade had to be challenged. Elizabeth Fry believed that prisoners too were made in the image of God: therefore inhumane prison conditions had to be opposed.

Man and woman were both equally made in the image of God. This language would have been familiar in the ancient world. Rulers often placed images of themselves in prominent places to represent them. Sometimes they appointed a vicegerent to rule on their behalf. God is invisible. He placed man and woman as his representatives on earth to rule on his behalf and to represent him. If you asked, 'What is the invisible God like?' the answer should be: 'Look at man — that points to what God is like!' Unlike all the other creatures, humans were given souls that would never die, the capacity for reason, the capacity to communicate and the capacity to relate to their Creator. They were able to create life — to have children who would in their turn fulfil the creation mandate. The other creatures, by instinct, would provide food and shelter for themselves. But men and women were not just to labour for the benefit of self and family. Rather they were to work to serve the greater good of others. Supremely, God created man and woman in his image to be holy. We were 'created to be like God in true righteousness and holiness' (Eph. 4:24, NIV).

The first man and woman failed miserably. And so have all their offspring. The rest of the Bible points to the sending of Christ as the 'true image' of the Father, the last Adam, who would succeed where the first Adam failed. But Adam's failure does not negate the truth that humans are made in the image of God. We are still given the creation mandate to fill and subdue the earth. So you are here today for a reason. God created you. Everything you do today is to bring glory to him. This can give purpose to the most mundane chores. As I prepare a meal for my family tonight, I can do that for the glory of God. As I work to keep my home well-ordered and comfortable, I reflect something of the orderliness and love of beauty of my Creator God. If I am in paid employment I strive to reflect the character of God and work hard to bring order out of whatever chaos may exist in my workplace, playing my part in 'subduing the earth'.

This world is God's arena; he made it 'very good'. He gave us the task of managing it. We are to be aware of, and concerned for, environmental issues and issues of social justice and world poverty. God has supplied our world with abundant physical resources. Greed and mismanagement mean that the vast majority in our world lack the very basics of clean water and sufficient food. If we are truly convinced that every human being is made in the image of God, surely we will care about these things.

Prayer: Lord, forgive me if I have despised any human beings made in your image. Help me today to live and work as accountable to you, and for your glory.

Text for the day:
> So God created man in his own image,
>   in the image of God he created him;
>   male and female he created them

(Gen. 1:27).

Work and worship

In Genesis 2, God lays out the foundational principles of human life: firstly, work and rest; secondly, our relationship with our Creator. Tomorrow we look at the final section of the chapter, dealing with marriage and family life.

The days of creation establish the principle of time, and how to use it. God 'rested' after the six days of creation. This was not a rest of exhaustion, but one of satisfied enjoyment of what he had done. God then 'blessed' the seventh day and 'made it holy' (2:3). This was the institution of a 'Sabbath' rest: one day in seven. It was later enshrined in the Ten Commandments, or moral law (Exod. 20:8-11). The Fourth Commandment refers back to creation: 'For in six days the LORD made heaven and earth ... and rested the seventh day. Therefore the LORD blessed the Sabbath day and made it holy.'

This creation ordinance reflects the fact that we were not designed to work non-stop. 'Workaholics' end up in slavery to their work. They make it an idol. But a day of rest enables us to take time to acknowledge our Creator, who gave us the strength and opportunity to work at all. We worship him, not the work. When the principle of a day 'off work' in every week is abandoned, productivity actually falls. God knows best! Am I faithful to this principle? Do I set aside one day a week to worship the God who gave me strength to work? Or do I just carry on with my projects and all my various responsibilities and fail to stop to rest and worship?

In the New Testament age, believers moved away from the observation of the seventh-day Sabbath. In honour of the resurrection they met to worship on the first day of the week. This came to be known as 'the Lord's day' (Rev. 1:10; Acts 20:7; 1 Cor. 16:2). But the creation principle of one day in seven was maintained.

In an age of ever-increasing consumerism, it is increasingly uncommon for Christians to keep the whole of the Lord's Day special. There is pressure to fill our lives with more and more expensive 'leisure' activities. There is the demand to work longer hours to pay for a higher and higher standard of living. But to set one day aside for the Lord (for meeting with other believers, prayer, giving hospitality, visiting the sick or elderly, or in personal Bible study and prayer) is liberating. It is a wonderful way of 'de-cluttering' from materialism.

The command given to the man (Gen. 2:16-17) establishes the principle of submission to the law of God. In chapter 1, man and woman were given authority over the rest of creation (1:28), but it was delegated authority. They were to rule '*over*' creation as vicegerents, or deputy rulers, *under* God their Maker. Continued obedience to the one (easy) command would express acceptance of their position as created by God. Rebellion against the authority of the Creator who gave them life would cut them off from the source of life (2:17). What is my attitude to the law of God? Do I, like the psalmist, 'delight' in it because it is an expression of God's glorious character? (Ps. 119:47). Am I submissive to the Word of God? Or do I feed rebellious thoughts?

Each of these fundamental areas of life was designed for our joy and delight. God placed the man in the garden to work it and keep it (Gen. 2:15). This was work in a paradise — a perfectly exquisite environment, with no frustration and no 'thorns'. The relationship between God and man was also to be one of delight and fulfilment, not clogged by sin or selfishness.

Prayer: Give thanks that all God's commands are intended for our good and happiness.

Text for the day: *I find my delight in your commandments, which I love* (Ps. 119:47).

Marriage

We are told today that 'Families come in all shapes and sizes' —
married or cohabiting, gay or straight. But these verses show that
God designed one man to be joined to one woman in exclusive
and faithful union. That is why they were originally one flesh, and
then reunited. Jesus Christ quoted these verses and explained:
'What therefore God has joined together, let not man separate'
(Matt. 19:5-6).

When Paul quotes this account, he explains the significance of
marriage: it was planned to illustrate a more profound reality.
From all eternity the triune God had a purpose for salvation for
sinful humanity. Central to this plan was the self-giving love of the
Lord Jesus Christ for his 'bride', the church. Marriage was to be a
signpost to point to this eternal reality. The husband's self-giving
protection of, and provision for, his wife was to mirror Christ's
love for his people. The wife's willing acceptance of the leadership of her husband was to reflect the church's submission to her
Lord and Saviour:

> *'Therefore a man shall leave his father and mother and
> hold fast to his wife, and the two shall become one flesh.' This
> mystery [marriage] is profound, and I am saying that it refers
> to Christ and the church* (Eph. 5:32).

The fall into sin brought about a tragic dislocation in the
marriage relationship (Gen. 3:16). Christ redeems us from the
curse. Believing husbands and wives are to seek God's help to
make their marriages fulfil the grand purpose: to reflect that
glorious relationship between Christ and the church. Husbands are
to forsake any tendency either to harsh domination or to passivity, and are to lead in a Christlike and self-sacrificial way. Wives
are to resist the temptation to dominate their husbands (or to be
passive 'doormats') and to support and affirm their husbands'
leadership role.

God created the woman to be a 'helper fit [or "suitable"] for
man'. This helper design is an exalted design. God has providentially

gifted women with many qualities complementary to those of men. Women tend to be better able to empathize with others, more intuitive, to have greater verbal ability. We have been given a 'maternal' instinct that can be fulfilled in many different callings and ministries even if we don't have biological children. Whether married or single, we can fulfil our helper design for the glory of God and the good of others.

All too often the phrase, 'It is not good that the man should be alone' (Gen. 2:18), is used to patronize singles. But it means, 'It is not good for a person to be solitary.' When God spoke these words, the man was literally solitary: alone with the angels above him and the animals below him. He needed human companionship.

Jesus was unmarried, but he was not solitary: 'My mother and my brothers are those who hear the word of God and do it' (Luke 8:21). Paul was single, but he was not solitary. He laboured alongside 'beloved' fellow workers of both sexes (Rom. 16:8,12) and dearly loved his spiritual 'mother' (Rom. 16:13). The church is to be family to those who are single, and Christ and Paul both commend those who forfeit marriage for the sake of the kingdom (e.g. by refusing to marry a non-Christian).

What is my attitude to marriage? God's design is for sexual desire to be fulfilled within marriage. Yet we live in a moral cesspit, where sexual desire is stirred up by advertising, clothes, magazines and television. Adultery and sex outside marriage are the norm. We are to be different. Whether married or single, we are to respect God's design. By God's grace we are to cultivate faithful, tender love to our own marriage partners. We are to respect and pray for the marriages of others. We are to seek *never* to be a stumbling block to the purity of others (Heb. 13:4).

Prayer: Pray that the marriages known to you (and your own if you are married) would reflect the beauty of the relationship between Christ and the church.

Text for the day: *This mystery [marriage] is profound ... it refers to Christ and the church* (Eph. 5:32).

'The dwelling place of God is with man'

Paradise! A world without sin, misery, violence, ugliness or pollution. A community of perfect harmony, total trust and uninhibited fellowship between God and his people. The first two chapters of the Bible describe paradise lost; the last two chapters predict paradise restored. The chapters in between describe the ugly reality of a once-perfect world wrecked by Satan and ruined by sin.

Today the marks of paradise lost are everywhere: terrorism, gross economic inequalities, domestic abuse, family break-up, emotional turmoil. Every individual and family is marked in some way by the effects of sin. This is not the way it was meant to be! The universe created by God was an exquisite setting for the crown of his creation — man and woman. The glories of nature were all 'good', but they were only the frame for the picture. Human beings were 'crowned ... with glory and honour' (Ps. 8:5) and placed as vicegerents of God, with stewardship on his behalf over the rest of creation (Ps. 8:6-8).

God created men and women to live in harmony. They were to cultivate and organize this new world, and produce offspring to begin to fill it. They had beautifully complementary roles, and they were to work in transparent and loving partnership. Most of all, they were to find joy in worshipping, obeying, loving and communicating with their Creator. Yes, they were given authority over the rest of creation. But it was authority given to them by the one who had authority over them. Paradise would only remain such while they freely submitted to and loved the God who had made it, and them.

That paradise was lost. The garden of uninhibited fellowship with God was closed. Access to the tree of life was prohibited by cherubim and a flaming sword.

At the end of the Bible we find the people of God in another paradise — not this time a garden, but a city. The once empty and unsubdued universe is now filled with the complete number of the elect of God. They have free access to the tree of life, and unbroken fellowship with each other and with God. The first paradise was lost through disobedience. The disobedient cannot enter this new city (Rev. 21:27). There will be no possibility of sin spoiling paradise restored.

The glories of the new heavens and earth, as described in Revelation 21 – 22, outshine even the glories of the first paradise. But at the heart of all the beauty is the one who is the source of all beauty, and there is the wonder of friendship with God himself:

> *Behold, the dwelling place of God is with man. He will dwell with them, and they will be his people, and God himself will be with them as their God. He will wipe away every tear from their eyes, and death shall be no more, neither shall there be mourning nor crying nor pain any more, for the former things have passed away* (Rev. 21:3-4).

The whole of the Bible between Genesis 1 – 2 and Revelation 21 – 22 points to Christ, and how he reopened the way into the paradise of eternal fellowship with our Creator. Until Christ returns, there is an open invitation: 'Let the one who is thirsty come; let the one who desires take the water of life without price' (Rev. 22:17). We are still in the day of opportunity, but this day will not go on for ever. Christ says, 'Behold, I am coming soon' (Rev. 22:12). Today we are one step closer to the return of Christ and the inauguration of paradise restored.

Prayer: O Lord, thank you for the glorious prospect of paradise restored!

Text for the day: *Surely I am coming soon* (Rev. 22:20).

The Fall

The man and his wife hid themselves from the presence of the LORD God (Gen. 3:8).

Today you may be enduring some ongoing frustration or grief, whether involving your family, employment, health or church. On the wider front, who can fail to be moved by the suffering all around us? Genesis 3 explains the source of all grief and pain. Satan set out in envy against his Creator to wreck God's glorious new creation. Clothing his hatred with disarming friendliness, he presented himself to Eve as her true friend. 'Did God actually say ...?' he asked, planting thoughts of mistrust and doubt (as he still does today). Submission to the Creator was, he implied, servitude. They would be far happier to be independent, to break free from acknowledging the authority of the Creator. The woman fell straight into the trap. Adam was with her and did nothing to stop her. She then persuaded him to eat with her.

Adam and Eve had enjoyed a relationship of perfect intimacy with God and with each other. They had been naked and un-ashamed. Now they hid. God called Adam to account first. Created to be the spiritual leader, he had failed. Instead of owning his responsibility he shifted the blame to his wife. The trust between man and wife was shattered. The woman tried blame-shifting as well, accusing the serpent of deception.

Each had wilfully rejected obedience to God, their Creator. The consequences unfolded inexorably. Satan was cursed. His victory would only be temporary. Eventually the 'seed of the woman' (Christ) would crush his head. Then judgement was pronounced on the woman. Her primary fulfilment was to have been found in marriage and childbearing. Now both would involve pain and frustration. Lastly the man was judged. His primary fulfilment was to have been found in cultivating the ground. This too would involve painful frustration. Man and woman were driven from the garden. Cherubim prevented access to the tree of life. This vividly symbolized the result of sin. Because Adam, as representative of all humanity, sinned, we are now separated from God. 'Sin came into the world through one man, and death through sin, and so death spread to all men because all sinned' (Rom. 5:12).

Before driving the couple from the garden, 'The LORD God made for Adam and for his wife garments of skins and clothed them' (Gen. 3:21). They had attempted to cover their own nakedness (3:7). Now God himself provided a covering. One of the meanings of 'atone for' in the Old Testament is 'to cover', and a recurring symbol of God's righteousness is 'clean clothes', as opposed to our 'filthy rags' of unrighteousness. God still had gracious purposes for man and woman and their children. (Note that the man and woman were not personally 'cursed' as Satan was: there is hope of salvation for them!)

In Eden — sad indeed that day —
my countless blessings fled away,
my crown fell in disgrace.
But on victorious Calvary
that crown was won again for me —
my life shall all be praise.

Faith, see the place, and see the tree
where heaven's Prince, instead of me,
was nailed to bear my shame.
Bruised was the dragon by the Son,
though two had wounds, there conquered one —
and Jesus was his name

(William Williams, trans. R. M. Jones).

Text for the day: *The LORD God said to the serpent, '... he shall bruise your head, and you shall bruise his heel'* (Gen. 3:14-15).

Cain and Abel

By faith Abel offered to God a more acceptable sacrifice than Cain (Heb. 11:4).

All of humanity can be divided between the 'seed of the woman' and the 'seed of the serpent'. In this chapter, we see representatives of both groups within a single family. Abel, who came to God in faith, was one of the 'seed of the woman' and the first of a whole multitude of martyrs (Matt. 23:35). Cain did not come with faith. He was one of the 'seed of the serpent', the first of those who blaspheme against God and oppose his true people.

When we come to worship God, whom do we aim to please? Ourselves (looking for what we can get out of it)? Others (worshipping because they would think badly of us if we did not)? Or God? Do we come wholeheartedly or half-heartedly? Do we bring our best energy, concentration, gifts and offerings? Or do we use our best time, strength and resources for ourselves and give God the leftovers?

We are to worship God in the way he prescribes (Exod. 20:4-6). Our giving must be carefully planned (1 Cor. 16:2) as well as generous and cheerful (2 Cor. 9:6-7). God sees our hearts. When the Pharisee went up to the temple to pray, only God knew the pride and self-sufficiency of his heart. And God knew the humility and dependence of the publican as well (Luke 18:9-14). In our worship, as in all of life, let us say that 'We make it our aim to please him' (2 Cor. 5:9).

> *You to please and you to know,*
> *these are my delight below;*
> *you to see and you to love,*
> *these are my delight above*

(Augustus Toplady).

Abel came to God in faith and humility, Cain in self-sufficiency and pride. May we never approach God with anything less than reverent awe!

Sin entered the world with one act of disobedience against God. Here we see sin expressed in Cain's lack of submission to God. God gave Cain the opportunity to repent, and warned him of the 'sin … crouching at the door' (Gen. 4:7). Cain gave in to sin and murdered his brother. His punishment was swift: banishment from the presence of God (4:14) and a curse from the very ground which had been the focus of his life (4:2).

The rest of the chapter points starkly to the divergence of the two seeds. From Cain came the ungodly line: his descendent Lamech (4:23-24) gloried in violence. But the righteous Abel was 'replaced' by Eve's son Seth, and from his descendants came those who '[called] upon the name of the LORD' (4:26).

Prayer: O Lord, as I worship you may I seek to please you alone!

Text for the day: *We make it our aim to please him* (2 Cor. 5:9).

The Flood

The LORD saw that the wickedness of man was great (Gen. 6:5).

Chapter 5 is a genealogy of the godly line — the ten generations of those 'sons of God' (Adam to Noah) who called on the name of the Lord. Chapter 6 introduces the corruption of the godly line. Men who worshipped God were seduced by the beauty of ungodly women. Intermarriage meant that there was no longer a bulwark against the vile practices prevalent at the time. (Here, as elsewhere in Scripture, it is clear that God's people are not to marry unbelievers — see Deut. 7:3-4; 1 Kings 11:1-4; Ezra 9:1-2; 2 Cor. 6:14). The Lord delivered an ultimatum. There would be 120 years more — then the judgement.

While the hearts of men were filled with wickedness, the heart of the Lord was filled with pain (Gen. 6:5-6). Violence prevailed; lust was unchecked; the corruption of human life was complete. The strongest men of the time exulted in their power to do evil. Their foul outrages were celebrated rather than abhorred (6:4). The Lord planned to blot it all out and start again. In the midst of such corruption, God set his favour on one man. Through Noah the 'seed of the woman' would be preserved. Because 'Noah found favour in the eyes of the LORD' (6:8), God determined to spare him and his immediate family from the flood. Building a massive boat in the middle of dry land demanded courage, hard work, huge financial resources and, above all, faith. Noah believed God about 'events as yet unseen' (Heb. 11:7).

We, like Noah, live in a world filled with corruption and sin. No boundaries are respected; the sinful arrogance of men and women knows no limits. Sexual perversion of all kinds is exalted; greed is praised; ungodliness is the cultural norm; violence is commonplace. The Lord is patient, and has extended the day of opportunity, not willing that any should perish. But his patience will not last for ever. The Day of Judgement will come:

As were the days of Noah, so will be the coming of the Son of Man. For as in those days before the flood they were eating and drinking, marrying and giving in marriage, until the day when Noah entered the ark, and they were unaware until the flood came and swept them all away, so will be the coming of the Son of Man (Matt. 24:37-39).

Noah was faithful in his generation. Are we faithful despite the cynicism and scepticism of those all around us? Will we, like Noah, have courage to warn others, emboldened by remembering what is unseen?

*The heroes of Scripture
with hearts full of faith,
their eyes on the city,
engaged in the race.
With hope in the promise,
encouraged to see
invisible glories
and joys yet to be.*

*Consider your mighty Saviour King
enduring the cross,
and run with a holy, joyful strength
the race to the last*

(John Tindall).

Prayer: O Lord, give me courage to warn others of the wrath to come, even as Noah did.

Text for the day: *[As] they were unaware until the flood came and swept them all away, so will be the coming of the Son of Man* (Matt. 24:36-39).

'God remembered Noah'

The phrase 'God remembered' means far more than the English verb 'to remember' conveys. When God remembers someone, he intervenes on their behalf, because he has committed himself to them. God had committed himself to Noah (Gen. 6:18). He now 'remembered' Noah (8:1) by bringing the flood to an end, and by inaugurating a new creation.

The bringing of Noah and his family safely through the judgement in the ark is a vivid picture of salvation. All was of grace — a fact underlined by the phrase, 'The LORD shut him in' (7:16). Noah going through the waters of judgement was a symbol of the believer going through the waters of baptism (1 Peter 3:20-21). Noah and his family alone had been spared, and were given a new beginning on a cleansed earth. The only fitting response was worship. Noah built an altar and offered up whole burnt offerings, representing his consecration, faith and submission. God had 'blotted out' the old community of humans who lived in arrogant disregard of their Maker. Now God started again with a worshipping and submissive community. He was pleased with the sacrifice, and with the one who offered it.

After the flood, God blessed Noah and his sons, just as he had blessed Adam and his wife, once more giving the 'creation mandate' to fill the earth (Gen. 1:28; 9:1). He had given Adam and Eve permission to eat every fruit in the garden, but with one prohibition. Now he gave Noah permission to eat all animals, but with a prohibition. Meat was not to be eaten with the lifeblood still in it. Later in the Old Testament, the blood of animals came to signify atonement for sin (Lev. 17:11-12). Now that the blood of Christ has secured final atonement for sin, all the various ceremonial food prohibitions of the Old Testament are done away with (1 Tim. 4:4). God then commanded that humans produce life (fill the earth) and protect life (he would demand accounting for life taken). Human life is precious to God, because he made man in his image.

Having given commands, God bound himself in a covenant. He would never again destroy all living things in a great flood.

The sign of this was to be the rainbow. The Hebrew word for 'bow' (the weapon) is the same as the word for 'rainbow'. God was hanging up his weapon of war and making peace. The flood was God's war; this was the treaty of peace and preservation. The regularity of the days, months, seasons and years would all signal God's faithfulness to this covenant.

He fills the sun with morning light,
he bids the moon direct the night;
his mercies ever shall endure,
when suns and moons shall shine no more

(Isaac Watts).

Prayer: Almighty God, thank you for your faithfulness, as seen in the perfect regularity of day and night and the seasons of the year. Thank you above all for Christ, and the safety promised in him when you do finally bring this world to an end.

Text for the day: *When the bow is in the clouds, I will see it and remember the everlasting covenant between God and every living creature* (Gen. 9:16).

Blessing and cursing

These early chapters of Genesis contain the whole Bible in microcosm: creation, sin, salvation, judgement and new creation. Blessing and happiness follow obedience to the Creator; cursing and misery follow disobedience. The first two chapters of Genesis are chapters of obedience and blessing; the next two are chapters of disobedience followed by cursing.

The following chapters trace the miserable effects of sin. Cain's descendant Lamech gloried in sinful violence (4:23-24). Another Lamech lamented the 'painful toil' resulting from the curse on the ground (5:29). Corruption increased on the earth to the extent that 'Every intention of the thoughts of [man's] heart was only evil continually' (6:5). God determined to blot out mankind, removing the 'breath of life' which he had given at creation (7:22). The 'seed of the woman' would, however, be preserved. God committed himself to making a covenant with Noah (6:18). After the flood there was a new creation. God sent out the living things from the ark to be fruitful and multiply once more (8:17). He promised 'never again [to] curse the ground because of man' (8:21) and blessed Noah and his sons (9:1).

Into the beautiful scene of new creation and God's blessing there intrudes this sordid story of drunkenness and shame (9:20-24). It echoes the account of the Fall. Even when conditions are perfect, the heart of man is still evil (8:21). Noah, the man of faith, is still a sinner. Within his own family we see the righteous ('the seed of the woman') who are blessed, and the wicked ('the seed of the serpent') who are cursed.

The meaning of this ugly incident was plain. Canaan son of Ham was cursed, and with him his descendants the Canaanites (10:15-20). In due time, their wickedness would reach a peak, and they would be 'vomited out' of the land which God was preparing for the people of blessing, the children of promise, the descendants of Shem (10:21-31; 11:10-32). Through Shem's descendant Abraham all families on earth would be blessed (12:3).

Today we are participants in that blessing! Christ has borne the curse which we deserved. He has secured for us 'every spiritual blessing in the heavenly places' (Eph. 1:3). But all around us we see evidence of God's curse on disobedience. Ham violated principles of respect for his elders and natural modesty — principles which seem to have been forgotten in our permissive society. But disregard of God's law does not bring freedom and happiness. It brings misery and God's curse. Lives all around us have been wrecked by sin. The gospel is the only ultimate answer.

> Blessings abound where'er he reigns:
> the prisoner leaps to lose his chains;
> the weary find eternal rest
> and all the sons of want are blessed.
>
> Where he displays his healing power,
> death and the curse are known no more;
> in him the tribes of Adam boast
> more blessings than their father lost

(Isaac Watts).

Prayer: Thank you, Lord Jesus, for bearing the curse in my place. Thank you that because of your perfect life and death I have been given every spiritual blessing. May I bring your blessing to others today.

Text for the day: *Blessed is everyone who fears the LORD, who walks in his ways!* (Ps. 128:1).

'Let us make a name for ourselves'

The theme of this section is human arrogance. God had commanded Noah's descendants to disperse and fill the earth (Gen.
9:1). Instead, the Shinarites united to 'make a name for ourselves'
(11:4). Their grandiose building project would, they believed,
secure their lasting fame. They were motivated by pride, disobedience and rebellion.

In the Old Testament context, this account supplied a polemic
against the pretensions of the 'superpower' of the day, Babylon.
Every major city in Babylon had a vast 'step-tower' or ziggurat.
The one in Nebuchadnezzar's sixth-century Babylon measured
ninety metres by ninety metres at the base, and was ninety metres
tall; such ziggurats had, it seems, been built for centuries. The
Babylonians considered their cities and towers to be of divine
origin. This account provides a cutting satire on such pretensions.
Here were men uniting to construct a tower to reach heaven. But
it was so small that God had to 'come down' to take a look.
Their scheme to unite was confounded. God confused their
languages and scattered them throughout the world.

These builders were archetypes of every civilization that seeks
to exalt itself without reference to God. Human pride will be
brought low. Every earthly empire will fall. All rulers will have to
bow the knee to Christ.

> Why do the nations rage
>   and the peoples plot in vain?
> The kings of the earth set themselves,
>   and the rulers take counsel together,
>   against the LORD and against his anointed, saying,
> 'Let us burst their bonds apart
>   and cast away their cords from us.'
> He who sits in the heavens laughs;
>   the LORD holds them in derision

(Ps. 2:1-4).

> *God has highly exalted him … so that at the name of Jesus every knee should bow, in heaven and on earth and under the earth, and every tongue confess that Jesus Christ is Lord, to the glory of God the Father* (Phil. 2: 9-11).

At a national level, the people of Israel were being warned. Any nation that rebels against God will fall. Would Israel submit and be blessed, or rebel and be cursed? On a personal level, we see the folly of seeking to make a name for ourselves without reference to God, the stupidity of seeking to take to ourselves the glory and renown that are due to God alone.

Multiplicity of languages has been one of the great barriers to the gospel. Zephaniah anticipated the time when people would be gathered from afar to speak one language (Zeph. 3:9-13). On the Day of Pentecost, the Holy Spirit empowered Jesus' followers to proclaim the gospel in many different languages (Acts 2:1-13). We look forward to the time when all nations will together be united in the service of the Lord God Almighty and of the Lamb (Rev. 21:24-26).

Let every kindred, every tribe,
on this terrestrial ball,
to him all majesty ascribe
and crown him Lord of all

                              (E. Perronet and John Rippon).

Prayer: Pray for those you know who are engaged in Bible translation, and pray for workers to be raised up to take the gospel to the many remaining unreached people groups of the world.

Text for the day: *Whoever exalts himself will be humbled, and whoever humbles himself will be exalted* (Matt. 23:12).

The triumph of faith

By faith Abraham obeyed when he was called to go out to a place that he was to receive as an inheritance. And he went out, not knowing where he was going (Heb. 11: 8).

The early chapters of Genesis record the ugly effects of the curse in the world, like ink spreading outwards to stain a clean garment. The call of Abram was the turning point. It was like a 'new creation'. The first man had been driven out eastwards from Eden (Gen. 3:24). Later, many nations had spread over the world (Gen. 10). Now God selects one man to begin one nation, and calls him to return westwards, back towards Eden. From his descendants would come the one who would reverse the effects of the curse. Through Abram 'all the families of the earth shall be blessed' (12:3). The word 'bless' or 'blessing' occurs five times in 12:2-3.

Abram grew up in a pagan environment (Josh. 24:2), in one of the finest cities of the greatest civilization of the time. His family had retained some knowledge of the one true God (Gen. 31:53). God told him to leave, and go to 'the land that I will show you' (12:1). He was commanded to leave the known for the unknown, the secure for the insecure, the comforts of settled life for all the discomforts of migratory life — for a lifetime. The promises that accompanied the command were breathtaking in their scope: Abram's descendants would become a great nation; they would be blessed by God, and they would be a blessing to the whole world.

Abram was not given any tangible guarantees. The promise that he would become a great nation seemed improbable. His wife was barren (11:30), and he was seventy-five by the time he left Haran. But he went, 'as the LORD had told him' (12:4). On arrival in Canaan, his faith was challenged by the stark reality that the land was already occupied by the Canaanites. The Lord renewed his promise: 'To your offspring I will give this land' (12:7). Despite the fact that there were still no offspring, Abram built an altar to the Lord (12:7) and obediently travelled on.

Genesis 11:27 – 12:9   Day 12

Again he built an altar and 'called upon the name of the LORD'
(12:8). Again, in faith, he moved on (12:9).

It is moving to imagine the simplicity of Abram's altars, in
comparison with the elaborate temples found back in Ur. An
onlooker might have assumed that real worship took place in the
stunning architecture and among the crowds of worshippers in
Ur. The reality was that God was with Abram and his simple
stone altars at the oak of Mamre and in the hill country of Bethel.

His call we obey
like Abram of old,
not knowing the way,
but faith makes us bold;
for though we are strangers
we have a good guide,
and trust, in all dangers,
'The Lord will provide'

(John Newton).

Abram's call was unique. But his obedience is a model. To
follow Christ in a secular society demands faith and courage. Will
we choose to trust and obey today? Or will we distrust God's
goodness and disbelieve his promises?

Prayer: O Lord, thank you for Abraham's great example of faith.
Help me today to trust you and obey you.

Text for the day: *Abram went, as the LORD had told him*
(Gen. 12:4).

The failure of faith

Scripture does not only record faith's triumphs; it tells of failures too. Abram's fear led to deception, which led to Sarai's purity being endangered. Abram's motives were honourable. He wanted to preserve his life. After all, if he were killed, the promises would fail. He did not expect that his wife would really be taken by another man. Saying that Sarai was his sister (a half-truth!) was intended to buy time. If she were known to be his wife, and another man desired her, Abram might have been killed. If she were thought to be his sister, the man would have to commence negotiations with her brother. This would give him time to escape.

Should Sarai have gone along with this? She is, after all, commended for her submission (1 Peter 3:6). But sin is sin. We are to obey those in authority over us, but not if they tell us to sin (Acts 5:29). Christian wives, Jesus is Lord — not your husband. We are to submit, but not if it means following our husbands into sin. Peter commended Sarah for the overall tenor of her life; he was not justifying everything she did.

Abram rationalized his deception. It is easy to believe that 'The end justifies the means'. It is tempting to 'cut a corner' if it appears that by our doing so God's kingdom will benefit. But God demands obedience to all his commands. As Samuel said to King Saul (who also made a 'spiritual' rationalization for disobedience), 'To obey is better than sacrifice' (1 Sam. 15:22).

Abram's ploy backfired. Instead of an ordinary Egyptian entering into negotiations for Sarai, Pharaoh saw her extraordinary beauty. As an absolute monarch, he did not have to bargain with anyone. He just took her. But if he had slept with her, God's promise to raise up a nation through Abram would have been endangered.

God intervened. Abram's failure of faith would not be allowed to compromise the divine promise. Pharaoh's household was struck with a supernatural plague. Pharaoh's indignation at Abram's untruthfulness put Abram to shame. Sarai's virtue was preserved. Abram escaped with his life and with his wife. He had been shocked and he had been shamed. But God had not only delivered them, he even allowed them to profit materially from this incident (Gen. 12:16; 13:2). The wealth so gained would, however, cause trouble in the future (13:6-7).

We may be fearful. Our faith may fail. We may rationalize our disobedience. We may bring shame on ourselves. God will not allow any of this to threaten fulfilment of his covenant. If we are 'in Christ' he has committed himself to keep us:

> *His oath, his covenant and his blood*
> *support me in the rising flood;*
> *when all around my soul gives way,*
> *he then is all my hope and stay.*
> *On Christ the solid rock I stand,*
> *all other ground is sinking sand.*
>
> *I trust his righteous character,*
> *his counsel, promises and power;*
> *his name and honour are at stake*
> *to save me from the burning lake.*
> *On Christ the solid rock I stand,*
> *all other ground is sinking sand*

(Edward Mote).

Prayer: Thank God for his covenant of grace to save his people from their sins.

Text for the day: *If we are faithless, he remains faithful — for he cannot deny himself* (2 Tim. 2:13).

Faith does not grasp the things that are seen

This account opens and ends with worship (Gen. 13:4,18). This underlines Abram's trust in God for material provision. The enormous wealth acquired in Egypt had brought its own problems. The land was unable to sustain Abram's and Lot's livestock. This time, when his faith was challenged, Abram's attitude was exemplary: 'Let there be no strife between you and me' (13:8). As the leader of the family, Abram had the right to determine where each of them should go. To avoid contention, he let his nephew have first choice.

By contrast, Lot failed to defer to his older relative. He looked out for himself. 'Lot lifted up his eyes and saw that the Jordan Valley was well watered everywhere like the garden of the LORD' (13:10). He looked only at the immediate prospect of prosperity, and did not consider the spiritual danger of living in close proximity to the cities of Sodom and Gomorrah. Grasping at the things that were seen would ultimately lead to disaster for his family.

As soon as Lot had left Abram, God reassured him. Lot had taken the best. Abram would be given it all.

Today, if we have faith in God we do not have to fight for our rights. There may be times when it is more important to say, 'Let there be no strife between us.' God will take care of our needs; he will vindicate us. Abram's example of self-renunciation points forward to Christ, the supreme example of one who did not 'grasp his rights' (Phil. 2:6-7).

Many people around us have no certain hope for eternity; they live for today. It is not surprising that they grab all the happiness they can in the here and now. Acquiring new and better clothes and household goods, enjoying better holidays, redecorating the house — these things fill the horizon of so many. Where is your heart today? Are your best energies going to be concentrated on what you can acquire for yourself and your family? Or are you going to spend your best energies in serving others to the glory of God? Are you dazzled by the things that are seen, or are you longing for the things that are unseen?

In Bunyan's *Pilgrim's Progress*, Christian was shown two children: 'Passion seemed to be much discontented, but Patience was very quiet.' Passion was given what he wanted — a bag full of treasure — but in a very short time, 'He had lavished all away, and had nothing left him but rags.' Patience, representing those who look forward to eternity, was willing to wait for the treasure that lasts.

Oh, let me feel you near me;
the world is ever near.
I see the sights that dazzle;
the tempting sounds I hear.
My foes are ever near me,
around me and within;
but, Jesus, draw still nearer
and shield my soul from sin!

(John E. Bode).

Prayer: Father God, thank you that your Son did not grasp his rights, but freely gave them up for me. Help me today not to grasp for my own advantage. Help me to be willing to put others ahead of myself. Protect me today from covetousness. Help me to be content and trust in you.

Text for the day: *Keep your life free from love of money, and be content with what you have, for he has said, 'I will never leave you nor forsake you'* (Heb. 13:5).

Faith trusts in God to provide

In ancient times it was common for rulers to extort tribute from weaker neighbours. Here, one eastern lord and his allies went to war against a group of vassal states who had failed to pay up. They swept through the Jordan valley, defeating the local kings and plundering their towns. Abram's nephew Lot (now living in Sodom) and his family were also captured. On hearing the news, Abram did not hesitate. He pursued the invaders with his own household men, plus allies (Gen. 14:13,24), attacked them by night and defeated them. He then recovered Lot and his possessions, together with all the other captives. God had promised to bless Abram and his family. It was God who gave success. God had promised that Abram and his seed would possess the promised land, and he empowered Abram to defeat those who invaded it.

On his triumphant return, Abram was greeted by two kings with two offers. The King of Sodom (14:17,21) offered Abram great wealth. The King of Salem (14:18-20) offered him a blessing. In his relief and excitement at winning a great victory, Abram was vulnerable. Would he remember that the victory was the Lord's and that the Lord would continue to supply all his needs? Or would he fall into the trap of thinking that as he had won the battle, he deserved his share of the plunder? He could have rationalized the latter choice by saying that God had given it into his hands!

The glorious blessing pronounced by the King of Salem put everything in perspective:

Blessed be Abram by God Most High,
  Possessor of heaven and earth;
and blessed be God Most High,
  who has delivered your enemies into your hand!

(14:19-20).

Abram was reminded that God is Creator and the owner of all wealth. He can distribute it as he pleases. God was the one who had won the victory. God was the one who had committed himself to bless Abram now and for ever. If Abram had been momentarily tempted to accept anything from the notoriously wicked King of Sodom, this reminder checked him. There was no need to take any blessing from an earthly, evil lord, when every blessing was guaranteed by his heavenly, righteous Lord.

This encounter with Melchizedek was a high point in Abram's life. This priest-king was not part of the elect family, but evidently served the one true God. Abram instinctively acknowledged him as his spiritual superior. In offering him a tenth of all the spoil, he was offering the first fruits of victory back to the God who had granted victory. In hearing the blessing pronounced over him by this godly man, Abram was inspired to greater faith in the promises of God and empowered to resist worldly temptation.

Elsewhere in the Bible, Melchizedek is regarded as a 'type' or forerunner of Jesus Christ, in that he was both a priest and a king (Ps. 110:4; Heb. 7:1-17) and also a king of righteousness and peace. He stands in complete contrast to the King of Sodom, who led a city of such overwhelming wickedness that God felt compelled to wipe it out altogether. For Abram to have accepted wealth from the King of Sodom would have compromised the truth that God, not man, had given the victory and the blessing. Abram's response to the King of Sodom was uncompromising. The allies could have their fair share, but he would accept nothing:

> *I have lifted my hand to the LORD, God Most High, Possessor of heaven and earth, that I would not take a thread or a sandal strap or anything that is yours, lest you should say, 'I have made Abram rich' (Gen. 14:22-23).*

Prayer: Pray for grace today to resist the temptation to run after the approval of those who reject God. Pray for faith to look to God for victory and provision.

Text for the day: *Put not your trust in princes... Blessed is he ... whose hope is in the LORD his God* (Ps. 146:3,5).

God's covenant with Abram

Abram had rejected the wealth offered by the wicked King of Sodom. God graciously reassured him afterwards: 'Fear not, Abram, I am your shield; your reward shall be very great' (Gen. 15:1). God's protection and provision would be all he needed.

Abram responded with a question. God had promised him a family. Where was it? Would his servant be his heir? God reassured him. Abram would have a son, and his descendants would be as numerous as the stars. Humanly speaking, this seemed ludicrous; but Abram believed God. God also reiterated his second promise: Abram would possess the land. Again, Abram found this hard to believe. How was he to know that he would possess it? As yet he did not legally own a single acre.

In response to this question, the Lord initiated a solemn covenant ceremony. Abram fell into a deep sleep and then became aware of a terrifying and supernatural darkness. At this point God revealed the future to him. Abram's descendants would be exiles and slaves in a foreign land for 400 years. After that God would rescue them, and bring them back to the promised land. Only then would the sin of the inhabitants of Canaan be so great that they should be removed. Abram himself would die in peace before these things happened. Then God himself (represented by the smoking fire pot and flaming torch) moved between the carcasses. This signified his unbreakable promise. If he failed to provide Abram with offspring, and if he failed to give them the land, then he himself would become like those carcasses.

This kind of ceremony was not unusual in ancient times. But usually both parties to the agreement passed between the dead animals (e.g. Jer. 34:18-19). They swore on their lives that they would keep the agreement. If they broke it, they could be killed as the animals had been. In the Hebrew language the phrase to 'make a covenant' is literally 'to cut a covenant'. Here, the covenant was one-sided. God made the promise. God committed himself to keep it.

The whole narrative relating to Abram underlines God's initiative. God called Abram and promised a son. No part of the promise seemed 'possible', for none of it could be fulfilled by natural means: the promised land was already occupied; Sarai was barren; Abram and Sarai were very old. Abram contributed nothing. All he could do was accept and believe in God's provision. God 'counted it to him as righteousness' (Gen. 15:6; Rom. 4:3; Gal. 3:6).

God's covenant with us is also one-sided; it is a covenant of grace. He took the initiative in our salvation. Christ secured it at Calvary when his body was broken (just as the animals were 'broken' in this account). God accepts us as righteous because of what Christ has done. We contribute nothing to our salvation. But as Abram believed God, so we are called to believe God. Our faith may be weak (even Abram questioned and doubted). We may cry out, 'I believe; help my unbelief!' (Mark 9:24). Our faith may be as small as a grain of mustard seed, but it is the power and reliability of the one in whom we put our faith that counts (Matt. 17:20).

Prayer: Worship the Lord for his covenant of grace!

> *He by himself hath sworn —*
> *I on his oath depend —*
> *I shall, on eagles' wings upborne,*
> *to heaven ascend;*
> *I shall behold his face,*
> *I shall his power adore,*
> *and sing the wonders of his grace*
> *for evermore*
>
>   (Thomas Olivers).

Text for the day: *And he believed the LORD, and he counted it to him as righteousness* (Gen. 15:6).

God sees, God hears and God looks after me

This brief chapter is stained with tears. Failure of faith led to tragedy on a personal level which would have devastating results throughout history.

Humanly speaking, we can identify with Sarai's frustration. God had promised Abram numerous descendants, but the years rolled on and nothing happened. There was a socially acceptable means for dealing with infertility. Sarai felt strongly that it was up to her to initiate it and it was her duty to act!

When faced with grief we can run to God and plead his promises. Or we can harden our hearts against him and blame him for our predicament. The stage is then set for us to give up on him and act on our own behalf. Instead of praying to God, Sarai blamed him for her predicament (Gen. 16:2) and decided to act for herself. She would give her servant Hagar to her husband, so that he could have a child through her.

Sarai was attacking the principle on which God's covenant was based. All was to be of divine initiative. Her barrenness (as that of Rebekah and Rachel after her) was not malicious neglect. God was highlighting the fact that when the sons were given, they were his gift.

Abram should have condemned this interference in God's plan. He was passive. He failed to prevent this faithless scheme and he failed to protect Hagar from the vicious treatment meted out to her by Sarai (16:6).

Hagar had little choice. She is the most tragic of the figures in this account — used and abused and finally thrown out. Her intense sufferings prefigure the agony of the people of God when, they, in their turn, were enslaved in Egypt (the word 'dealt harshly' in verse 6 is that used in Genesis 15:13 to describe the sufferings of the Israelites in bondage).

God saw Hagar's tears, listened to her laments (16:11) and came to her help. He thus revealed himself to her as the God who sees, the God who hears and the God 'who looks after me' (16:13). His command seemed harsh: Hagar was to return to the woman who had so ill-used her. But he promised Hagar a son, who was to be called Ishmael and who would have numerous descendants. Hagar responded in faith. She called on the name of the Lord: 'You are a God of seeing.' This God sees all things, and he had seen her. 'Truly here I have seen him who looks after me' (16:13). She proved her faith by her obedience. She returned and evidently told Abram about God's appearance and his instructions, so that when the son was born he was called Ishmael (meaning 'God hears').

Prayer: The following words of Patrick (c. 389–461), the great Irish Christian, vividly express trust in the God who sees, the God who hears and the God who looks after us. Use them as your prayer today:

> I bind unto myself today
> the power of God to hold and lead,
> his eye to watch, his might to stay,
> his ear to hearken to my need;
> the wisdom of my God to teach,
> his hand to guide, his shield to ward;
> the word of God to give me speech,
> his heavenly host to be my guard
>
> (Patrick, trans. C. F. Alexander).

Text for the day: *You are a God who sees me... Truly here I have seen him who looks after me* (Gen. 16:13, ESV alternative reading).

'I will ... be God to you and to your offspring after you'

Abram was seventy-five when God called him and promised him numerous offspring, the land and that all nations would be blessed through him. At the age of eighty-five, impatient at the delay in fulfilment of the promise, Abram took Hagar, who bore him Ishmael. This faithless act may have contributed to the delay of thirteen years before God appeared to Abram again. Now, when Abram was ninety-nine, God revealed himself as *El Shaddai*, the almighty, all-sufficient God. Before confirming the covenant again, God reaffirmed Abram's call to a life of faith: 'Walk before me, and be blameless' (Gen. 17:1).

'Walk before me' evokes the picture of an Eastern shepherd and his flock. We are God's people, his flock, and we take directions from him alone. Each day, each hour, each moment our heart cry is to be: 'Lord, what do you want me to do? What shall I say now? How would you have me to act?' If we walk before him in this close relationship of guidance, protection and love, then our walk will be 'blameless'.

The heart of the covenant was relational. God promised 'to be God to you and to your offspring after you' (17:7). What God is in himself, he promises to his people. We have his power to protect us, his wisdom to make us wise and his righteousness reckoned to our account. Supremely, we have his love, demonstrated to us in the gift of his Son. The promise of 'Canaan, for an everlasting possession' (17:8) spoke of an eternal relationship. Abram himself saw beyond the physical reality of the land to the heavenly country to come (Heb. 11:10) where we are God's people and he is our God. The New Testament makes it clear that the land of Canaan was a temporary picture of the promised land which we shall enjoy for all eternity (Rev. 21:3-4).

The promises were repeated, but made even more glorious. Abram's own wife Sarai would bear the son of promise, to be called Isaac. God would establish an eternal covenant with his descendants, and from him kings would be born. This covenant was confirmed by two signs, both of which demanded costly and immediate obedience. Abram and Sarai were to adopt new names, as a perpetual reminder of God's promises. It took faith and courage to do this. For the elderly Abram, with one son, to take the name 'father of a multitude' was to invite mockery. But God's promise was so certain that he said, 'I *have made* you the father of a multitude of nations' (17:5, emphasis added). The second sign, that of circumcision, was painful, but Abraham obeyed that very day.

We are to be obedient in participation in the signs of the new covenant (baptism and the Lord's Supper). And as we 'walk before' the Lord in daily obedience, we have that wonderful promise that he will 'be God to' us (17:7).

Twice in this chapter Abraham fell on his face before the Lord (17:3,17). The reality of communicating with God Almighty compelled the utmost reverence. Yet he laughed on hearing that his ninety-year-old wife would conceive and bear a child. The words of our Lord suggest that this was the laughter of joyful amazement rather than the cynical laughter of unbelief (John 8:56). Paul writes of this encounter:

> *He did not weaken in faith when he considered his own body, which was as good as dead (since he was about a hundred years old), or when he considered the barrenness of Sarah's womb. No distrust made him waver concerning the promise of God, but he grew strong in his faith as he gave glory to God, fully convinced that God was able to do what he had promised. That is why his faith was counted to him as righteousness* (Rom. 4:19-22).

Prayer: Praise God that his plan has always been to be gracious to 'a multitude of nations' (Gen. 17:5), and pray today that the gospel would soon be taken to the remaining unreached peoples.

Text for the day: *I am God Almighty; walk before me, and be blameless* (Gen. 17:1).

'Is anything too hard for the LORD?'

In ancient times, the making of a covenant often culminated in a meal (e.g. Gen. 26:28-30). How would this work when the initiator of the covenant was Almighty God? When the Lord himself appeared in human form along with two angels at Abraham's tent, was Abraham expecting a divine visitation? Did he realize the identity of the three immediately? Or did it dawn on him as the conversation progressed that these were no ordinary men? We cannot tell. But he knew by the time 'the LORD said, "I will surely return to you about this time next year, and Sarah your wife shall have a son"' (Gen. 18:10).

Abraham's faith and obedience were rewarded. Thus he is called 'the friend of God' (2 Chr. 20:7; Isa. 41:8; James 2:23). This description fits one who was honoured to provide a meal for the Lord himself and share the intimacy of discussing his plans (Gen. 18:17). Some suggest that this visitation was an appearance of the pre-incarnate Christ.

The description of the preparation of the meal (18:4-8) builds up to the central drama of this section: the announcement to Sarah that she would bear a son (18:10). There are parallels with other 'annunciations' in Scripture, notably to Samson's parents (Judg. 13:2-20), the Shunammite woman (2 Kings 4:8-17) and Mary (Luke 1:26-38). In this case Sarah overheard the announcement rather than hearing it face to face. Given her extreme age, the barrenness that had afflicted her during the normal childbearing years and the extreme age of her husband, it is hardly surprising that she laughed.

But God is the God of wonders. His rebuke to Sarah literally reads: 'Is anything too wonderful for the LORD?' God, by definition, is all-powerful, the God who does wonders (Ps. 77:11; 136:4). It is no problem for the one who created the universe to create new life in an elderly barren woman. When the Lord appeared to Manoah and his barren wife to tell them of the birth of Samson, Manoah offered a sacrifice to 'the LORD, to the one who works wonders' (Judg. 13:18-19). God delights to do the 'impossible'. Sarah's infertility and age were ordained to highlight the fact that her son would be God's gracious provision.

The wonder of providing a son to the aged, barren Sarah foreshadowed the greater wonder of providing a son to the virgin Mary. And that provision opened the way for the greatest wonder of all: God's free gift of pardon to his enemies, his gift of grace to the undeserving. Truly, our God is a God who does wonders.

Prayer: Praise God for his wonders of grace:

> *Great God of wonders! All thy ways*
> *are matchless, godlike, and divine;*
> *but the fair glories of thy grace*
> *more godlike and unrivalled shine:*
> *Who is a pardoning God like thee?*
> *Or who has grace so rich and free?*
>
> *In wonder lost, with trembling joy,*
> *we take the pardon of our God:*
> *pardon for sins of deepest dye,*
> *a pardon sealed with Jesus' blood:*
> *Who is a pardoning God like thee?*
> *Or who has grace so rich and free?*

(Samuel Davies).

Text for the day: *Is anything too hard for the LORD?* (Gen. 18:14).

'Shall not the Judge of all the earth do what is just?'

The themes of justice and righteousness dominate this section. The sins committed in Sodom and Gomorrah were blatant. The Lord heard the outcry provoked by the injustice, cruelty and immorality of the people. Their callous disregard for the poor and needy finally provoked God to act (Ezek. 16:49). God informed Abraham of his plans because Abraham was going to pass on God's ways of justice and righteousness to the next generation (Gen. 18:19).

Abraham knew that the Lord would not treat the wicked (who reject God and his laws) and the righteous (who live according to God's will) in the same way. He was primarily concerned for his nephew Lot. But given that he had rescued some of the inhabitants of Sodom from marauding intruders, we may assume that his concern extended beyond his own family.

The interchange between the Lord and Abraham was extraordinary. It concluded with God assuring Abraham that if he found just ten righteous people within Sodom, he would spare the city. This is a reminder of the difference that God's people make in the world. Until we reach heaven, we shall never know how many judgements have been deferred for their sake. It is also a powerful reminder of the power of intercessory prayer. Abraham did not limit his prayers to his own family; he pleaded boldly for the entire community.

Would the Lord find ten righteous? The next ugly episode shows that he would not. When the two angelic visitors arrived at Sodom to investigate, Lot insisted on their staying the night in the safety of his home. But then 'the men of the city, the men of Sodom, both young and old, all the people, to the last man' (19:4) surrounded the house and demanded to sleep with the two visitors. Depravity was universal. Lot was the only man in the city who regarded homosexual rape as evil. Even Lot had been compromised by living there for so long. To offer his two virgin daughters to be raped by the townsmen was breathtakingly immoral. The angelic visitors intervened to protect the family and themselves. But this night of horror sealed Sodom's doom. Even when the men of the city were struck with a supernatural blindness, they did not hesitate, but continued to seek to fulfil their evil designs. Judgement was certain.

The extent to which Lot had been morally compromised by living in Sodom was seen in his reluctance to leave. The angels had to pull him and his wife and daughters away. Even then he begged pathetically to be allowed to stay nearby. It was only the Lord's mercy (19:16) and Abraham's intercession (19:29) that ensured his deliverance.

Today, the gross evil of society around us matches that of Sodom. There is no shame, and few constraints. The outcry reaches the Lord. Yet, as God's covenant people, we are called on to intercede for those around us.

Prayer: This is still the day of gospel opportunity! Pray that God's mercy in Christ should be extended to the salvation and transformation of even the most depraved.

Who can stand before your anger,
who can face your piercing eyes?
For you love the weak and helpless,
and you hear the victims' cries.
Yes, you are a God of justice
and your judgement surely comes:
upon our nation, upon our nation
have mercy, Lord!

(Graham Kendrick).

Text for the day: *Shall not the Judge of all the earth do what is just?* (Gen. 18:25).

'Remember Lot's wife'

Scripture presents the overthrow of Sodom as a powerful picture of God's justice in destroying the wicked. It prefigures the great judgement, when all evil will finally be destroyed (2 Peter 2:6-10).

We cannot comprehend what Abraham was thinking as he watched the smoke rising from where just hours before thousands of people had gone about their daily business. But he knew that God had assured him that if only ten righteous were found the cities would be spared. And for his sake, though he may not yet have known it, the Lord had spared Lot (Gen. 19:29).

Lot had been sickened by the violent lawlessness that he witnessed in Sodom every day (2 Peter 2:7-8). The destruction of Sodom and Gomorrah, and the rescue of Lot, shows that the Lord is able to 'rescue the godly from trials, and to keep the unrighteous under punishment until the day of judgement, and especially those who indulge in the lust of defiling passion and despise authority' (2 Peter 2:6-10). The prevailing attitude of the citizens of Sodom had been one of refusal to respect any authority and of total sexual licence. Nothing was off limits. Does this not describe Western culture today? If Lot was 'tormenting his righteous soul' (2 Peter 2:8) over the vice that surrounded him, it is a dangerous sign if we are comfortable in our culture. If we are not shocked by those advertisements, TV shows and films that 'defile passion and despise authority' then we have been desensitized to sin. Sodom was also guilty of being 'arrogant, overfed and unconcerned' and 'did not help the poor and needy' (Ezek. 16:49, NIV). This too is an alarmingly accurate description of the Western world today: 20% of the world's population consume 84% of the world's resources, and overindulgence is a major cause of disease.

It is sobering that even though Peter describes Lot as a 'righteous' man, he had been terribly compromised by living in Sodom. There was the feeble capitulation to the violence and lust of his neighbours when he offered them his daughters. There was the pathetic lingering when commanded to leave, so that the angels had physically to drag him out. And at the end of the account we find him hiding in a cave, drunk and violated by his own daughters. What a warning! Even if we think we are maintaining a clear testimony, we may be absorbing the mindset of those around us.

The Lord Jesus delivers the most sober warning of all: 'Remember Lot's wife' (Luke 17:32). Angels had brought her safely out of the doomed city, but her heart was back with her home, her possessions, her friends, her 'security'. In disobeying the clear command not to look back, she betrayed unbelief in the Word of God, and was turned into a pillar of salt. What a terrible monument to worldliness and distrust!

Where is your heart today? It is so easy to be mesmerized with the here and now: job, home, possessions, family, friends, 'security'. This account is a vivid reminder that there is no security apart from looking to Jesus (Heb. 12:2). Don't look back!

Prayer: Use the words of this song as your prayer:

Each hindrance discarded
and sin laid aside,
with patient endurance
see Christ as your prize.
The hardships you suffer,
your sorrows and care,
though painful at present
will righteousness bear.

Consider your mighty Saviour King
enduring the cross,
and run with a holy, joyful strength
the race to the last

(John Tindall).

Text for the day: *Run with endurance ... looking to Jesus, the founder and perfecter of our faith* (Heb. 12:1-2).

The gift of grace

At last the promised son was born. There was tension right up to the end: Abraham once again failed in faith and lied about Sarah, with the result that she had been taken into the harem of a foreign ruler (Gen. 20). God had again intervened to preserve Sarah's purity and the promised child. This failure on Abraham's part (a repetition of his sin in Egypt — see Gen. 12), underlined the fact that Isaac was a child of grace. God did not give him to Abraham and Sarah because they were 'deserving' parents. If Abraham's sin is highlighted in chapter 20, Sarah's cruelty to Hagar and Ishmael is starkly portrayed in this chapter (21:10). Isaac's parents were not only physically incapable of bearing children; they were also sinners.

Their reaction to this incredible gift of God was the laughter of delight, relief and astonishment (21:6-7); and the name they gave their son expressed their joy ('Isaac' means 'laughter'). It is only when we become conscious of our own sinfulness in the eyes of God that we begin to appreciate the incredible gift that God has given us. As long as we think that we 'deserve' salvation, we cannot laugh with astonishment and joy at the 'inexpressible gift' of the Lord Jesus Christ. When it sinks in that we are naturally unable to save ourselves, and morally incapable of pleasing God, then we are simply awestruck at God's wonderful provision of pure grace.

The account of Isaac's birth is followed by the tragic expulsion of Hagar and Ishmael. The painful family tensions leading up to it are only hinted at. There was sin on both sides. Sarah had failed in faith, taken matters into her own hands and arranged for her husband to sleep with her maidservant. Unsurprisingly, she had been jealous of Hagar ever since. Ishmael's reaction to the birth of a younger brother (who would take his place as the primary heir) was unsurprising, but his laughter was cruel and taunting. Yet, through all the human sinfulness, God was working out his purpose. His plan was that the line of grace (through Isaac) was not to be compromised. There was to be a clear distinction between his own chosen people and the other nations. Moses' great concern in writing the Pentateuch was the establishment of boundary markers, distinguishing Israel from pagan peoples. They were to stay separate and pure. That was the purpose of including the sordid account of Lot's incest with his daughters at the end of Genesis 19. The impure origins of the Moabites and Ammonites were an object lesson to the Israelites: God wanted Israel to be different — a beacon of holiness in an evil world.

Although Abraham was naturally devastated at the loss of his elder son, and rightly concerned for Hagar, God reassured him. He could let Sarah banish Hagar and Ishmael. A separation had to take place. There had to be no mistake about it: 'Through Isaac shall your offspring be named' (21:12). In the New Testament, the story is interpreted allegorically: Sarah and her son represent the promise of God and freedom; Hagar and her son represent human effort and slavery (Gal. 4:21-31). Moreover, Paul looked back at Ishmael's taunting of Isaac as typical of the kind of persecution which the people of the world employ against the people of God (Gal. 4:29).

Despite the fact that God purposed to fulfil his promises through Sarah and Isaac, we see his compassion extending to Hagar and Ishmael. He provided for their physical needs and gave them hope for the future. God does not only deal kindly with his elect people; we see daily examples of his loving care extended to others also.

The message of this chapter is clear: God deals with his people on the basis of pure grace, and he expects us to be separated from the world.

Prayer: Almighty God, thank you that you do not deal with me on the basis of my own 'merit'. I have none. I praise you for the inexpressible gift of your Son and for salvation by grace alone. I pray that I may live as one of your people this day, and have courage to be different from those around me.

Text for the day: *Thanks be to God for his inexpressible gift!* (2 Cor. 9:15).

Abraham believed God

This was the supreme test of faith. God called Abraham to 'Take your son, your only son Isaac, whom you love' (Gen. 22:2) and offer him up as a burnt offering. Abraham's response was utterly submissive: 'Here am I' (22:1,11). The command to sacrifice the son of promise cut right against the grain of all his natural affections and of all that he knew of God. God had promised this son, miraculously provided him and covenanted that through him all nations would be blessed. It was as if, from being Abraham's closest friend, God had become his worst enemy. Yet Abraham did not argue; he obeyed. He reasoned: 'I do not understand why the Lord wants me to do this. It is a terrible command. But because I trust the Lord, I will obey him.' He even reckoned that perhaps the Lord planned to raise Isaac from death, and fulfil his purpose in that way:

> By faith Abraham, when he was tested, offered up Isaac, and he who had received the promises was in the act of offering up his only son, of whom it was said, 'Through Isaac shall your offspring be named.' He considered that God was able even to raise him from the dead, from which, figuratively speaking, he did receive him back (Heb. 11:17-19).

God was testing Abraham. Was God the ultimate reality in his life? Or was Isaac?

There will be many times when the Lord calls us to go through dark times which seem to make no sense. God wants us to understand that while the trial may seem incomprehensible, humanly speaking, and while it may seem even to destroy our usefulness in the kingdom of God, yet his purposes do not depend on us, but only on him. What he blesses is obedience. What or who is biggest, most real, most valuable and most significant to you? Those times when all else is stripped away test whether we really mean it when we sing, 'All to thee, my blessed Saviour, I surrender all.'

Abraham came through the test. His faith in God was proved real (James 2:21-23). The anguish he suffered in anticipating the death of his only beloved son was a pale shadow of the incomprehensible anguish suffered by the Father when he gave his Son for us. In being willing to give his son, Abraham was obeying God's command. But there was no external compulsion to force God the Father to give his Son: it was motivated purely and freely by love: 'He who did not spare his own Son but gave him up for us all...' (Rom. 8:32).

Prayer: Thank you, Father, that for all eternity past you planned the costly plan of salvation and that you freely gave your only Son. Thank you, Lord Jesus, that you willingly gave your life for my salvation. Thank you, Holy Spirit, for opening my eyes to my need for this sacrifice.

Text for the day: *Behold, the Lamb of God, who takes away the sin of the world!* (John 1:29).

Hope in the face of death

These all died in faith, not having received the things promised, but having seen them and greeted them from afar, and having acknowledged that they were strangers and exiles on the earth (Heb. 11:13).

Abraham and Sarah had seen the beginning of the fulfilment of the promise in the gift of Isaac. But what about owning the land and having descendants as numerous as the stars? These promises still seemed impossible. Abraham and Sarah were just 'sojourners', temporary residents. When Sarah died, she was the first to die without seeing the promises fulfilled. Abraham now faced, not only natural desolation at the death of his wife, but a renewed challenge to his faith. In that culture it was vitally important to bury your dead in your ancestral home. The family tree in Genesis 22:20-24 highlights the fact that all his family roots were back in the east. Would he now return to his ancestral home to bury his beloved wife? The decision to purchase an ancestral burial spot within the land of Canaan was Abraham's way of saying 'Yes' to the promises of God. He would not go back. Purchasing the land and burying his wife there bound his descendants to this land. In turn he would be buried there, as would Isaac, Rebekah, Jacob, Leah (Gen. 49:29-32; 50:13) and Joseph (Gen. 50:25; Exod. 13:19).

Abraham responded to Sarah's death with faith. Death, the breaking of precious earthly relationships, is our greatest opportunity to demonstrate our faith in God. Without an eternal hope, death can bring only despair. But Jesus said, 'I am the resurrection and the life.' God is the God of Abraham, Isaac and Jacob, and he is the God of the living (Mark 12:26-27). They live today! Sarah's body may have rotted in the cave of Machpelah, but her spirit is with the Lord, and one day her body will be raised, incorruptible, to rejoice for all eternity at the fulfilment of all God's promises. We do not mourn as those who have no hope!

Abraham and Sarah died 'in faith', looking ahead. Praise God that his promises to them have now been fulfilled in Christ.

We can take great encouragement also from the way the New Testament looks back at Sarah's life. Her faults are not white-washed in the Genesis narrative. We see her disbelief at God's promise, her mistaken effort to secure the promised son by giving her servant to her husband, her subsequent jealousy of, and cruelty to, Hagar. Yet in Hebrews Sarah is commended as a woman of faith (Heb. 11:11), and Peter commends her as a godly role model and a wife who honoured her husband (1 Peter 3:5-6). How wonderful that the grace of God covers our sins and failings!

Prayer: Pray for those you know who mourn, that they would not mourn as those who have no hope, but would have the eternal perspective that alone can bring real comfort.

Lives again our glorious King;
where, O death is now your sting?
Once he died our souls to save;
where's your victory, boasting grave?

Soar we now where Christ has led,
following our exalted Head;
made like him, like him we rise,
ours the cross, the grave, the skies

(Charles Wesley).

Text for the day: *Jesus said to her, 'I am the resurrection and the life'* (John 11:25).

'As for me, the LORD has led me'

Sarah's death spurred Abraham on to look to the future and provide a wife for his heir, so that the line of promise could continue. The family tree in Genesis 22:20-24 introduces Rebekah, the wife God chose for Isaac. Not that Abraham knew this ahead of time. He had to act in faith. He knew that for Isaac to marry a Canaanite would not be the right way to continue the line of blessing. He had to seek a wife for his son from among his relatives. The quest was full of unanswered questions. Would there be a suitable young woman? How would he find her? Would she agree to leave the known for the unknown? Abraham 'did not waver' in his faith. He sent off his servant with this confidence:

> *The LORD, the God of heaven, who took me from my father's house and from the land of my kindred, and who spoke to me and swore to me, 'To your offspring I will give this land', he will send his angel before you* (24:7).

The Lord leads and guides his people. He weaves all the tiny details of our lives together. This beautifully constructed narrative describes God's perfect plan. The drama of the quest for a wife for Isaac is magnificently portrayed by skilful use of repetition. When Abraham commissioned his servant to travel all the way back to Paddan-Aram (in north-west Mesopotamia) to find a wife for Isaac, one can fully understand the man's hesitation. 'Perhaps the woman may not be willing to follow me to this land' (24:5). Abraham, however, had no doubts. The Lord would provide an angel to go ahead of him. As the story unfolds, we see that this was indeed the case. The servant was guided to the right place and to the right woman. When the details of his journey were recounted to Rebekah's family, they could only conclude: 'The thing has come from the LORD' (24:50). The family consented to the match. Rebekah agreed to leave her family and friends and travel a vast distance to marry a man she had never met.

God's guidance is the major theme in this account. But neither Abraham nor the servant abdicated their responsibilities. Abraham did not just wait for a suitable bride for Isaac to arrive. He organized a hugely expensive expedition and sent his most trusted servant. The servant obeyed Abraham's instructions implicitly and prayed for a wife who would demonstrate kindness, hospitality, hard work, modesty and humility. God had already chosen Rebekah. He overruled every circumstance to ensure her marriage to Isaac. But he worked through the active, intelligent, prayerful obedience of Abraham and his servant.

In all our decisions, whether large or small, we are to be obedient to God's revealed will, as found in his Word. We are to pray for guidance. We are to act in faith. And then we are to be thankful for God's provision.

All the way my Savour leads me:
what have I to ask beside?
Can I doubt his tender mercy
who through life has been my guide?
Heavenly peace, divinest comfort
here by faith in him to dwell!
For I know, whate'er befall me,
Jesus doeth all things well

(Frances J. van Alsyne).

Prayer: Thank you, Lord God, for your wonderful providence, as illustrated so powerfully in this account. I pray that you would give me confidence that you have every detail of my life worked out for my good and for your glory.

Text for the day: *The LORD will guide you continually* (Isa. 58:11).

'Blessed are the dead who die in the Lord'

When the time came for Abraham to die, he could have been discouraged. Compared with the magnificent sweep of the promises, so little had come to pass. God had promised him the land; he only owned a burial field. God had promised a vast number of descendants; Isaac had no children. Looking back at his own life, Abraham had at times failed badly. But we are told that he died 'in faith'. He had not seen the things promised, but he believed that they would come to pass. His confidence did not rest in himself, but in God.

We often feel discouraged. Perhaps when we were converted we had great ideas of how the Lord could use us. But we may now feel that we have failed the Lord so often, that our lives have been so ordinary and that we have seen few of the great blessings we used to pray for so boldly. Maybe when we come to the end of life, we shall question whether it has counted for very much at all.

The perspective of faith is to look up to the Lord and see that he has ordained our lives as part of his great purpose. We are all links in a chain. Each of us has been called to praise and obey God where we are. It is comforting to remember that we are part of a worldwide church, and one that spans the ages:

As o'er each continent and island
the dawn leads on another day,
the voice of prayer is never silent,
nor dies the strain of praise away.

The sun that bids us rest is waking
our brethren 'neath the western sky,
and hour by hour fresh lips are making
thy wondrous doings heard on high.

So be it Lord! Thy throne shall never,
like earth's proud empires, pass away,

thy kingdom stands, and grows for ever,
till all thy creatures own thy sway

(John Ellerton).

Abraham could not see at the time how significant he was in the history of salvation, but he died believing that God would yet keep his promises. God did bless Isaac (Gen. 25:11); he is faithful to his word. We need to remind ourselves of the promises. God is bringing all things into subjection to Christ, the King of kings and Lord of lords. And so, however small our own part seems to be in the wider picture, we are given a beautiful assurance:

Therefore, my beloved brothers, be steadfast, immovable, always abounding in the work of the Lord, knowing that in the Lord your labour is not in vain (1 Cor. 15:58).

'Blessed are the dead who die in the Lord from now on.' 'Blessed indeed,' says the Spirit, 'that they may rest from their labours, for their deeds follow them!' (Rev. 14:13).

Abraham was willing to live the life of an alien and stranger, looking forward to the fulfilment of the promises. If we have that perspective, we will not hoard worldly goods now; we will be open-handed, investing in eternity, knowing that our real inheritance is in heaven. We will be ready to die.

Prayer: Lord, I worship you for the example of Abraham, the man of faith. I pray that I would live by faith today, and remember that I am only an alien and stranger in this world. Thank you for my inheritance in heaven.

Text for the day: *Blessed are the dead who die in the Lord* (Rev. 14:13).

'It depends not on human will or exertion, but on God, who has mercy'

God fulfils his promises by supernatural power. Ishmael, the son born by human contrivance, bore many children (Gen. 25:12-16). Isaac, the son of promise, was unable to have children for twenty years. As in the case of Sarah, when Rebekah conceived it was clearly a divine gift.

The account of Esau and Jacob is a powerful illustration of God's election. Justice would seem to demand that twins be treated equally. The bizarre struggle within her womb provoked Rebekah to ask the Lord what was going on. She was told that the younger son would take precedence and inherit the blessing. As Paul later pointed out, this was determined before either of them had done anything good or bad. We would have been unable to distinguish between the two unborn babies. God had their destiny mapped out. His choice of the 'number two' son went counter to the human tradition.

This account is brutally honest about the sinfulness of each member of the founding family. Esau lived for the moment. When he was hungry, he ignored any commitment to his inheritance. In selling his birthright (the pre-eminent place in the family) he showed himself to be a godless man (Heb. 12:16). His pagan wives made life a misery for his parents (Gen. 26:35). His life is a terrible warning for those of us who have been brought up with spiritual privileges. If we take them lightly, we can easily be sucked into living for the here and now, making material and physical comfort a priority. Esau eventually realized, too late, that he had lost the blessing for ever (Gen. 27:38).

Although Jacob was the son of God's choice, by nature he was no better than his brother. In many ways, his character was even less attractive. He took advantage of his brother's need in persuading him to give up his birthright. Later he brutally exploited his father's age and blindness. He tricked Isaac into giving him the blessing, aided by Rebekah, who showed no scruples about deceiving her husband.

Isaac does not come out of this story with any glory either. Despite God's firm promises of blessing (26:3-5) he showed himself willing to deceive Abimelech exactly as his father had done (26:7-9). Like his father he had to accept reproof from a pagan ruler (26:10). All this highlights the fact that God's covenant was a covenant of grace. God blessed Isaac with extraordinary prosperity, not because of any virtue, but because of his promise (26:4-5,12-13,24).

Despite his sins, Isaac showed himself to be a man of faith. God commanded him not to go down to Egypt at the time of famine, but to stay in the promised land (26:2). While he stayed in the land God prospered him. This provoked the jealousy and hostility of the Philistines, and yet Isaac persevered (26:18). God is sovereign, but we are responsible to obey. God chose Abraham out of sheer grace, but Abraham persevered and stood in the place of God's blessing (26:5). Isaac received the promises because of grace alone, but he too persevered and stayed in the place of God's blessing despite hardships. We have been saved by grace, but we must stand firm to the end (Matt. 10:22).

> *Your mercy, my God, is the theme of my song,*
> *the joy of my heart and the praise of my tongue;*
> *your free grace alone, from the first to the last,*
> *has won my affections and bound my soul fast*
> ('J. S.' in the *Gospel Magazine*, 1776).

Prayer: Almighty God, thank you that you choose to save and use sinners. Thank you for your free grace to me.

Text for the day: *It depends not on human will or exertion, but on God, who has mercy* (Rom. 9:16).

The blessing procured by deceit and trickery

If we have been familiar with this narrative since childhood, we may no longer be shocked at just how sinful and dysfunctional the chosen family was. Later in Israel's history some Jews were tempted to feel pride in their spiritual heritage. This account shows that there were no grounds for this!

When we look at Rebekah, it is no surprise that Jacob turned out to be a deceiver. She hatched the plot to cheat Esau. She may have rationalized the lie by remembering that Jacob was to be the son of blessing, but true faith would have left it to the Lord to work out. Jacob willingly went along with his mother's instructions. He was only anxious about being found out. He didn't care about the sin of deceiving his father or worry about what the Lord would think. Their plan was crude and almost laughably obvious. But it is an awful warning about how successfully we can excuse sin to ourselves.

For his part, Isaac ignored the oracle of God, which had specifically said that the blessing was to go to the younger son. He planned to give the blessing to his favourite, Esau. Moreover, he was driven by greed. Note the repeated emphasis on his love of delicious food (Gen. 27:4,7,9,14,17,31). Esau had shown his attachment to earthly priorities (red stew) over heavenly priorities (the birthright and associated blessing), but his father did not come far behind. It is tragicomic to see him anticipating the tasty stew so eagerly. It is also ironic that this man, so fond of taste and smell, was deceived by those senses into blessing his younger, less favoured son. Isaac also showed himself weak in not taking a lead in the family at an earlier point to provide suitable wives for his sons, a weakness deeply resented by his wife. His weakness and passivity were easily exploited by his devious wife and younger son.

When Isaac realized that he had been tricked by Jacob, his grief was intense, but he knew that this was from the Lord. God had intended that the blessing should go to the younger son. He accepted the Lord's will. Herein lay faith — not a heroic, un-tainted or consistent faith, but faith nevertheless. As Jesus says, if we have faith as a grain of mustard seed we shall prevail. The important thing is the one in whom we place our faith. We are weak, but he is mighty. The Lord's blessing was founded on his covenant promise to Abraham and his seed after him — on the promise, not on the virtue (or otherwise) of the recipients of the promise. The Lord's sovereign purposes would prevail, even working through human unbelief, greed and deceit. How encouraging it is that in the New Testament Isaac's sin is passed over and his faith is celebrated: 'By faith Isaac invoked future blessings on Jacob and Esau' (Heb. 11:20).

But sin does have consequences. This deceit would bear bitter fruit for the rest of Rebekah's life. She feared that the insanely jealous Esau would murder Jacob as soon as the elderly Isaac was out of the way. Pragmatism drove her to suggest what Isaac should have initiated earlier. Jacob must leave, and find a wife from her home country. She would never see her favourite son again. The deceit would also bring bitter consequences for Jacob. In the short term he may have thought he had got away with it. But Laban, a man even more deceitful than himself, was awaiting him. Jacob's deceit was to be turned back on him with a vengeance.

Prayer: O Lord, forgive me for rationalizing sin. Holy Spirit, please shine the spotlight of truth into my heart and mind to convict me of deceit and untruthfulness. Help me not to exaggerate, and not to embellish the truth so as to put myself (or those I love) in a good light. Help me not to exaggerate the failings of those I dislike.

Thank you for your grace in working in and through such sinners as Isaac, Rebekah and Jacob. Help me to remember that, like them, I am only ever a sinner saved by grace.

Text for the day: *So put away all malice and all deceit and hypocrisy and envy and all slander* (1 Peter 2:1).

'This is the gate of heaven'

God appeared to Jacob in a vision on his way out of the promised land, and then again on his way back. These appearances
bracketed his long years of exile. On both occasions the Lord
reassured Jacob. He would be the one to receive and pass on the
blessing promised to Abraham. His seed would inherit the land.
And both times Jacob responded in worship.

The first appearance of the Lord came in a dream. Exhausted
after a hard day's travelling, Jacob slept. As he slept he dreamed.
A stairway reached up to heaven, with angels ascending and
descending. At the top was the Lord. Jacob's eyes were opened to
the reality of the constant interchange between heaven and earth.
God continually sends his angels to minister on earth; they are
usually unseen. But whether or not we see it, the Lord has been, is
and will be sovereign in all the affairs of the world. He occupies
the supreme place. He is at the head of the stairway.

The Lord Jesus alluded to this incident in his words to Nathan-
iel: 'Truly, truly I say to you, you will see heaven opened, and the
angels of God ascending and descending on the Son of Man'
(John 1:51). Jesus Christ himself is the stairway, the only mediator
between God and man.

And he is always there for us. The stairway to heaven is never
closed. 'This is the gate of heaven' can be true for you at this very
moment, wherever you are. And at any time of day or night,
when you lift your heart to the Lord, praying in and through the
Lord Jesus, you can know that 'This is the gate of heaven.'

> Beneath the cross of Jesus
> I gladly take my stand:
> the shadow of a mighty rock
> within a weary land;
> a home within the wilderness,
> a rest upon the way,
> from the burning of the noontide heat,
> and the burden of the day.

Oh, safe and happy shelter!
Oh, refuge tried and sweet!
The appointed place where heaven's love
and heaven's justice meet!
As weary Jacob in his sleep,
that wondrous dream was given,
so seems my Saviour's cross to me —
a ladder up to heaven

(Elizabeth Clephane).

Prayer: Lord Jesus, I worship you that you came from heaven to earth to bring us from earth to heaven. I praise you that I can approach the Father in your name wherever I am and at any time. I pray that I would consciously live in the presence of God today because of what you have done for me.

Text for the day: *This is the gate of heaven* (Gen. 28:17).

The deceiver deceived

As Jacob fled for his life, he had been given wonderful promises and a glorious vision of God. These encouraged him as he continued his journey eastwards. Then, in a remarkable repetition of God's provision for Isaac, Jacob was led to exactly the right place and exactly the right family from which he could choose a wife. Everything seemed to be going so well. He showed his strength and initiative in rolling the heavy stone away from the well and watering the flocks for his beautiful cousin; her father gave him the warmest of welcomes, and within a month he had negotiated a marriage settlement. Yes, the terms were high: he would have to serve his uncle Laban for seven years. But 'They seemed to him but a few days because of the love he had for her' (Gen. 29:20).

Maybe it seemed to Jacob during these years that he had got away with the double deception he had perpetrated on his brother. After all, God had told his mother before their birth that the elder (Esau) would serve the younger (Jacob), so it was all within the plan of God. He worked his seven years, eagerly anticipating his marriage to the lovely Rachel.

But God had not forgotten Jacob's sin. Yes, he had brought Jacob to Rachel. But he had also brought Jacob to Rachel's father — a man who was even more adept at deception than Jacob. One can hardly imagine Jacob's helpless fury as he woke up after his wedding to find that he had been given Rachel's older sister, Leah. What an awakening! Laban had cleverly exploited Jacob's drunkenness, and the custom of taking brides fully veiled to their new husband's tent.

Just as Jacob himself had entered his father's tent, tricking Isaac into thinking he was the firstborn, so Leah had entered his own tent, tricking him because she was the firstborn. 'Why then have you deceived me?' demanded Jacob (29:25). Did he remember his father's words: 'Your brother came deceitfully and he has taken away your blessing'? (27:35). Jacob was trapped. He had slept with Leah, and he was landed with her. Yes, he could have Rachel as well, but would have to work seven more years for the crafty Laban and would always have to live with two rival wives, competing with each other for his attention. This was not a recipe for domestic happiness, as the following chapter shows.

The lesson is very clear. Even while God may bless us, if there are sins in our lives for which we have not repented, God will act to bring these to light. His aim is our holiness. He may bring very difficult people into our lives, but we should ask ourselves what lessons he wants us to learn through them. And when God disciplines us, he may ensure that we feel for ourselves the harm we have done to others.

Prayer: O Lord, I pray that you would show me if there are sins in my life for which I have not repented. I pray that you would show me if I have sinned against others and not resolved the issue. I pray that you would guard me from the evil of deceit. Help me to be honest and straightforward in all my dealings with others.

Text for the day: *Do not be deceived: God is not mocked, for whatever one sows, that will he also reap* (Gal. 6:7).

The birth of the patriarchs

Jacob had been brought up in a home where his parents had each favoured one son. The result had been constant sibling rivalry between him and his brother Esau. Now he had to live in a situation of constant sibling rivalry all over again, as Leah and Rachel vied for his attention. He had to face up to his own sin, seeing it now in close up. He had to experience like for like. There was an elegant justice about it.

Jacob was a consummate schemer. He had inherited this from his mother's family. Laban, his mother's brother, was more than his match. Rebekah, his mother, had plotted and schemed to get the birthright for Jacob. His cousins (now his wives), Leah and Rachel, showed the same ruthless capacity for manipulation. Each was determined to protect her own interests. This was not a happy household to live in. One can only imagine the bickering between the children of the rival wives in the early years. The bitter fruit was fully demonstrated in the pitiless treatment of Joseph by his brothers later on.

At the end of reading this somewhat sordid section, we might be tempted to ask, 'Did we have to know all this?'

The book of Genesis was written by Moses to explain to the nation of Israel how they had come into existence. They had nothing to be proud of. The patriarchal leaders had been born into a sinful family, as bargaining counters for rival wives to play off against each other. But the account makes it clear that God gave each of these children. God is sovereign over birth and death. Even in the midst of the rivalry between Leah and Rachel, we see a measure of faith in God shining through.

The lesson is exactly the same for the church. We are no better than anyone else. We have not been chosen because of our virtue or noble lineage. We are each chosen as sinners. We are each saved by grace. There is no room for pride.

The second lesson for the nation of Israel was that they had been born in strife. The constant tension between Leah and Rachel was played out in the lives of their sons. It was not surprising that the history of Israel was characterized by tribal

strife. This was tragic when we remember that the context for all
this was the glorious promise given to Abraham. The promise was
now being fulfilled; his seed was being multiplied. The purpose
was the blessing of all the nations, so we should surely have
expected harmony, unity and common purpose. Instead there
was squabbling.

But from the line of Leah's fourth son, Judah, the Prince of
peace would eventually be born. The *nation* of Israel failed to
fulfil God's purpose of bringing blessing to the nations, but
through the *seed* of Israel the 'true Israel' would come — Christ
and all united with him. In Christ all the promises to Abraham
would be abundantly fulfilled.

This brutally honest account shows the Lord using sinners to
fulfil his purposes. In the midst of these squalid family quarrels
God was driving forward his plan. He could have given up on
these selfish women, who used their slaves to further their own
ends. But he didn't. In all this, the seed of Abraham was multiplied and the foundations of the twelve tribes were laid.

Praise God that he uses sinners for his glory. That means he
can use you and me.

Prayer: Almighty God, I worship you that your wonderful
purpose of salvation was never allowed to fail. Thank you for
your grace to sinners. Thank you that you use sinners to drive
forward your plans. Thank you that you heard and answered the
prayers of Leah and Rachel, even though they were so unworthy.

Text for the day: *God chose what is low and despised in the
world, even things that are not, to bring to nothing things that are,
so that no human being might boast in the presence of God* (1 Cor.
1:28-29).

Met by angels

Twenty years earlier, when Jacob was leaving the promised land, the veil between heaven and earth had been lifted. He had seen the angels of God and, indeed, the Lord himself (Gen. 28:10-13). The Lord had confirmed the covenant promises to Jacob — that his offspring would possess the land and that all families on earth would be blessed through them (28:13-15). Jacob in his turn had affirmed his confidence in God, trusting God to bring him back to his father's home in peace (28:21).

Now the Lord had overruled, through the hostility of Laban, and had forced Jacob to return home. But his sin against Esau lay heavy on Jacob's conscience. Fear of Esau's hostility tormented him. He had said that he would trust the Lord to bring him back to his father's home 'in peace', but he felt no peace.

At the point of his re-entering the promised land, angels met Jacob. Angels are 'ministering spirits sent out to serve for the sake of those who are to inherit salvation' (Heb. 1:14). 'The angel of the LORD encamps round those who fear him, and delivers them' (Ps. 34:7). God promises to 'command his angels concerning you to guard you in all your ways' (Ps. 91:11).

> The hosts of God encamp around
> the dwellings of the just;
> deliverance he affords to all
> who on his succour trust.
>
> Fear him, ye saints, and you will then
> have nothing else to fear;
> make you his service your delight,
> your wants shall be his care
>
> (Nahum Tate and Nicholas Brady).

Jacob's eyes were opened to the reality of this normally unseen host. But he still panicked when he heard that his brother was fast approaching with his own host of retainers. He resorted to his own devices and his own wealth, sending ahead lavish gifts to try to pacify Esau. He was, in effect, attempting to give back the blessing he had stolen, even though in the sovereignty of God it had been made plain that he was heir.

Thus far, Jacob was a man who had trusted his own wits, made his own way and often resorted to manipulation and deceit. Now his desperate prayer did acknowledge that all his family and wealth had been the gift of God (Gen. 32:9-12), but his attempts at appeasement (32:13-21) revealed that he had not yet abandoned his own scheming. He was not yet humbled. He needed a final climactic encounter with God.

Prayer: O Lord, open my eyes. Thank you that you send angels to protect your people. Help me to trust in you alone, and never to resort to my own scheming to get me out of trouble.

Pray, specifically, for those you know who are ministering in difficult and dangerous situations. Pray that they too would be aware of divine protection and provision today.

Text for the day: *Are they [angels] not all ministering spirits sent out to serve for the sake of whose who are to inherit salvation?* (Heb. 1:14).

Wrestling with God

As a baby, Jacob had wrestled with his twin before birth; he came from his mother's womb grasping the heel of his elder brother. Hence his name, 'Jacob' (meaning, 'He takes by the heel' or 'He cheats'). God had told his mother that 'The older shall serve the younger' (Gen. 25:23), but instead of trusting God to fulfil this, Jacob twice cheated his brother Esau, once for the birthright (25:29-34) and then for the blessing (27:1-29).

Although he met his match in Laban, Jacob got the better of Laban too. He had begun to recognize that he owed his great prosperity to the Lord, but there had been a lot of scheming and manipulation along the way.

As the heir to the covenant blessing, Jacob had to acknowledge that the blessing was a gift of God. He had to renounce his old ways of scheming. At the end of this never-to-be forgotten night he lost his old name of 'deceiver'. Jacob had spent his life 'wrestling' against others. He had relied on his native wits and only intermittently relied on the Lord. Now the Lord met with him on the eve of his re-entry into the promised land. He wrestled with him by night, so that Jacob only gradually apprehended that it was a supernatural figure with whom he fought.

The climax of this mysterious and violent encounter was when the Lord dislocated Jacob's hip, marking him with a permanent reminder of his weakness and dependence. Jacob would always limp now. It was a physical sign of internal humbling. Then God renamed Jacob, giving him the new name Israel ('He strives with God' or 'God strives'). He also gave Jacob the blessing for which he had held on so long (32:26,29). Jacob then renamed the place Peniel ('The face of God').

Every Christian has to come to the point of recognizing that we have no strength apart from the Lord. It may not be through a single crisis experience, as with Jacob. It may involve a longer process of humbling. But, like Jacob, until we recognize our own utter weakness and dependence, we shall not receive the blessing.

Prayer: Use these three verses of Charles Wesley's great twelve-stanza poem on Jacob as your own prayer:

> Yield to me now; for I am weak,
> but confident in self-despair;
> speak to my heart, in blessings speak,
> be conquered by my instant prayer;
> speak, or thou never hence shalt move,
> and tell me if thy name is Love.
>
> I know thee, Saviour, who thou art,
> Jesus, the feeble sinner's Friend;
> nor wilt thou with the night depart,
> but stay and love me to the end;
> thy mercies never shall remove:
> thy nature and thy name is Love.
>
> Contented now upon my thigh
> I halt, till life's short journey end;
> all helplessness, all weakness, I
> on thee alone for strength depend;
> nor have I power from thee to move:
> thy nature and thy name is Love

(Charles Wesley).

Text for the day: 'Not by might, nor by power, but by my Spirit,' says the LORD of hosts (Zech. 4:6).

The rape of Dinah

Godly manhood should be exercised for the protection of others. All too often sin twists it towards lust, passivity or violence. The young girl Dinah was a victim of all three: the lust of Shechem, the passivity of her father and the violence of her brothers. Once she had been raped, she was regarded as 'spoiled goods' and no other man would want her. At least in this case (unlike that of Tamar, cf. 2 Sam. 13:1-20) Shechem subsequently wanted to marry her. But then he was murdered by Simeon and Levi. One can only imagine the subsequent sadness of Dinah's life — probably unmarried and without children, a situation which was despised and pitied. Dinah was not necessarily totally free of blame. To socialize with the pagan Canaanites was a recipe for disaster (Gen. 34:1). That, of course, did not excuse her violation.

Jacob, as head of the family, should have protected his daughter from pagan influences. Instead of showing godly leadership, he was passive and weak. He was spiritually compromised at this time. In Genesis 28:20-22 he had made a vow that if God cared for him, he would return to Bethel and give thanks. By the end of chapter 33 God had fulfilled all his promises to Jacob. But Jacob failed to return to Bethel. He settled down in Shechem and bought land (33:19). He did make some effort at acknowledging the Lord (33:20) but, as so often happens, prosperity led to complacency.

Having lived close by Shechem for seven or eight years, it seemed so natural for Dinah, the only daughter among many sons, to mix with the local girls. Of course she also met the local young men. Her father was too passive to protect her. She fell prey to the lust of the son of the local prince, who then wanted to marry her. This opened the whole scenario of intermarriage between God's people and the Canaanites. If the godly seed intermingled with the ungodly seed, the line of salvation would be jeopardized.

Jacob should have acted decisively and refused the marriage offer. He was paralysed by fear. His sons were furious at the failure of their father to protect the family honour, and they took a terrible revenge. To kill and loot a whole settlement because of the sin of one man was a grotesque injustice, but even after that Jacob was feeble in his protestations. Dinah saw her 'honour' being protected in a hideous way — a tragedy still played out in cultures where the men of a family see it as their 'duty' to protect female virtue, even when it means killing their own sisters or daughters.

This dark chapter warns of the danger of spiritual compromise. If we enjoy a time of peace, plenty and security, we need to beware of backsliding. It can have terrible effects.

This chapter also points to the need to protect our young people. All too often young teenagers are not given firm boundaries. They lose their virginity, with bitter consequences — emotionally, physically and spiritually.

It reminds us of the care we need to take in mixing with unbelievers. Too much socializing with those who reject biblical standards can lead to spiritual compromise, even entangling us into marriage with a non-Christian, which the Bible forbids.

This chapter leaves us without any clue as to Dinah's subsequent fate. Mercifully, elsewhere in Scripture, hope is offered to those women who suffer the violation of rape. The Old Testament law said that when a woman was violently raped, the man was guilty; she was innocent (Deut. 22:26). Godly women who have themselves been raped (such as Helen Roseveare, a missionary in the Congo) have been able to bring comfort to others by assuring them that in the eyes of God their inner purity is untouched. We can only trust that as the Lord showed mercy to Jacob (35:1), bringing him back from backsliding, so Dinah was included in the family repentance and restoration (35:4).

Prayer: Pray for wisdom to live 'in the world but not of the world'.

Text for the day: *'Go out from their midst and be separate from them,' says the Lord* (2 Cor. 6:17).

Repentance and restoration

After all the traumas of his earlier life, Jacob had settled down in Shechem. He had bought land and his family had become accustomed to mingling with the local idol-worshippers. His wife Rachel had never fully abandoned the idolatry of her father's home. Her theft of her father's household gods (Gen. 31:19) had gone undetected. It seems that the whole family was compromised by spiritual complacency, idolatry and backsliding. The tragedy of Dinah's rape had triggered off the appalling violence against the Shechemites, and Jacob feared their revenge (34:30).

How sad that good times often result in backsliding! Sometimes it takes a crisis to drive us back to the Lord. How gracious of God to receive us back in such circumstances! The Lord now reminded Jacob of the vow he had once made, to return to Bethel and worship there (35:1; 28:18-22). Jacob responded in repentance and faith. Idols and other charms were buried and clothes were ceremonially washed. God then protected the group from attack all the way back to Bethel.

God had met with Jacob at Bethel on his way out of Canaan. He had promised to give Jacob land, descendants, blessing to the nations through his family and protection (28:13-15). Now the return to Bethel brought Jacob's story to a natural conclusion. God had kept his promise and again promised future blessing. The command to 'be fruitful and multiply' (35:11) echoed the command given to the man and woman in the garden (1:28) and to Noah and his sons after the flood (9:1,7). In verse 15, when Jacob called the place Bethel, this confirmed the name actually given twenty years earlier. Similarly, when Jacob wrestled with the Lord at Peniel, he had been given a new name, Israel, 'He strives with God' (rather than Jacob, 'He cheats'). This new name was now confirmed (35:10).

The whole saga shows God's grace in choosing, calling, keeping and restoring a flawed and sinful man. We can take heart from this. We may look at our lives and ask how we can possibly expect a place in heaven. We may be painfully aware of disobedience, complacency and backsliding. Just as God enabled Jacob and his household to repent and return to him, so we are summoned today to the cross. We are never to say, 'I'm too sinful to return.'

The deaths of Deborah (Jacob's mother's nurse, who had been with the family for many years), Rachel and Isaac all pointed to the fact that an era was coming to an end. Rachel's death was especially poignant. It may have been a bitter reminder to her husband of her angry threat: 'Give me children, or I shall die!' (30:1). Even more terribly, unaware of his wife's deception, Jacob had invoked the curse of death on the one who stole his father-in-law's gods (31:32). The joy of the birth of another son was thus overshadowed by the death of the little boy's mother.

Jacob then had to suffer the treachery of his first son. Reuben, eldest son of Leah, resented the favour shown to Rachel's sons Joseph and Benjamin. When the head of a family died, it was the custom for the firstborn to take his concubine. Sleeping with Bilhah was Reuben's desperate ploy to assert his right as the firstborn. (Remember how his own father, Jacob, had been ruthless in asserting his claim to the birthright.) God would punish Reuben for this gross violation. The position he so badly craved was denied him (49:3-4). Yet, as one of the twelve patriarchs, he still had a special place in God's plan. As the saga of Jacob comes to a close, we are reminded again of the sinfulness of this founding family, and we marvel at the grace of God in choosing and using sinners such as them — and such as us.

Prayer: Praise God for his grace, that he always welcomes us back to the cross.

Just as I am, without one plea
but that thy blood was shed for me
and that thou bidd'st me come to thee,
O Lamb of God, I come

(Charlotte Elliott).

Text for the day: *Whoever comes to me I will never cast out* (John 6:37).

Faithful over God's house

Verse 1 of Genesis 37 really belongs with the previous chapter. If you glance quickly through chapter 36 you see a rather obscure list of ancient names. This is a record of the descendants of Esau, showing that this ungodly line achieved great power and fruitfulness incredibly quickly. A deliberate contrast is drawn between the dramatic prosperity of Esau (36:1-43) and the comparative obscurity of Jacob (37:1).

When Isaac blessed his two sons, he said that Jacob was the one who would carry forward the promises (27:29). Esau would 'live by the sword' and eventually 'break the yoke' of his brother from his neck (27:40). After Esau and Jacob met to bury Isaac (35:29), they separated. Esau moved south to the hill country of Seir (36:8). He and his sons and grandsons quickly became overlords of the various tribes in that region. He prospered; he 'broke the yoke' of Jacob from his neck; he lived by the sword. His father's oracle was fulfilled to the letter.

When Jacob tricked Esau by giving him red stew in exchange for the birthright, we are told that Esau was 'called Edom', which sounds like the Hebrew for 'red' (25:30). The name 'Edom', then, can mean three different things: Esau himself (36:1,8,19); the territory occupied by his descendants; and the Edomites who were descended from his sons and the Horite tribes they conquered. The Israelites were to understand that when the Edomites showed them bitter hostility (as when they were refused permission to go through Edom on the way back to the promised land — Num. 20:14-21), these people were the descendants of Esau.

The Israelites were also to learn from the fact that Esau seemed to prosper in every way (Gen. 36), while his brother Jacob was still just a sojourner, with very little outward status (37:1). God's people are often called on to be patient and faithful, while the wicked around them prosper (Ps. 73). At those times, do we trust God? Or do we succumb to bitterness and envy? We must remember that outward prosperity can increase rapidly, but it vanishes with death.

With the account of Jacob rounded off (37:1), the narrative then shifts its focus to Joseph, the son who was chosen to carry forward the purposes of God. The outstanding theme of Joseph's life was faithfulness to God in every circumstance. Whether exalted or despised, he trusted God. He was thus a type of the Lord Jesus, who was 'faithful over God's house as a son' (Heb. 3:6).

Israel (Jacob) was undoubtedly foolish to favour Joseph so blatantly. The gift of the richly ornamented cloak was probably a sign that he regarded Joseph as his heir, especially as Reuben, his firstborn, had forfeited the blessing by sleeping with his father's concubine (Gen. 35:22). Joseph's dreams, confirming that he was to be the leader in the family, compounded his brothers' hostility against him. They already hated him because he had 'brought a bad report of them to their father' (probably reported as an act of faithfulness, rather than a trivial case of tale-bearing).

The brothers could not see that the pre-eminence they so envied would be inextricably linked with suffering. Nor did they know that Joseph had been chosen by God in order to bring about their own salvation from famine.

These first few glimpses into Joseph's life introduce the theme of faithfulness despite opposition. The opposition Joseph faced was not from outside the people of God. It came from his own family. We may be faithful, and find that the opposition that hurts most comes from within the church.

Today, whether we are tempted to resent the prosperity of the wicked, or whether we are tempted to envy the pre-eminence of other believers, let us remember those words of Christ: 'What is that to you? You follow me!' (John 21:22).

Prayer: Almighty God, please help me to be faithful to you, and to be liberated from seeking the approval of others.

Text for the day: *What is that to you? You follow me* (John 21:22).

'See to it that ... no "root of bitterness" springs up'

If this account is familiar to you, try to imagine again the sheer horror of a group of older brothers ganging up on their second-youngest brother — not to taunt or tease, but to kill him. And consider that these were not just any brothers: they were the founding fathers of Israel, the representatives of God's old-covenant people, whose names are said to be inscribed on the gates of heaven (Rev. 21:12). Yet these men had become so consumed with bitterness and envy that they were ready to justify murder.

Given the brothers' open hatred, it was unwise of Israel to send Joseph on the mission to Shechem, but Joseph obeyed. 'Here I am' (Gen. 37:13) has poignant overtones of being willing to be offered up as a sacrifice. Moreover, he could easily have justified returning home when the brothers were not found at Shechem, but he persevered in the quest, fulfilling not only the letter but the spirit of his father's instruction.

The brutal cruelty of the brothers is highlighted in the account of Joseph's abduction. Having stripped him and thrown him into the pit, they sat down to a meal and then sold him for just twenty pieces of silver. Many years later, Joseph's desperate cries of distress still echoed in their ears (42:21). But they hardened their hearts and cynically deceived their father, using Joseph's robe dipped in blood. Once again, we see Israel's former deception of Esau (using the skins of young goats) coming back to haunt him. The brothers had grown up in a family where deception was endemic. It came only too naturally to them. Israel was deceived. He believed Joseph to be dead and was inconsolable.

The brothers' treatment of Joseph clearly foreshadows the treatment of Christ by his 'brothers' the Jews. Christ's own parable echoes the story of Joseph:

> But when the tenants saw him, they said to themselves, 'This is the heir. Let us kill him, so that the inheritance may be ours.' And they threw him out of the vineyard and killed him (Luke 20:14-15).

The exchange of Joseph in return for silver also foreshadows Christ's betrayal.

Cain murdered his brother Abel. Ishmael taunted Isaac. Esau hated Jacob and plotted to kill him. But Cain, Ishmael and Esau were not of the chosen line. Jacob's sons were within God's line of purpose. This is a terrible picture of hatred *within* the people of God. And what a sombre warning to us! If we begin to allow any root of bitterness or envy to fester in our minds, it can turn to hatred. Unless it is put to death, sin grows. All too often we nurse resentment against those who should be dearest to us: our spouse, our siblings, our fellow church members. We need to remember Jesus' warning that, as far as God is concerned, hatred is equivalent to murder (Matt. 5:21-22). Here and now let us repent of any resentment against others.

The news of Joseph's supposed death left Jacob in utter despair (Gen. 37:35). And yet, unbeknown to him, Joseph was on the first stage of a journey that was to lead to unthought-of elevation. How often we are in the place where all seems dark, when we are tempted to despair! And yet we have the whole of Scripture which teaches that God is absolutely sovereign. Nothing and no one is outside his control. His purpose in this world will go forward. God takes the worst sins, the most ghastly tragedies, and uses them for his greater glory. Weeping may last for a night, but there is joy in the morning. We may be discouraged, but we are never to despair.

Prayer: O Lord, forgive me for bitterness, resentment and anger. Cleanse me and fill me with your love for others. Thank you for your great grace and love towards me, in that while I was still full of enmity towards you, you set your love on me.

Text for the day: *See to it that ... no 'root of bitterness' springs up and causes trouble* (Heb. 12:15).

Judah's sin and Joseph's self-control

Chapter 38 is an unsparing account of Judah's sinfulness. The beginning of this chapter is something of a 'flashback'. It was a convention in Hebrew narrative to take an entire episode and place it in parallel alongside other episodes. Chronologically they may run in parallel like train tracks.

Judah decided to leave his father's household and set up home with a Canaanite at a relatively young age — sixteen or so. Here was a case of teenage rebellion. Instead of waiting patiently for his father to arrange a suitable match (as Isaac had done) he disobeyed God's clear command and risked the purity of the godly line by intermarrying with an idol-worshipper.

The point of this story is that, although God was raising up Joseph to lead his brothers and to save the whole family from extinction, it was through Judah that the line of the Messiah was to come (Gen. 49:8-12). But the line risked extinction when Judah's wicked first son was put to death by the Lord. Judah's second son avoided fathering an heir and was also put to death by the Lord. Judah's duty was then to give his widowed daughter-in-law to his third son, so that the family line could continue. He failed to do so (38:26). Tamar, in desperation, disguised herself in order to sleep with Judah and become pregnant. Judah at first hypocritically condemned her. When confronted with the fact that he was the father, he acknowledged that she was 'more righteous than I' (38:26). She alone had taken seriously the sacred duty of preserving the family line.

What amazing condescension that this incestuous union was part of the genealogy of Christ! (Matt. 1:3).

The theme of God's electing grace is further underlined by the birth of the twins. The 'younger' son, Perez, literally pushed the 'older' one out of the way, and thus took his place as the firstborn.

Judah had done wrong in taking a pagan wife; he had compounded his sin by failing to do the right thing for his daughter-in-law. He then used a prostitute, but hypocritically condemned Tamar for immorality when she conceived out of wedlock. It is a pitiful saga of lust, unfaithfulness and selfishness. It stands in stark contrast to the virtue of Joseph in chapter 39. He maintained his integrity when tempted by Potiphar's wife, insisting on his duty to be faithful to his master and to God.

The theme of Joseph's life was that the Lord was with him (39:2,21). This was the key to his success. It was awareness that God was with him that strengthened him to resist the temptation that could have wrecked his prospects of future usefulness (39:12). 'How then can I do this great wickedness and sin against God?' he asked (39:9). It is only a sense of the presence of God that equips us to resist the temptations of Satan. A moment-by-moment sense of the reality of his presence can only be maintained when we are obedient. Obedience may not 'pay' in the short term. For Joseph the consequence was to be thrown into prison. But the Lord was with him there as well.

These chapters also paint a dramatic contrast between two women. Tamar, from a pagan background, still had an overriding sense of responsibility to maintain the family line. She had not been paralysed into inactivity and despair by her plight as a childless widow. She seized the initiative. At the end of Ruth the people who gather to congratulate Boaz on his marriage say, 'May your house be like the house of Perez, whom Tamar bore to Judah' (Ruth 4:12). The wife of Potiphar, by contrast, had no sense of responsibility at all. She was driven by lust and selfishness. She ignored her responsibility to her husband. When spurned by Joseph, she was ruthless in condemning him to appalling punishment. She is the epitome of the 'foolish woman' as so dramatically portrayed throughout the book of Proverbs.

Prayer: O Lord, help me to see sin as that thing which you hate, and help me to fear displeasing you above all else. 'Keep back your servant ... from presumptuous sins; let them not have dominion over me!' (Ps. 19:13).

Text for the day: *How then can I do this great wickedness and sin against God?* (Gen. 39:9).

The way up is down

Life seems so unfair sometimes! Cruelly treated by his brothers, Joseph had been raised from a pit only to be sold into slavery. Then, having worked his way up to a position of respect, he found himself the subject of malicious false accusation and thrown into a dungeon along with criminals. Slavery was bad; imprisonment was worse. It looked as though God had abandoned him.

Now, truly, the 'iron entered into his soul' (Ps. 105:18, *Young's Literal Translation*). Joseph still wept for the loss of his father, the rejection of his brothers and, now, for his loss of reputation and freedom. But he did not fall into the despair of inactivity. He did not disdain the menial work assigned to him. He worked so faithfully that he found favour in the eyes of the warder, and he was given even greater responsibilities. Here, in the prison, as in Potiphar's household, the Lord gave him success in everything (Gen. 39:20-23). Far from being consumed with self-pity, Joseph looked out for the interests of others and enquired about the well-being of his fellow-prisoners. This brought the opportunity to seek the Lord's help in interpreting their dreams. Joseph proved faithful in passing on the interpretation, even when it cannot have been easy. But what an encouragement to Joseph when the interpretations proved to be exactly correct in every detail! In the ongoing darkness of the long years of imprisonment, this knowledge that God still spoke to him gleamed like a golden thread through the gloom.

For even the certain revelation from God of the meaning of the dreams, and Joseph's plea to the released cupbearer, did not bring immediate release. Joseph had to go on waiting. The chapter ends so poignantly: the cupbearer 'forgot him'. It must have seemed as if God had forgotten him too. But Joseph waited patiently. This is the meaning of faith: going on serving, obeying, believing — even when everything seems against us. True faith perseveres despite the bleakest circumstances.

This chapter's theme is plain: faithful service in the small things and patiently waiting God's time for release. Joseph foreshadows the supreme faithfulness and patience of the Lord Jesus Christ.

Joseph was unjustly accused; so was Jesus. Joseph was cruelly treated; so was Christ. It seemed as if God had forgotten Joseph. 'My God, my God, why have you forsaken me?' cried our Lord on the cross.

> For to this you have been called, because Christ also suffered for you, leaving you an example, so that you might follow in his steps. He committed no sin, neither was deceit found in his mouth. When he was reviled, he did not revile in return; when he suffered, he did not threaten, but continued entrusting himself to him who judges justly (1 Peter 2:21-23).

Whatever you are suffering today, remember that God has promised: 'I will never leave you.' And if you are suffering unjustly, remember that we are to leave judgement to God. He judges justly. Be faithful. Be patient.

> Trouble may break with the dawn,
> and evil may come and darkness will fall;
> clouds will appear in the sky
> and tears in our eyes and pain in the soul.
> But God stands at his people's side,
> gives them a place to hide,
> rescues and saves them, takes them to heaven
> and in his own dear Son he brings them home
> > (Malcolm Macgregor).

Prayer: Almighty God, keep me faithful. And keep me patient. Thank you for the supreme example of the faithfulness and patience of the Lord Jesus Christ.

Text for the day: For to this you have been called, because Christ also suffered for you, leaving you an example, so that you might follow in his steps (1 Peter 2:21).

God's control of the nations

Who is in control of the world today? The media would have us believe that politicians, business leaders and multi-national corporations are pulling the strings. They call on economic forecasters, scientists and political spin doctors for wisdom. In the 1890s BC, Pharaoh of Egypt was the most powerful international figure of his day. He trusted astrologers and magicians for advice. But in this chapter we see him at a loss. He had a dream which unnerved him, leaving him feeling ignorant and powerless. It dawned on him that he was not as in control as he imagined. His advisers were helpless. What was going to happen to him? And what was about to overshadow his kingdom?

This is the moment for which God had prepared Joseph. He came before Pharaoh, unabashed at the glory and splendour around him. He was calm and confident. He knew he was servant of the Most High God, the Maker and Sovereign of Pharaoh and all his court. He explained that he could not interpret Pharaoh's dream, but he knew that God would (41:16,28,32). God had revealed the future so that wise plans could be set in place to protect the peoples of the earth from appalling famine.

Today the nations are in darkness regarding the truth of God. Scientists, researchers, economic forecasters, politicians, business leaders — none predict the future with certainty. God has revealed what we need to know of the future. He speaks today through his Word just as clearly as he spoke then through his servant Joseph. Pharaoh took the warning that was given. But will our leaders today listen?

> Why do the nations rage
>   and the peoples plot in vain?
> The kings of the earth set themselves,
>   and the rulers take counsel together,
>   against the LORD and against his anointed, saying,
> 'Let us burst their bonds apart
>   and cast away their cords from us.'

He who sits in the heavens laughs;
the Lord holds them in derision

(Ps. 2:1-4).

Pharaoh acknowledged the Lord's words and recognized that Joseph should take leadership of the nation through the years of plenty and then of famine. Raised to the highest place, Joseph demonstrated statesmanship, organizational ability and political skill. Egypt not only successfully came through the seven terrible years of famine, but managed to supply the surrounding nations as well. In all this Joseph never became proud. Blessed with wealth, recognition and a family, he gave his sons Hebrew names, and attributed all his success to the Lord (Gen. 41:51-52). He still bore the scars of the rejection by his brothers, but the Lord had eased the pain (41:51). Clearly Joseph did not forget his family; he was desperately anxious to enquire about his father when his brothers arrived in Egypt. But the wounds of the past were being healed.

It seems so extraordinary that the younger son of an obscure family should find his way through slavery and prison to take the place of highest authority. But that is God's way: a small nation, an insignificant family, a stable in Bethlehem, a carpenter who was crucified — and this man exalted to be King of kings and Lord of lords, the one to whom every knee will bow!

Whatever the local, national and international situation today, what a glorious assurance that the affairs of the nations are all being superintended by the Sovereign Lord! Not only so, but he is directing all things for the good of his people, and for his own glory.

Prayer: Praise the triune God for his sovereign control of all things. Praise him that he is overruling every detail of your life today. Take time to commit all your plans to him.

Text for the day: *You alone are holy. All nations will come and worship you* (Rev. 15:4).

Awakening conscience

When Joseph was just a youth God had revealed that he would one day lead his family. Through all the hardship of the intervening years, Joseph never lost his faith in the Lord. When brought to stand before the most powerful leader in the world, he expressed total reliance on God (Gen. 41:16). He demonstrated complete humility (he could not interpret dreams, but God could), but also total confidence (God was in control of his destiny, and that of Pharaoh and the whole nation). That combination of humility and confidence were the hallmarks of his extraordinary leadership. He remained as totally dependent on the Lord as he had been in the pit, in the slave caravan and in the prison.

As the years rolled on, the fulfilment of his dreams grew nearer. Joseph wisely stewarded the vast resources of Egypt during the seven years of plenty. Then, when famine bit Egypt and the surrounding nations, he was given the responsibility of organizing and selling the reserves of grain. God gave him wisdom so that many lives would be spared, especially the lives of the covenant family. Eventually Jacob sent his sons (minus Benjamin) to buy grain from Egypt. Jacob's dread that something might befall Rachel's only remaining son must have stirred up once more the brothers' memories of their heinous treatment of Joseph.

When the ten brothers bowed before Joseph with their faces to the ground, the dreams of long before were at last fulfilled. Joseph knew it. But he did not enlighten his brothers. He was called by God to be the leader of his family. As a true leader, he was not interested in merely asserting authority over his brothers. He did not want terror and fear; he did not want to exact revenge. He wanted to see changed hearts. He longed for genuine repentance, which was a necessary prerequisite for real reconciliation. Joseph carefully managed each scene so as to awaken the consciences of his brothers. They were given a taste of the various experiences he had suffered: false accusation, imprisonment, the feeling of powerlessness. If these men had been hardened it would have been a waste of time. But they rapidly realized that

God was punishing them for the sins committed against Joseph twenty years earlier. They remembered Joseph's cries of anguish and their own callous refusal to listen (42:21). The mystery of their money being replaced in their sacks added to their sense of foreboding and guilt. Their respect and concern for their father contrasted with their earlier resentment. They now accepted that Benjamin was special, as he was the only remaining son of Rachel (42:37).

The process of bringing Joseph's brothers to true repentance took two long years. Joseph, no doubt, longed to see his father and Benjamin more quickly. He could have made himself known straight away. A quicker, superficial 'reconciliation' would have resulted. But he would never have really known the true state of his brothers' hearts. They would have said all the right things, simply because Joseph was now in a position of power and wealth. Twice in this chapter the brothers protest: 'We are honest men' (42:11,31). Twice Joseph says that he will test them to see whether they are indeed 'honest men' (42:19,33). This testing would, necessarily, take time. As a wise leader, Joseph was willing to wait.

Joseph's wisdom is a reminder that, in our desire to be Christlike, we need not be foolish or naïve. For example, if an abusive husband is beating up his wife, often the first instinct is to call for 'reconciliation'. But if the man is unrepentant (something that has to be tested by time, as all too many abusers are all too plausible with words), that wife should not be sent back into danger. Separation for the sake of her safety and that of the children may be needed, and the aim is to bring the husband to true repentance.

Prayer: Father God, I pray that you would show me any unconfessed sin in my life, and give me true repentance.

Text for the day: *Repent, and do the works you did at first* (Rev. 2:5).

The testing of the brothers

The whole point of the events of these two chapters was to test the brothers for jealousy. First of all, Benjamin was given special treatment at the banquet (Gen. 43:34). If this had happened to Joseph twenty years previously, the brothers would have been consumed with rage. Now they did not resent Benjamin's special treatment. Back at home they had already accepted that Benjamin was their father's favoured son. Judah had personally guaranteed his safety (43:9) as, previously, had Reuben (42:37).

When the brothers arrived in Egypt, they were amazed to be invited to the ruler's house for a meal (43:16-18). God had been stirring their consciences. They were feeling so guilty that anything, whether good or bad, made them feel that their sins had been remembered. 'It must be the silver,' they thought. They had professed to be honest men and now wanted a chance to clear their names.

Perhaps today you are feeling guilty about something. It may be a sin against others, or it may be a private matter which no one else knows about. If conscience is nagging, this is a gift of God. It should drive us back to the Lord, not away from him. Here, once the issue had been brought out into the open, the brothers were reassured: 'Your God and the God of your father has put treasure in your sacks for you' (43:23). The steward was saying, 'Evidently your God wants you to have your silver, because my accounts are fine.' Their consciences were pacified at that level.

Then the real test came. The cup was placed in Benjamin's sack. It looked as though he had stolen it, and the steward demanded that he return to Egypt as Joseph's slave. If the brothers' hearts had been unchanged, they would have given Benjamin over into slavery and accepted the free pardon held out to them. But they were different men from what they had been when they sold Joseph into slavery. They could not conceive of putting their father through that suffering again (44:13). Judah was true to the guarantee he had given his father (43:9). He offered to serve as Joseph's slave in place of Benjamin (44:33). He spoke with true feeling of the love his father had for Benjamin. His speech demonstrated the genuine transformation which had taken place in his own life and that of his brothers (44:18-34).

Instead of the animosity they once showed towards Joseph, there was now self-sacrifice. Judah's pledges in 43:8-9 and 44:33-34 form the beginning and end of this section. These were changed men. The trial had worked. Their confession was plain (44:16). They were not spies, nor was Benjamin a thief, but through these false accusations they had been forced to acknowledge their real guilt. There is much 'discovery' in this section about 'hidden cups', but it is the brothers who have been uncovered.

Now the true nature of repentance is revealed. It is not simply feeling sorry, nor even a confession of sin. It is a complete turning around, a change of mind and heart. Before there was animosity; now there is love. Before, hatred was prepared to sacrifice a brother; now loyalty is prepared to sacrifice self rather than the brother. These are brothers wholly committed to unity now. The foundations are laid for a true nation, not a squabbling rabble.

In contrast to their earlier selfishness and hatred, the brothers have shown responsibility (willingness to take the blame for any disaster); integrity (making restitution for money in their sacks); unity (retrieving their brother from prison) and gratitude for provisions (even when another was favoured above them).

Prayer:
  Search me, O God, and know my heart!
    Try me and know my thoughts!
  And see if there be any grievous way in me,
    and lead me in the way everlasting

                                          (Ps. 139:23-24).

Text for the day: *Search me, O God, and know my heart!* (Ps. 139:23).

Reconciliation

This is a delightful account, full of human warmth. It is all about
family reconciliation. This was only possible on the basis of
genuine repentance. Joseph had patiently waited as the reality of
the brothers' changed hearts was demonstrated. There was no
doubt now. The forgiveness he offered was full and free. For a
man so wronged, he showed remarkable absence of rancour.
There was a genuine love for the brothers (Gen. 45:2,4). He
wanted them all to move to Egypt. Their sin against him was put
behind them (45:5). That is real forgiveness: treating the offender
as if he had never sinned.

I wonder if when we forgive, we forgive like this. But we
should remember how the Lord forgives us. He gives us that
warm and welcoming embrace, like the father of the prodigal
come back home again. That is the standard of forgiveness which
is expected in the Christian church.

But while it is quite simple to understand, all of us must
acknowledge that to offer forgiveness of this quality is far from
simple in practice. What about all the painful memories? How did
Joseph manage to put those behind him? His secret against
bitterness was an understanding of the sovereignty of God
(45:5,7). Did this mean that the crime of the brothers didn't really
matter because it resulted in good? Did he say that they hadn't
really committed a crime and that repentance wasn't necessary?
No, not at all. The brothers had sinned, and that demanded real
repentance and real forgiveness. But Joseph was saying that he
was not bitter about what had happened. He would not hold it
against the brothers now that there was repentance, because God
had used it for good.

Imagine that someone has offended against you. Maybe even
a crime has been committed against you. But you are also able to
say that all of this has happened within God's sovereign purpose.
This event has made you ultimately more humble, it has made
you more dependent on the Lord in some way. It has put you in
a situation where your faith has been tested. And by the end of it,
you are able to say, 'Whatever that offender meant by hurting me

in that way, I can see that in the providence of God it has been used for some good in my life.'

It was easier for Joseph in one way, because he saw the repentance, the change in his brothers. Sometimes we never do receive an apology, either because the person is unaware even of having done wrong, or is too thick-skinned to think about it. What then? Can we accept it without bitterness? Or what of the offender who does say 'Sorry', but then offends again? What did Jesus say? 'Forgive us our sins, for we also forgive everyone who is indebted to us' (Luke 11:4). What strong words those are! Yet here is Joseph as a picture of God's own forgiveness. He wanted to make them feel accepted again; he wanted them to forget the crime, to know that they were unreservedly forgiven. He gave them gifts and the promise of a new future with him in Egypt.

This is a lovely picture of God's acceptance of us in Christ, possible because Christ himself prayed: 'Father, forgive them, for they do not know what they are doing' (Luke 23:34, NIV).

Prayer: Father, thank you for your wonderful love and grace. Help me to forgive others, even as you have forgiven me.

Text for the day: *Forgive us our debts, as we also have forgiven our debtors* (Matt. 6:12).

God's blessings for his people, and for the Egyptians

We can hardly imagine the astonishment and joy Jacob felt when he heard that his beloved son Joseph was not only still alive, but in such an exalted position. Preparations were made immediately for the trip down to Egypt and the reunion of father and son.

But leaving the promised land was not a step to be taken lightly. Jacob was apprehensive and offered sacrifices to the Lord at Beersheba, the southernmost part of the land of Israel. Once he left Beersheba, he would be entering Gentile territory. Would God still be with him? The Lord spoke to reassure him (Gen. 46:2-4). He repeated the promise given to Abraham: Jacob's family would become a great nation. But that growth would take place down in Egypt. In the providence of God, this would be the place where they would have the room and the resources to grow and flourish and prosper as a nation. God would bring them back up to the promised land when (as he had explained to Abraham) the sin of the Amorites was complete.

God had carefully planned everything for the good of his people. He prepared the land of Egypt for them, and even the prejudice of the Egyptians against shepherds was overruled to keep the chosen people pure, away from danger of intermingling with the Egyptians. The sending of Joseph down into Egypt and his exaltation and wise leadership were all designed to further God's purposes for his covenant people. Although this family of seventy people didn't seem to be that significant on the international scene, they were actually at the very centre of God's great purpose for the world (45:5,7). Joseph was used to save very many lives — not only his own family, but also vast numbers of Egyptians and other nationalities too. But it was his family which was closest to the heart of God.

The riches and pride of Egypt are deliberately contrasted with the earthly insignificance of the chosen family. Jacob, who had for years humbly tended flocks, assumed the spiritual authority to bless Pharaoh, the greatest world leader of his day (47:7,10). Eternal treasure outweighs earthly treasure. In God's plan, that

Genesis 46 - 47   Day 44

particular pharaoh is not even remembered by his own name.
Jacob's new name, Israel, became the name of God's chosen
people; it is still the name of an earthly nation, but still more
significantly, the church is named as the 'Israel of God'.

God's purpose was always to bless many nations through his
chosen people: 'In you all the families of the earth shall be
blessed,' he promised Abram (12:3). When Pharaoh promotes
Joseph and then shows favour to his family, God blesses him in
return (47:13-26). Egypt prospered as long as the chosen people
were treated well. But later on, when God's people were oppressed, Egypt suffered as a result.

This account points to the sovereignty of God in ruling the
nations for the good of his covenant people (45:7-8). As we pray
for our world today, is this our hope? God is building a kingdom
for his Son, and every local, national and international event is
part of his great purpose. As Joseph pointed out to his brothers,
even their sin had been overruled by the Sovereign Lord (45:5,8;
50:20).

*Kings shall bow down before him
and gold and incense bring;
all nations shall adore him,
his praise all people sing:
to him shall prayer unceasing
and daily vows ascend;
his kingdom still increasing,
a kingdom without end*

(James Montgomery).

Prayer: Sovereign God, I worship you for your great plan to
bring blessing to all nations in Christ.

Text for the day: *All the ends of the earth have seen the
salvation of our God* (Ps. 98:3).

'God meant it for good'

God's programme for his covenant people was being fulfilled (Gen. 15:13-14). He had saved his chosen family from starvation by taking them safely down to Egypt. He would keep them there, separated from intermingling in the region of Goshen, until the clan of seventy people had multiplied into a great nation. His purpose was that they should then return to the promised land. Jacob's burial alongside Abraham, Sarah and Leah signalled faith in this promise (49:29-32; 50:13). Similarly, Joseph declined the state funeral in Egypt that would have been his by right and ordered that his body should be kept and carried up into the promised land at a later date (50:25; Exod. 13:19; Josh. 24:32).

The writer to the Hebrews gives a poignant reminder of the turning point in Jacob's life in quoting the Septuagint (Greek) translation of Genesis 47:31, describing Jacob as 'bowing in worship over the head of his staff' (Heb. 11:21). When the Lord wrestled with Jacob and touched his hip, Jacob was left limping for the rest of his life. Leaning on a staff for support was a daily reminder of the lesson he learned that night to abandon his own scheming and rely on God alone. His self-reliance had cost him years of suffering (Gen. 47:9). His later years saw faith rewarded, and he could die in confidence that God's purposes for his offspring would indeed be fulfilled.

A key theme in the patriarchal narratives is the way that the Lord subverts the natural order of things to demonstrate that blessing is given by grace. God planned to bless the younger son, Jacob, ahead of the elder son, Esau. Instead of waiting patiently, Jacob had interfered, seeking to bring it about by his own deceitful scheming, something for which he had paid dearly. But in the last years of his life he acknowledged the Lord's sovereign right to prefer the younger ahead of the older. In obedience to divine guidance he blessed his younger grandson Ephraim ahead of the older grandson Manasseh, despite Joseph's protest (48:17-20).

The prophetic oracles delivered by Jacob to his sons in the last hours of his life also demonstrate his strong faith. Each of his twelve sons was blessed. Each would produce offspring who would return to the promised land. The eldest three had forfeited the chance of the birthright by means of sin. (Reuben had slept with his father's concubine as a premature attempt to grasp leadership in the family; Simeon and Levi had been appallingly violent in revenging the rape of their sister). Judah, despite the sin outlined in chapter 38, had proved himself a worthier son. His genuine repentance for his part in the sin against Joseph had been proved when he offered to sacrifice himself in the place of Benjamin (44:18-34). Although the primary blessing and birthright were reserved for Joseph, it was from Judah that the line of kings would come: David, Solomon and, ultimately, Christ (49:10).

These concluding chapters highlight Joseph's wisdom, as he continued to administer Egypt (47:13-26), his generosity of spirit, as he confirmed his full forgiveness of his brothers' sin against him (50:15-21) and his strong confidence in the promises of God, as he ordered that his bones be carried up into the promised land (50:24-25). Most of all, we see his unshakeable trust in the sovereignty of God: 'You meant evil against me, but God meant it for good, to bring it about that many people should be kept alive' (50:20).

Prayer: Almighty God, I worship you and praise you that you work all things together for good for those who are called according to your purpose. Please increase my confidence in your sovereignty today.

Text for the day: *And we know that for those who love God all things work together for good, for those who are called according to his purpose* (Rom. 8:28).

Two midwives stand against the king

This book records God's mighty deliverance of his covenant people from Egypt. (Exodus means 'departure'.) It is a direct continuation of Genesis. God had told Israel on his way down from Canaan to Egypt that he would make his family into a great nation while they stayed in Egypt, but that he would then restore them to the promised land (Gen. 46:3-4). So Exodus 1:1 picks up the story of Israel's sons in Egypt, and then we hear of the amazing multiplication of his family.

The Israelites were in Egypt for 430 years altogether (Exod. 12:40-41). The period between Joseph's death and the rise of the 'new king' (1:8) was over 200 years. During that time, the small clan of seventy had multiplied into a great nation. God's promise had been fulfilled. For a long time, life had been pleasant. While the memory of the wise ruler Joseph lingered, they had been favoured. Eventually, that memory faded and the Hebrews were reduced to cruel slavery. All this was part of God's plan. Without this oppression, they would never have chosen to leave.

The oppression grew systematically worse: first the extortion of forced labour, ultimately the attempt to wipe out the people by murdering their baby boys. The 'seed of the serpent' was attempting to eliminate the 'seed of the woman' (Gen. 3:15), but God would never let this happen. He was with his people through these years of suffering, thwarting all attempts to wipe them out and blessing them with numerous offspring (Ps. 105:24). Outwardly, Pharaoh would have seemed to be perhaps the most powerful man on earth at the time. But in fact he was a pawn of Satan. And this book shows the way in which he was confronted by a far greater King, before whom he was impotent.

When the mighty King of Egypt summoned Shiphrah and Puah into his presence and commanded them to tell the other midwives to kill the Hebrew baby boys, they faced a stark choice. They could obey Pharaoh — or God. Shiphrah and Puah knew that, whatever Pharaoh might do to them, God was greater and must be obeyed. Their faith was precious to God, and he protected them from the wrath of Pharaoh. When they were summoned back to explain themselves, God overruled so that the story they came up with satisfied the king sufficiently to ensure that they were not punished. And he rewarded them with children of their own.

In Egypt, the pharaohs loathed the idea that when they died their memory might be forgotten. Hence the massive pyramids named after them and the elaborate rites to embalm and preserve their bodies. But today we have to search hard to find out the name of this king! By contrast, Shiphrah and Puah are still honoured by all those who read the Bible, because they made a stand for God in a generation which hated him and persecuted his people. In the midst of very ordinary lives, when faced with a conflict of loyalty, they chose to obey God rather than men (Acts 4:19; 5:29). God was kind to those women. Are you facing a conflict of loyalty at the moment? Will you obey God or men?

The faithfulness of Shiphrah and Puah is still reflected today in those Christian nurses and doctors who are disadvantaged and discriminated against for their refusal to take part in abortion and infanticide in hospitals. But God is pleased with them. We must take courage from this chapter to fear God and make a stand for him, even in the mundane and ordinary details of our lives. When God's people remain loyal and faithful in a generation which hates him and hates his people, he will honour them.

The chapter ends on a dark note. Foiled in his efforts to intimidate the midwives, Pharaoh commanded that the baby boys were to be drowned. This was the lowest point of Israel's oppression. It may have seemed that God had deserted them. But in fact their deliverance was already planned out. The following chapters record the outworking of that plan.

Prayer: O Lord, please help me to be faithful and obedient to you today, whatever the cost.

Text for the day: *We must obey God rather than men* (Acts 5:29).

God heard, God remembered, God saw and God knew

The birth of God's deliverer (Exod. 2:2) was fraught with suspense. Would Pharaoh's edict be obeyed? Once again, Pharaoh was thwarted by women — Jochebed, Miriam and his own daughter. Moses' mother was determined to save her child, whatever the risk. Her initiative is highlighted. She hid him in defiance of the king's edict. She devised the scheme to place him in a papyrus basket in the Nile. She set his sister to keep watch. God wonderfully overruled so that she was paid to nurse her own child. Once again, Pharaoh was made to look very foolish. Not only had this Hebrew boy not been killed, but the resources of Pharaoh's own household were used for his maintenance and eventually he was brought up as a prince of Egypt.

God planned every detail of Moses' life, so that he was completely prepared for his great task. The fact that he was a beautiful child contributed to his mother's determination to save him and the princess's resolve to adopt him. The employment of his own mother as nurse gave him an early grounding in the worship of the one true God. Education as an Egyptian prince equipped him with the literary skills needed for the writing of the first five books of the Bible. It also provided the leadership and military skills needed for taking the people out of Egypt and through the wilderness (Acts 7:22).

But the most important factor was his being brought up to love and fear the Lord. For, when Moses had grown up, he had to make a momentous choice. He had experienced the wealth and privileges of royalty. The Hebrew people were dreadfully oppressed. Would he remain at court, to enjoy its pleasures and comforts? Or would he stand with his own people? (Heb. 11:24-26). His choice was based on the knowledge of God that he had seen in his parents, that he had been taught in his earliest years and had not forgotten. 'One generation shall commend your works to another, and shall declare your mighty acts' (Ps. 145:4).

What a testimony to the importance of godly parents! If God blesses us with children, we have the privilege and responsibility to teach them about him, not only in words, but by our whole life. In just a few years Moses' parents instilled into their son a love and fear of God that could not be erased by many years of pagan education and ungodly influence. It is fitting that they take their place among the heroes of faith (Heb. 11:23).

God had much to teach Moses before he was ready to lead the people. His catastrophic failure to deliver his people in his own strength led to forty years of exile. He endured this period of physical preparation, acquiring exact knowledge of the terrain in which he was to lead the people for the next four decades. He also underwent equally important spiritual preparation. As this highly educated Egyptian prince shepherded flocks in the wilderness he learned humility and patience.

After eighty years, Moses was ready to deliver the covenant people. In many ways he foreshadowed the one who would deliver his people from spiritual slavery and bring them to freedom. As infants, both Moses and Jesus were threatened with death by evil rulers; both were supernaturally delivered. Jesus was taken down into, and then brought up out of, Egypt (Matt. 2:13-15), which evoked memories of the Exodus. The word 'exodus', translated 'departure', is deliberately used of his mission in Luke 9:31.

Both Moses and Jesus were sent on a rescue mission by the covenant-keeping God, who saw the plight of his people, and determined to save them. As the Hebrews groaned under inhumane conditions, he 'heard', he 'remembered', he 'saw' and he 'knew' (Exod. 2:24-25).

Prayer: If you are a parent, take time to give thanks for the great privilege of commending God's works to your children, and pray for wisdom in fulfilling this task. If not, pray for children and young people you know, that they may learn of God's works.

Text for the day: *One generation shall commend your works to another, and shall declare your mighty acts* (Ps. 145:4).

'I will be with you'

This day dawned like any other, but it was to be the turning point in the history of God's people. 400 years had passed without any direct communication from God, but now the Lord met with Moses and commissioned him for his great task. Nothing that Moses might have experienced if he had remained at the court of Pharaoh compares to this — a meeting with the living God. God revealed himself in the form of fire, symbolizing his perfect holiness. When Moses approached, he removed his sandals to show reverence for God's purity. He instinctively covered his face.

The message the Lord gave Moses was one of grace. He had heard his people's cries; he was going to rescue them, and Moses was going to lead them (Exod. 3:10). Moses' reaction was one of incredulity: 'Who am I...?' (3:11). God replied, 'I will be with you' (3:12). As Adoniram Judson, the great missionary to Burma, once said, 'Nothing is difficult for omnipotence.' It was not Moses who was going to do the rescuing. It was God.

Moses' next three questions conveyed a deep sense of personal inadequacy.

Firstly, how would the people of Israel know that he really had been sent by God? How was he to describe the God who had spoken to him? In reply, the Lord used the same verb as in verse 12. God's name in verse 14 could be translated either as 'I will be what I will be' or 'I am who I am', but it goes alongside the assurance of verse 12 that 'I will be with you.' It is not only the existence of God that comforts his people, but his commitment to be there for them and with them. 'I am', or YHWH, is translated 'the LORD' (capitalized). This used to be rendered 'Jehovah'. It is now thought that a more accurate rendering is 'Yahweh'. It is the personal name which signifies that God is committed to his people. He promised to save his people and bring them out of Egypt triumphantly, loaded down with booty (3:20-22).

Secondly, Moses asked, what if the people just did not believe him? (4:1). In response, the Lord gave Moses the power to perform three miraculous signs which showed that God, not the Egyptian idols, had power over all. These signs (as also the plagues) point to God's power over creatures, over men and over nature, including the Nile itself.

Thirdly, what about Moses' sense of inadequacy in speaking? (4:10). The Lord dismissed this. He had already promised to be with Moses (3:12), and now promised: 'I will be with your mouth' (4:12).

Finally the real truth came out: 'Please send someone else' (4:13). Moses was terrified. He had left Egypt in fear of his life. That may have left an indelible scar (God reassured him about this in 4:19). But his fear represented a failure of faith. The Lord then revealed that he had already provided a support for Moses. Aaron, his older brother, still fluent in the Egyptian language, was on the way to meet him, and would speak for him (4:14-16). Moses' reluctance to undertake this awesome task was under-standable. But the assurance, 'I will be with you,' should have been sufficient. And so with us. We may flinch at the cost of obedience. But the Lord says, 'I will never leave you nor forsake you' (Heb. 13:5; quoting Josh. 1:5). He promises to be with us, even through the fires and the floods (Isa. 43:2).

When through fiery trials thy pathway shall lie,
my grace all-sufficient shall be thy supply;
the flame shall not hurt thee: I only design
thy dross to consume, and thy gold to refine.

The soul that on Jesus hath leaned for repose,
I will not, I will not desert to its foes;
that soul, though all hell should endeavour to shake,
I'll never, no never, no never forsake!

(K in *Rippon's Selection*, 1787).

Prayer: Pray for courage to stand for the Lord today, whatever the cost, knowing that God is with you.

Text for the day: *I will never leave you nor forsake you* (Heb. 13:5).

'Israel is my firstborn son... Let my son go'

An eighty-year old man sets out, accompanied by his wife and two sons on a donkey. Their mission: to defy the absolute ruler of the superpower of the ancient world. It would have been laughable were it not that 'Moses took the staff of God in his hand' (Exod. 4:20). With this staff he would bring plague after plague to devastate Egypt's prosperity and security. If Pharaoh did not release the Lord's firstborn son, the Lord would strike down Pharaoh's own firstborn son, along with the firstborn of all the Egyptians.

God outlined his plan before Moses arrived in Egypt. Moses was to request permission for his people to go and worship their God. Pharaoh would refuse. God would 'harden his heart'(4:21). After the first five plagues Pharaoh hardened his own heart; it is after the sixth plague that we are told that the Lord hardened his heart. The Lord's hardening was, in effect, the removal of any gracious softening influences. Pharaoh was set more and more inexorably on the wicked course he had already chosen. The deliverance of the Israelites was to be seen as a mighty act of the Lord, not as Pharaoh's decision. The succession of plagues was a striking demonstration of the Lord's superior power over the false gods of Egypt. Pharaoh was told explicitly that the Lord had raised him up 'for this purpose ... to show you my power, so that my name may be proclaimed in all the earth' (9:16).

The incident in the lodging place on the way back to Egypt underlines the vital importance of total obedience to God. Moses was God's chosen instrument of redemption, but he had neglected to circumcise his son. Probably his wife Zipporah had objected to circumcision, and Moses had felt unable to force the issue. But he nearly paid with his life for this disobedience. It seems that the resultant tension led to separation between him and his wife (18:2). We are reminded that it is never safe and never right to hinder others in their obedience to God. In this case, wilful disobedience led to great suffering. Only after Moses' son had been circumcised could Moses resume his journey.

When Moses and Aaron shared God's message with the Hebrews, the people believed and worshipped. That was encouraging.

But when the message was conveyed to Pharaoh he refused to let the people go and brutally increased their workload. The Hebrew foremen blamed Moses and Aaron. Far from bringing them deliverance, they had made a bad situation worse! Moses turned to the Lord in prayer. He had been obedient, but his mission had led to even greater suffering for the people of God. What was going on?

Obedience is not always instantly rewarded. God's people often pay a high price when they make a faithful stand. We must expect opposition from the world; we may even receive opposition from the believers we try to serve. But the Lord told Moses that although all seemed dark in the short term, his plan was going to be accomplished (6:1). He was not going to abandon his 'firstborn son' (4:22).

God's promises to us are equally certain. If we are 'in Christ' we have been adopted as God's children. He will never abandon us. Our obedience may result in persecution. We may be perplexed at hard providences. But our loving heavenly Father is in control.

God moves in a mysterious way
his wonders to perform,
he plants his footsteps in the sea
and rides upon the storm.

You fearful saints, fresh courage take;
the clouds you so much dread
are big with mercy and shall break
in blessings on your head

(William Cowper).

Prayer: Praise God that all his plans will certainly be accomplished.

Text for the day:
'I will be a father to you,
*   and you shall be sons and daughters to me,'*
says the Lord Almighty

(2 Cor. 6:18).

'I will ...'

Moses was bewildered. He had obeyed God, but the consequences had been dire: '[Ever] since I came to Pharaoh to speak in
your name, he has done evil to this people, and you have not
delivered your people at all' (Exod. 5:23).

God assured Moses that the vicious hostility of Pharaoh was all
part of the plan. Pharaoh would never voluntarily let the people
go. But, equally, the Hebrews had been so subjugated by the years
of oppression that they would never summon up the courage to
leave of their own volition. So God would push Pharaoh to the
point where he would drive them out of Egypt (6:1).

The rest of this passage outlines the Lord's covenant commitment to his people, couched in the form of a magnificent series of
'I will's.

> *I will bring you out from under the burdens of the Egyptians*
> (6:6).
> *I will deliver you from slavery to them* (6:6).
> *I will redeem you with an outstretched arm* (6:6).
> *I will take you to be my people* (6:7).
> *I will be your God* (6:7).
> *I will bring you into the land* (6:8).
> *I will give it to you for a possession* (6:8).

These promises were given alongside the assurance: 'I am the
LORD' (6:2,6,7). The Israelites' King was declaring his authority
over them and his care for them. These were the people who
would be privileged to witness the outworking of the covenant
promises made so long ago. Abraham, Isaac and Jacob had
known the name 'Yahweh' in one sense, but the Hebrew usage of
'know' is not just hearing something but experiencing it. The
patriarchs had heard the promises, but this particular group of
people was to experience their fulfilment (6:3).

When Moses communicated this covenant assurance to the
people, they wearily dismissed him. They were exhausted,
dispirited and hopeless. Yet we, who know the end of the story,

know that each of the 'I will's came to pass. God's covenant commitment would inexorably be carried through, whatever the weakness, failure and sin of his people.

That is our assurance today. God has bound himself to his people by a covenant. Because of what Christ has done, God says:

I will make my dwelling among them and walk among them...
I will be their God...
I will welcome you...
I will be a father to you...

(2 Cor. 6:16-18).

We may feel discouraged and disillusioned. The Hebrews felt that the power of Pharaoh was more 'real' than the promises of God. We may feel that the (ungodly) world view that surrounds us is more 'real' than the Word of God. Our feelings are actually irrelevant. God's promises are sure. All the promises of God find their 'Yes' in Christ (2 Cor. 1:20).

Prayer: Praise the triune God that he is faithful to his covenant and keeps all his promises.

Text for the day: *All the promises of God find their Yes in him* (2 Cor. 1:20).

'How long will you refuse to humble yourself before me?'

Chapters 7-12 of Exodus describe ten devastating plagues on Egypt, each of which demonstrated the supreme power of God. We see Pharaoh engaging in customary Oriental bargaining. He kept increasing his 'offer' from allowing the people to sacrifice within Egypt (8:25), to allowing them to sacrifice out in the desert (8:28), to allowing the men to go (10:11), to allowing all the people but no livestock (10:24). Moses and Aaron stood firm: the Lord's command was non-negotiable.

The Exodus account does not go into details about precisely how these plagues occurred. Clearly 'natural' phenomena were unleashed by God, with supernatural and terrifying intensity. The Egyptians worshipped a whole pantheon of gods. The plagues demonstrated that the Lord was supreme over each one: 'On all the gods of Egypt I will execute judgements: I am the LORD' (12:12). For example, each morning the Egyptians would worship the sun god Ra. For the three days of thick darkness, Ra was shown to be impotent.

As plague followed plague (water turning to blood, infestations of frogs, gnats and flies, a plague on livestock, boils, hail, locusts, darkness and the death of the firstborn) Pharaoh witnessed the systematic devastation of his kingdom. At any moment he could have halted the destruction. But, as with all wicked dictators, he was more concerned for his own reputation than for the well-being of his people. To give in and release the Hebrews would have been a loss of face for him. The Lord demanded: 'How long will you refuse to humble yourself before me?' (10:3). Even his advisers grew impatient with his blind intransigence. They risked breaking all the rules of protocol to challenge him very directly (10:7).

God warned Pharaoh time after time. If Pharaoh had relented he could have been spared the final plague. But time after time he hardened his heart, and the Lord gave him up to his own wickedness. By then Pharaoh's power was decisively broken — a foreshadowing of the final judgement when every knee will bow to

Christ (Phil. 2:10). Evil rulers may mock the Almighty now, but the futility of their resistance to God is laughable.

> *Why do the nations rage*
> *and the peoples plot in vain?*
> *The kings of the earth set themselves,*
> *and the rulers take counsel together,*
> *against the LORD and against his anointed...*
> *He who sits in the heavens laughs;*
> *the Lord holds them in derision*
>
> (Ps. 2:1-4).

The question, 'How long will you refuse to humble yourself before me?', is not only posed to evil dictators. It is posed to all who have not yet submitted to the Lord's kingship. God may whisper the question gently. He may, as C. S. Lewis memorably put it, use the 'megaphone' of painful circumstances to shake the tranquillity of our lives. But how tragic if we refuse to humble ourselves before him! Such stubbornness leads inevitably to catastrophe, not only in this life but for eternity as well.

Prayer: Pray for those believers suffering under cruel and tyrannical regimes. Pray that they would have the faith to know that their oppressors will have to bow the knee to Christ at the Last Day. Give thanks that God's power over all evil was demonstrated in the victory over Pharaoh, but even more decisively at the cross.

Text for the day: *God opposes the proud, but gives grace to the humble... Humble yourselves before the Lord, and he will exalt you* (James 4:6,10).

The Passover and Exodus

'At midnight the LORD struck down all the firstborn in the land of Egypt' (Exod. 12:29). This was the end of the road for Pharaoh. He begged Moses and Aaron to leave and revoke God's curse (12:32). The people of Egypt also urged the Hebrews to go, showering them with gifts — perhaps in an effort to stave off more disaster. While other countries celebrate their independence by commemorating the heroism of those who fought for it, this independence was secured by God alone:

> On the day after the Passover, the people of Israel went out triumphantly in the sight of all the Egyptians, while the Egyptians were burying all their firstborn, whom the LORD had struck down among them. On their gods also the LORD executed judgements (Num. 33:3-4).

It is fitting that the drama of the escape is briefly told (12:29-42), and placed between detailed instructions about the Passover Feast and associated Feast of Unleavened Bread (12:1-28,43-49). All the symbolism was designed to help the Hebrews remember the unilateral action of God in delivering them. The deliverance was so mighty that in future years they were to take seven days to commemorate it. The Passover would mark the beginning of the calendar year. The Hebrews could not pride themselves on their courage or initiative. While they sat still in their own homes, God moved inexorably to strike their enemies.

The direction to put blood on the doorposts of the Hebrew homes showed that their salvation was an act of grace. They, like the Egyptians, were sinners. Without the shedding of blood there is no forgiveness for sin (Lev. 17:11; Heb. 9:22). The offering of the Passover sacrifice (12:27) was the means by which God's wrath against sin was averted. God was not only delivering his people from the wicked tyranny of Pharaoh, he was saving them from death. The shedding of blood symbolized atonement and accept-ance into a saving relationship with God. This new relationship was celebrated by the Passover meal, which was only to be taken by those who had entered into covenant with God (12:43-48).

The New Testament teaches that the Passover was a signpost, pointing forward to the great and final sacrifice to take away sin: 'For Christ, our Passover lamb, has been sacrificed' (1 Cor. 5:7). Peter says that we have been ransomed 'with the precious blood of Christ, like that of a lamb without blemish or spot' (1 Peter 1:19; cf. Exod. 12:5). The writer to the Hebrews says, 'How much more will the blood of Christ, who through the eternal spirit offered himself without blemish to God, purify our conscience from dead works to serve the living God' (Heb. 9:14). John the Baptist pointed to Christ and declared: 'Behold, the Lamb of God, who takes away the sin of the world!' (John 1:29). And the apostle John saw the vision of 'a Lamb standing, as though it had been slain' (Rev. 5:6).

The Lord Jesus celebrated the Passover Feast with his closest disciples on the night before his death. He himself was about to be taken and offered up as the one, perfect, final Passover Lamb. This inaugurated the new feast of celebration, the 'Lord's Supper'. Paul wrote:

> *The Lord Jesus on the night when he was betrayed took bread, and when he had given thanks, he broke it, and said, 'This is my body which is for you. Do this in remembrance of me.' In the same way also he took the cup, after supper, saying, 'This cup is the new covenant in my blood. Do this, as often as you drink it, in remembrance of me.' For as often as you eat this bread and drink the cup, you proclaim the Lord's death until he comes* (1 Cor. 11:23-26).

Prayer: Praise God for providing the perfect Lamb.

Text for the day: *Christ, our Passover lamb, has been sacrificed* (1 Cor. 5:7).

The pillar of cloud and fire

The pillar of cloud by day and the pillar of fire by night did not depart from before the people (Exod. 13:22).

Having saved his people from the grip of tyranny, the Lord did not leave them to their own devices. He knew their weakness, and that the first sign of trouble would sent them running back to slavery (13:17; cf. 14:11; 16:3). He guided them, showing them each day where to go. 'God did not lead them by way of the land of the Philistines... But God led the people round by way of the wilderness' (13:17-18). They did not necessarily know the dangers from which he preserved them this way — they were just to follow his leading. He was acting as their Shepherd King.

God's presence took the form of a pillar of cloud by day, and a pillar of fire by night (13:21). This verse could be rendered: 'The LORD went before them as a pillar of cloud to lead them along the way, and by night as a pillar of fire to give them light.' This was a glorious manifestation of the Lord's glory. It reassured the people of his presence with them, to protect, to illuminate and to guide. We may understand this as one pillar, not two. It was, to quote John L. Mackay, 'a fiery core enveloped by clouds. In daylight the cloud's brightness was rendered less intense by the shining of the sun, but in darkness the inner radiance of the fire shone through and lit up the surrounding area.'

Today God's people are not led by the 'fiery cloudy pillar' but we know that he is with us always. Today he leads us by his Word and by his Spirit:

> *I will ask the Father, and he will give you another Helper, to be with you for ever, even the Spirit of truth ... he dwells with you and will be in you. I will not leave you as orphans; I will come to you... If anyone loves me, he will keep my word, and my Father will love him, and we will come to him and make our home with him* (John 14:16-18,23).

We also have confidence that the sovereign God is in control of all the events that befall us; nothing is outside his control. Sometimes we may question a certain providence: 'Why has this happened to me?' Rather, we should be grateful for the ceaseless ways in which our Shepherd acts to protect us from dangers, including those we encounter through our own folly.

The Israelites, on the run from Pharaoh, did not dare to move forward without the clear guidance of God. We have an enemy far more powerful than Pharaoh, who would love to see us fall. We dare not move out into a single day without knowing that God is with us and for us. We need him with us to protect us from unseen dangers and sudden temptation. We need him with us because, unless he blesses, all our work will come to nothing. 'Commit to the LORD whatever you do, and your plans will succeed' (Prov. 16:3, NIV).

> For you are my rock and my fortress;
>   and for your name's sake you lead me and guide me;
> you take me out of the net they have hidden for me,
>   for you are my refuge.
> Into your hand I commit my spirit;
>   you have redeemed me, O LORD, faithful God
>
> (Ps. 31:3-5).

Prayer: Take time to commit your plans for the coming days to the Lord. It is also good sometimes to set aside an extended time for prayer to review plans for the longer term.

Text for the day: *For your name's sake you lead me and guide me* (Ps. 31:3).

'The Egyptians shall know that I am the LORD'

After the escape from Egypt, instead of leading the people immediately to freedom, God deliberately led them into what appeared to be an inescapable trap. Instead of moving further away from Egyptian-controlled territory, and towards freedom, they turned back. They found themselves trapped between water on two sides and Pharaoh's chariots on the third. The Egyptians concluded that these runaway slaves did not really know where they were going or what they were doing and jumped at the chance of recapturing them. The people of Israel concluded that God had abandoned them and railed furiously against Moses (Exod. 14:11-12).

The Lord's priorities are so different from ours! God didn't just want to take the people to the land of milk and honey as quickly as possible. That was what they wanted, of course. No, God wanted them to increase in faith and trust. He wanted their holiness. It is just the same for us. God's priority is not for us to get through life as easily and comfortably as we can. Humanly speaking, that's just what we want! But his purpose is for us to become like Christ. Sometimes he leads us into hard places, where it may seem as if he has abandoned us. All too often we reason: 'Because my life is so unbearable at the moment, the Lord must have forgotten me!' But sometimes the Lord does deliberately lead us to these hard places. We then learn to rely utterly on him.

At this critical moment, the people reached the point where there was absolutely nothing they could do to fight against the Egyptians. But the Lord had it all in hand. He told Moses to stop crying out to him, and simply step out in faith (14:15). Sometimes we arrive at a point where to continue to agonize in prayer about something can be a way of evading our responsibilities. We simply have to get on with our duties for the day, and trust God for the result. The Lord was controlling events so as to provide an unmistakable demonstration of his power: 'I will get glory over Pharaoh and all his host, and the Egyptians shall know that I am the LORD' (14:4). He fought for his people, and his weapons were the wind and the waves. He comprehensively defeated the whole

Egyptian army; he saved every single one of his own people, and none of them had to do so much as strike a blow: 'The LORD will fight for you, and you have only to be silent' (14:14).

Throughout the Old Testament the sea is seen as a symbol of the surging of evil and sinister forces. The Lord triumphs over them all. Egypt itself often symbolizes earthly powers who oppose the Lord Almighty. The nation of Egypt is sometimes portrayed in the Old Testament as a sea monster, which in turn sometimes symbolizes the Evil One himself. This mighty victory over Pharaoh's chariots and horsemen came to typify God's mighty victory over evil in every age.

The crossing of the Red Sea is alluded to throughout the Old Testament as God's great sign that he was 'for' his people. With the Exodus from Egypt, it formed the basis for God's claim to his people's loyalty. He had delivered them. And so for us, the greater victory over the forces of evil, secured by Christ at the cross, forms the basis for God's claim to our loyalty today. He has shown once and for all that he is 'for' us. Whatever the seemingly impossible situation that you are in today, once you have committed it to the Lord, you can simply get on with your duties knowing that if God is for you, who can be against you? (Rom. 8:31).

Prayer: O Lord, thank you for the great victory you secured over sin and evil at the cross. Forgive me that so often when I'm in a hard place, I doubt your love. Remind me throughout the day that, if you are for me, who can be against me? And help me simply to get on with the duties before me in a spirit of peaceful trust.

Text for the day: *The LORD said to Moses, 'Why do you cry to me? Tell the people of Israel to go forward'* (Exod. 14:15).

'The LORD will reign for ever and ever'

This great victory was celebrated in song by Moses, Miriam and the Israelites once they were safely across the Red Sea. 'The LORD is a warrior' (Exod. 15:3, NIV). When evil powers attack the people of God, he intervenes on their behalf. Satan and his hosts are powerful, and they work in and through evil earthly rulers, but the Lord is infinitely more powerful. When God threw the Egyptian chariots and officers into the sea, this foreshadowed his final victory over all evil: 'The LORD will reign for ever and ever' (15:18).

This wonderful song was sung every Sabbath during the period of temple worship. It reminded the people that, in the words of Alfred Edersheim, Israel was 'surrounded by the hostile powers of this world, that there must always be a contest between them, and that Jehovah would always himself interpose to destroy his enemies and deliver his people'. They were part of a 'big picture' — the conflict of good against evil. God had decisively intervened to proclaim the victory of good.

How tragic when Christianity becomes viewed as merely a matter of 'personal devotion'! Of course it is that, but much more! We are part of the worldwide body of Christ. The people of Christ are surrounded by hostile powers. There is conflict, but the victory has been won, in principle, at the cross. We await the Second Coming and the final outworking of that victory. Now, and to all eternity, we, as Christ's body the church, sing the Song of Moses (celebrating the victory which prefigured the cross) and of the Lamb (looking back to the cross). Remember today that you are part of the 'big picture'. If you are 'in Christ' today, you are part of his kingdom, on the victory side. Sing and give thanks!

Once Moses had led the people in song, his elder sister Miriam led the women in song and dance. Miriam was gifted as a prophetess. She, along with Moses and Aaron, was privileged to receive direct words from God for the people. For this reason, the prophet Micah acknowledges the role played by Moses, Aaron and Miriam in leading the people of Israel (Micah 6:4). Miriam is not the only prophetess in Scripture: we hear also of Deborah,

Isaiah's wife, Huldah, the daughters of Philip and the women of Corinth (1 Cor. 11:5). The prophet Joel rejoiced that in the New Testament age the Holy Spirit would be poured out on all flesh, and that both sons and daughters would prophesy.

It is notable that, although women in the Old Testament were generally assumed to be wives and mothers, there is no hint in Scripture that Miriam was married or that she had children. This foreshadows the honoured place given to those single women who are devoted to the Lord's service in the New Testament age (1 Cor. 7:34). Although women in the Old Testament age were usually confined to the domestic sphere, it is quite clear that Miriam was a 'public' figure and respected by the community. Indeed, later on she aspired (wrongly) to co-leadership with her brother Moses (Num. 12) and was publicly shamed.

Many today would read too much into Miriam's ministry. Evangelical feminists use her to buttress their argument that there should be no role distinctions between men and women. But there was never any doubt that Moses was the leader of the people. In the vast majority of places Moses and Aaron are named, without any mention of their sister (e.g. Exod. 16:2,6; 18:12; 24:1,9; 34:31; Lev. 11:1, Num. 2:1; 3:1; 4:1,34,45; 14:2,5; etc.). There is consistency in the Bible. Women can be given the gift of prophecy without negating the overall principle of male leadership. This lovely vignette of Miriam leading the women gives a glorious foretaste of the far greater freedom and opportunity for women in the era of the gospel, where men and women alike can share the task of evangelism, and where in Christ 'there is neither male nor female' (Gal. 3:28).

Prayer: Praise God through the words of the song in this chapter.

Text for the day: *The LORD will reign for ever and ever* (Exod. 15:18).

'I am the LORD, your healer'

The people had been delivered in such a dramatic way that, for the second time, they thought their troubles were over. But when God saves us, he does not lift us straight to glory. He leads us through hard times to deepen our dependence on him. The wilderness wanderings were all about building up a relationship of trust between the people and God. Time after time when difficulties presented themselves, the people grumbled and complained; they failed to turn to the Lord.

So, in this case, they travelled for three days without finding fresh water. When eventually they found water, the disappointment of discovering that it was undrinkable was overwhelming. The people turned on Moses, blaming him for their misery.

When we find ourselves in an impossible situation, the correct response is not to grumble, not to panic, but to pray to the God of the impossible. 'Nothing is impossible for God.' Moses exemplifies this correct response. He cried to the Lord. The Lord answered his prayer. The bitter waters were made sweet.

The whole episode had, of course, been designed to test the people's faith and teach them a lesson in dependence. They were to rely on the unseen God, rather than what they could (or could not) physically provide for themselves. After this powerful demonstration of the Lord's good provision, the lesson is driven home. If the people submit to the Lord as their King, then they will not be punished for rebellion, as the Egyptians were. The judgements on Egypt were also warnings to Israel. Refusing to submit to God will be punished.

How often, in our experience, what appears to be bitter can be made sweet by the grace of God! Time after time, we call out to him, and he transforms situations and people in a remarkable way.

His purposes will ripen fast,
unfolding every hour;
the bud may have a bitter taste,
but sweet will be the flower.

Blind unbelief is sure to err,
and scan his work in vain;
God is his own interpreter,
and he will make it plain

(William Cowper).

All too often we take health for granted and when problems arise we place our trust in human means. Rather, we should remember that the Lord is the giver of life, the granter of health and the healer from sickness. We are utterly dependent on him. Of course we are to use appropriate medical help, but we should always pray that God himself would work through it. Living in a fallen world, we know that we are not immune from sickness, accident and death. Immediate physical healing may not be God's will for us. But the death of Christ has secured our spiritual healing in this life, and glorified bodies which will never suffer illness, pain or death in the next. Praise God that he is 'the LORD, your healer'.

Prayer: Pray for grace to obey and trust God even when we are taken into situations that appear to be very bitter.

Text for the day:
But he was wounded for our transgressions;
   he was crushed for our iniquities;
upon him was the chastisement that brought us peace,
   and with his stripes we are healed

(Isa. 53:5).

Daily bread

Once again the people of Israel faced a crisis: their food supplies were running out. Once again, instead of praying, they grumbled (the word is repeated seven times in five verses) and turned against their leaders. Instead of being thankful for what God had provided so far, they looked back to the food they ate in Egypt.

Worse, they insulted what the Lord had done for them:

> Would that we had died by the hand of the LORD in the land of Egypt, when we sat by the meat pots and ate bread to the full, for you have brought us out into this wilderness to kill this whole assembly with hunger (Exod. 16:3).

They would have preferred to die in the plagues that fell on Egypt, or else remain as slaves. Their ingratitude is amazing.

Yet more breathtaking is the response of the Lord:

> I am about to rain bread from heaven for you, and the people shall ... gather a day's portion every day... At twilight you shall eat meat, and in the morning you shall be filled with bread. Then you shall know that I am the LORD your God (16:4,12).

Not only would the Lord provide for their needs (when they had not even asked him), but he would do so in such a way as to teach them the lessons they so badly needed to learn. While the provision of meat was temporary, the provision of bread would be an ongoing provision until they reached the promised land. There would only ever be enough for a day. The exception was the sixth day, when enough would be provided for the Sabbath as well.

The Lord was teaching his people the lesson of humble dependence. They had to learn the attitude: 'Give us [each] day our daily bread' (Matt. 6:11). And so do we. All that we have comes from God. At any moment, he could withdraw his gracious provision. We are to live in daily dependence on him, not only for our physical needs, but also for our emotional and spiritual needs. Just as we do not eat one large meal and then wait a week until the next one, but eat regularly, so we need to feed on the Word of God constantly. To neglect regular intake of the Word of God is to despise the provision God has given us:

And he humbled you and let you hunger and fed you with manna, which you did not know, nor did your fathers know, that he might make you know that man does not live by bread alone, but man lives by every word that comes from the mouth of the LORD (Deut. 8:3).

Ultimately, the bread from heaven pointed forward to the Word incarnate, Jesus himself:

Truly, truly, I say to you, it was not Moses who gave you the bread from heaven, but my Father gives you the true bread from heaven. For the bread of God is he who comes down from heaven and gives life to the world... I am the bread of life; whoever comes to me shall not hunger, and whoever believes in me shall never thirst (John 6:32-33,35).

Whatever our needs today, we can cry out to God, who will 'supply every need of yours according to the riches of his glory in Christ Jesus' (Phil. 4:19).

Prayer: Lord, forgive me that when I come into hard places I so often grumble, rather than praying. Help me to depend on you for my every need today and every day.

My every need he richly will supply,
nor will his mercy ever let me die;
in him there dwells a treasure all divine,
and matchless grace has made that treasure mine
                                        (William Gadsby).

Text for the day: *And my God will supply every need of yours according to his riches in glory in Christ Jesus* (Phil. 4:19).

Water from the rock

The people had been delivered from Pharaoh and brought miraculously through the Red Sea. They had been given the pillar of cloud and fire to lead them and daily manna to feed them. But when they came to a place where there was no water to drink, instead of praying to God, they rebelled against Moses: 'Why did you bring us up out of Egypt, to kill us and our children and our livestock with thirst?' (Exod. 17:3). Their anger was so intense that Moses feared for his life: 'They are almost ready to stone me' (17:4).

The hearts of the people had not yet been changed. They were physically free, but trapped in a slave mentality. The wilderness experience was God's way of training them. They had to learn to trust him. But their lack of trust was held up to later generations, and to us, as a dreadful object lesson:

> Do not harden your hearts, as at Meribah,
>   as on the day at Massah in the wilderness,
> when your fathers put me to the test
>   and put me to the proof, though they had seen my work.
> For forty years I loathed that generation
>   and said, 'They are a people who go astray in their heart,
>   and they have not known my ways.'
> Therefore I swore in my wrath,
>   'They shall not enter my rest'
>
> (Ps. 95:8-11).

In this case, God did graciously and abundantly provide water from the rock. But he was angry with the people, and ultimately he judged them and condemned them to forty years of wilderness wandering. Only the next generation would enter the promised land. The writer to the Hebrews quotes this incident and this psalm as a direct warning to believers who may be tempted to turn back (Heb. 3:7-11), and adds:

*Take care, brothers, lest there be in any of you an evil, un-
believing heart, leading you to fall away from the living God.
But exhort one another every day, as long as it is called 'today', that none of you may be hardened by the deceitfulness of
sin* (Heb. 3:12-13).

We are in a far more privileged position than the Israelites.
They received water from the rock. It provided for their physical
needs. But it also pointed forward to God's ultimate provision for
all his people's needs: Christ. We have received the spiritual
reality to which the water pointed. As Paul wrote, 'For they
drank from the spiritual Rock that followed them, and the Rock
was Christ' (1 Cor. 10:4).

Having received Christ, how much more careful we should be
to guard against unbelief and a complaining spirit! Paul wrote:

*These things happened to them as an example, but they
were written down for our instruction, on whom the end of the
ages has come. Therefore let anyone who thinks that he stands
take heed lest he fall* (1 Cor. 10:11-12).

We don't know what may suddenly happen to try our faith at
any time. Whatever happens, let us guard against a complaining
spirit. Let us be careful not to doubt God. When in trouble, let us
not grumble, but pray, knowing that the one who provided
water from the rock can also provide abundantly for us.

Prayer: O Lord, forgive me for all those times when I have
doubted you, grumbled and complained about my spiritual
leaders. Thank you for your abundant provision of water from
the rock for the Israelites, and your much more abundant provision of pardon in Christ.

Text for the day: *Today, if you hear his voice, do not harden
your hearts* (Heb. 3:7-8,15; 4:7).

'Whenever Moses held up his hand, Israel prevailed'

While Israel was encamped near Mount Sinai, the Amalekites were grazing their livestock in the area. They began to attack the Israelites, wanting them to move away from Amalekite watering holes. Amalek was the foremost of the heathen nations and symbolized all the enemies who would stand against Israel. So the people must learn this lesson well and apply it to all the battles which were still to come (Exod. 17:14). Moses commanded Joshua to lead some men into the attack (17:9). And while the fighting was going on, Moses, Aaron and Hur were on the hill with hands raised to the Lord (17:9-12).

This is fundamentally a lesson in dependence. The Lord provided manna and water, and now physical security and protection. The battle was to be won not simply by force of arms, but by intercession and faith in God. If Israel will trust in the Lord and see that the battle is the Lord's, then they will have the victory. The work is his and the victory is his.

Moses, as the leader of the people of God, was the mediator with the solemn obligation to bring the needs of the people before the face of the Lord. Note the role of the staff (17:9), the symbol of his calling (4:1-2,20). Moses stood and pleaded for the victory of the Lord, and by standing there guaranteed the triumph of Israel. Jesus at Calvary cried out for the salvation of his people, and by dying there guaranteed the final victory. (There is even a visual correspondence between Moses interceding with out-stretched arms and the Lord Jesus crucified between two thieves.)

Moses also foreshadowed Christ's ongoing work of interces-sion in heaven, where he holds out his hands towards the Father, displaying the wounds of Calvary and pleading for his people who are engaged in fearful combat in the valley below: 'Father I have died. I have paid the penalty for sins.' The one decisive victory of Calvary is the guarantee that all other battles will be won. But if Moses was a type of Christ he was an inadequate shadow of the Saviour. Fallible and weary, he needed Aaron and Hur to hold up his hands (17:12). Compare the perfection of Christ (Heb. 7:25).

Dependence on the Lord did not exempt Israel from the need to go into battle. The ordinary Israelite soldiers were simply summoned to fight. They could not see the big picture; they would not have known at any given moment how the whole battle was going. But, in the distance, maybe they glimpsed Moses on the hill with his hands upraised. They were to persevere, knowing that the Lord would grant victory in the end.

For us, being a Christian today is just like being a foot soldier in the heat of the battle. It would be great to be 'on the hill with Moses', in order to see the big picture. What is the Lord doing in the world, in our nation, even our town? What effect are we having on the enemy? But we don't have that privileged position. As foot soldiers we must be faithful in the small role the Lord has given us. We must not give up, even when we are discouraged or wounded. And if we do feel like giving up, let us remember to lift up our eyes. Jesus is interceding for us. The battle will be won in the end.

Wonderfully, Joshua, as well as Moses, is a type of Christ. Jesus knows what it is like to be a foot soldier! He endured all the pain of this earthly strife. He even gave his own life in the battle to ensure the final victory for his people. And now he calls you into his army, and he instructs you to fight under the banner of the cross. There must be prayer. In this account it is Moses who prays, but we live in the days of the new covenant, when all believers are 'priests'. We are all to engage continually in prayer: 'Apart from me you can do nothing' (John 15:5). And there must be real combat. Fight on. Keep going. And look to Jesus in the fight.

Prayer: O Lord, please help me to be humbly dependent on you throughout the day. Forgive me for self-reliance and pride.

Text for the day: *Do not be afraid and do not be dismayed at this great horde, for the battle is not yours but God's* (2 Chr. 20:15).

'The LORD is greater than all gods'

At first sight this seems to be a very ordinary incident: Moses receives a visit from his father-in-law.

When Jethro arrived at Sinai, ostensibly he came to bring back Moses' wife and sons. It would appear that Moses had sent Zipporah back to Jethro after the conflict over the circumcision of their son. Moses now met Jethro with every mark of honour and respect (Exod. 18:7,24). Despite his position as undoubted leader of Israel, Moses exhibited meekness and humility. All too often conversion and commitment to Christian service can lead to a disrespect for relatives and a neglect of family responsibilities. And this, in turn, can bring the gospel into disrepute.

When this Midianite high priest sacrificed and ate in the presence of the Lord (18:12), it pointed forward to God's ultimate purposes for the world. God's covenant with Israel focused on a single nation, but his ultimate purpose was to bring salvation to all nations (Gen. 12:3). In acknowledging that Jehovah alone is the Lord (18:10-11), Jethro was a foretaste of the Gentiles who will bow the knee to the Lord.

This stood in stark contrast with the fearsome opposition Israel had just encountered from the Gentile nation of Amalek. The people of God will always attract this twofold response of opposition and acceptance. Jethro reminds us that God's heart is for the world. The blessings of salvation are going to overflow to every tribe and people and tongue and nation.

This chapter also describes Moses' leadership of the people. At this point God's people did not have written Scriptures. There were oral traditions from the time of the patriarchs. But they had become confused with all the pagan and idolatrous ideas they had been taught in Egypt. So the people relied on their leader Moses, the single and unique channel through whom they received revelation from heaven (18:16; cf. 20:18-21). Moses sat alone on his judgement seat before the people. If the people wanted to know what God said, they had to come to him.

Jethro was wise enough to point out that the situation was impractical. It just did not work to have one man as the source of all wisdom for the whole nation of Israel. There had to be delegation. But even with the appointment of lesser judges, they still had to refer the more difficult cases to Moses, and in all matters the people were to regard him as the only lawgiver and teacher (18:19-20). The lesser judges had authority only in so far as it was delegated to them by Moses, and in so far as they taught the same truths as Moses.

How different the situation is now, in the era of the new covenant! Now many believers may read God's Word for themselves, and all Christians have the Holy Spirit to guide them (Col. 1:9-10). Yes, there are those who are called to lead the church — elders who govern and teach (1 Tim. 5:17). But at the same time, every believer is to understand the will of God from his Word (Jer. 31:33-34). When elders exercise authority, it is not their own; it is the authority of the Word of God. And we need to pray that all Christians, in all countries of the world, may have free access to the Bible.

Moses in this chapter prefigures Christ, the source of the knowledge and wisdom of God. He laboured selflessly on behalf of the people, making the will of God known to them. 'Moses was faithful in all God's house as a servant ... but Christ is faithful over God's house as a son' (Heb. 3:5-6).

Prayer: Lord God, thank you for your infallible Word. Thank you that I have free access to it. And thank you that, through Christ, I have free access into your presence.

Text for the day: *I will put my law within them, and I will write it on their hearts* (Jer. 31:33).

'If you will … keep my covenant, you shall be my treasured possession'

'I bore you on eagles' wings and brought you to myself' (Exod. 19:4).

He found him in a desert land,
    and in the howling waste of the wilderness;
he encircled him, he cared for him,
    he kept him as the apple of his eye.
Like an eagle that stirs up its nest,
    that flutters over its young,
spreading out its wings, catching them,
    bearing them on its pinions,
the LORD alone guided him…

(Deut. 32:10-11).

The image is of a mother eagle teaching her young birds to fly, but swooping to catch them on her wings if they fall. It poignantly conveys the heart of God towards his people. They had been rescued in order to enjoy an intimate relationship with God, like that between parent and child. They had been chosen, out of all the peoples on earth, to be his special people. This exclusive relationship was secured by a covenant (or agreement).

On his side, God had rescued them and he would continue to protect and provide for them as his 'treasured possession'. We may treat many of our possessions carelessly, but our very 'treasured' possessions we guard jealously. God would 'treasure' this people. For their part, they were to live as a 'holy nation', set apart to live for a holy God. This chapter, describing the awesome and terrifying power and holiness of God, comes before the detailed commandments, rules and regulations that followed. The theophany, or appearance of God, demonstrated to the people the nature and character of the God with whom they were entering into covenant. All the commandments would fall into place when they grasped something of the holiness of God: 'You shall be holy, for I the LORD your God am holy' (Lev. 19:2).

The end goal of this covenant was inclusive, not exclusive. God had a missionary purpose in selecting Israel. They were to function as priests in the world (Exod. 19:6). They were to display God's glory to the other peoples, acting as a light for the nations.

The overwhelming message of this chapter is the holiness of God. God does not change. The only way we can approach him is by 'Jesus, the mediator of a new covenant' (Heb. 12:24). The end goal of the new covenant is the same as that of the old. God has chosen a people for himself:

> But you are a chosen race, a royal priesthood, a holy nation, a people for his own possession, that you may proclaim the excellencies of him who called you out of darkness into his marvellous light (1 Peter 2:9).

The purpose of the new covenant, like that of the old, is a missionary purpose. We, as God's chosen people, are to proclaim his glory to the nations: 'Go therefore and make disciples of all nations' (Matt. 28:19).

Prayer: Pray that we, the people of God in our day, would fulfil our missionary purpose and take the gospel to the remaining unreached people groups.

Text for the day: *But you are a chosen race, a royal priesthood, a holy nation, a people for his own possession, that you may proclaim the excellencies of him who called you out of darkness into his marvellous light (1 Peter 2:9).*

The Ten Commandments

Chapters 19-24 of Exodus are all about the establishment of a covenant, or agreement, between God and his people. Chapter 19 sets the scene: God in his majesty, glory and holiness summoned the people into his presence. Chapters 20-23 set out the conditions of the covenant: the laws that the Lord expected his people to keep if they were to remain in relationship with him. Chapter 24 is about the confirmation of the covenant. The people together agreed to its terms and their leaders were invited to celebrate a covenant meal in the presence of the Lord.

The covenant stipulations begin with the Ten Commandments. Then comes a selection of laws for the religious and civil life of the people. There are further laws found in the remaining books of the Pentateuch, something over 600 in all. We may find it surprising that such a wide variety of laws are all mixed in together, but this simply reflects the fact that the Lord was concerned about every detail of his people's lives — all aspects of life were to be 'holy to the LORD'.

We are all familiar with the difference between rules that are relative and rules that are absolute. When we visit different homes, for example, we adjust our behaviour according to the custom of that home. Some hosts may expect us to remove our outdoor shoes; others will not. There is nothing 'absolute' about such customs. But whatever home we are in, it would be wrong to steal any of the contents! Stealing is always wrong. The Ten Commandments are a summary of God's moral requirements for all time. The principles apply to all people in all places at all times. The 'civil' and 'ceremonial' laws that follow are not absolute. They were designed to regulate Israelite social and religious life in that particular historical context. Certainly we can learn from them, as the principles behind them reflect something of the character of God. But we do not have to keep them, as they are now fulfilled in Christ.

The Ten Commandments begin with the people's relationship with God, and then move on to their relationship with each other. As Jesus summed it up:

You shall love the Lord your God with all your heart and with all your soul and with all your mind. This is the great and first commandment. And a second is like it: You shall love your neighbour as yourself. On these two commandments depend all the Law and the Prophets (Matt. 22:38-39).

Our relationship with God comes first. Without his grace and help we cannot live ethically pleasing lives. True morality is not 'self-help'. But once we are in relationship with God, he enables us to love our neighbours and to behave properly towards other people.

By ourselves we cannot love God or our neighbour. The New Testament perspective is that the law was given at Sinai to 'lead us to Christ'. The people of Israel failed from the start to keep the covenant. Centuries of failure demonstrated that they needed a Saviour — one who would keep the law perfectly on their behalf. When we look at the Ten Commandments we acknowledge our total failure to keep them. We acknowledge our need of forgiveness and our need of a Saviour. We look to Jesus, who kept the whole law perfectly, and we trust in what he did at Calvary to secure our forgiveness for breaking the law. We look to the Holy Spirit to come and live within us and empower us to love God and want to keep his commandments.

Prayer: Lord, I pray forgiveness for my constant failure to keep your moral law. Thank you for the Lord Jesus, who kept your law perfectly and died so that I might be forgiven. Please enable me by your Spirit today to love you and love your law, and empower me to obey it.

Text for the day: *So the law was put in charge to lead us to Christ that we might be justified by faith* (Gal. 3:24, NIV).

'You shall have no other gods before me'

'You shall have no other gods *before* me' suggests the meaning: 'You shall have no other gods *in my presence*.' As the Lord is everywhere, this forbids the worship of any other gods at all. An alternative translation is provided in the ESV footnote: 'You shall have no other gods *besides* me.' This is not saying that we can have other gods as long as we give our best praise to the Lord. No. There is only one true God in the universe — the Creator of all things, and that is the God of the Bible. We are to worship him alone. He is to be the Lord over all other authorities in our life. If we are called on to disobey him, whether by political authorities, an employer, husband, parent, or church leader, 'We must obey God rather than men' (Acts 5:29).

This command goes totally against the pluralism of today. It is a condemnation of all non-Christian religions. It is popular today to say that different religions are alternative paths to truth. Modern church leaders preside over 'interfaith' services, with representatives of all the different faiths. Such people are breaking this First Commandment. Various different faiths may contain some aspects of truth, but their worship is not acceptable to the one true God. He has revealed Christ as the only way by which we can offer acceptable worship: 'I am the way, and the truth, and the life. No one comes to the Father except through me' (John 14:6).

The people to whom the command was given faced huge pressures to worship gods other than the Lord. Egyptian culture was based around the worship of many gods. In Canaan it would be the same. Other gods are worshipped when human beings turn away from allegiance to the one true and living God. This happened first of all in the Garden of Eden, when Adam and Eve followed Satan, a created being, rather than their Creator. They believed a lie: 'You will be like God.' Every religion that fails to worship the one true God through his Son is the product of satanic activity. Romans 1 depicts the ensuing unravelling of the creation order. Instead of having rightful dominion over all living things, mankind stooped to worshipping created things rather than God. The result is moral chaos. We are told that it is 'unloving' to refuse to recognize the validity of other religions, other lifestyles — other gods. The Bible tells us that it is truly loving to offer others the salvation that can be found in Christ alone. The worship of false gods is at the root of all human problems. The call to repentance is the mission of the church: we call people back to worship of the Lord alone.

Today we may not be tempted to bow at the shrines of Baal or Moloch, but we are tempted to bow to the false gods of materialism and covetousness. Paul tells us to 'put to death … covetousness, which is idolatry' (Col. 3:5) and describes those who covet as idolaters (Eph. 5:5).

This command has a positive application. We are told *not* to worship other gods, but we *are* to worship the Lord alone. He is to have the place of pre-eminence in our lives. He is to be Lord of every aspect of our lives. He is the one who gives us our life and such strength as we have. We desire to use all that we have and all that we are for his glory.

> *Fill all my life, O Lord my God,*
> *in every part with praise;*
> *that my whole being may proclaim*
> *your being and your ways.*
>
> *Praise in the common things of life,*
> *its goings out and in;*
> *praise in each duty and each deed,*
> *exalted or unseen*

(Horatius Bonar).

Prayer: O Lord, help me to worship you alone. I need your Holy Spirit to show me where I love or value anything more than you.

Text for the day: *You shall have no other gods before me* (Exod. 20:3).

'You shall not make for yourself a carved image, or any likeness...'

The First Commandment calls us to worship God alone; this commandment relates to *how* we worship him. When the people made the golden calf, they thought they were still worshipping the one true God who had redeemed them from slavery. But their understanding of him was too small. They thought they could make an image to represent his strength (a bull is a symbol of strength) and that if the image was of costly materials (gold) and skilled workmanship, then it would honour God. But their image only represented God's strength; it did not convey anything about his moral character. So their worship quickly degenerated into a drunken orgy. The episode illustrates powerfully that any attempt, however sincere, to represent the transcendent God by means of created things will be hopelessly inadequate. And this command shows that any such attempt is forbidden.

Moslems interpret this command as prohibiting all artistic representations of the created order. But given that God himself directed the Israelites to craft such things as almond buds and cherubim in the tabernacle, this cannot be correct. What is forbidden here is making any image of God. We are not to make images of God the Father, God the Son or God the Holy Spirit.

The Roman Catholic and Orthodox Churches have traditionally argued that if Jesus has revealed himself as a visible man, then visual representations of the man Jesus are acceptable aids to worship. But Protestants have traditionally held that all such representations fall hopelessly far short of the majesty and glory of Christ. Images or pictures (sometimes called icons) are not to be used in worship. We learn and worship using the plain words of Scripture, by which the Spirit speaks to us and shows us Christ.

Many Protestants would still hold this view as regards worship, but would be very relaxed about pictures of Jesus in books, especially for children, or about portrayals of Jesus on screen or stage. However, leaders such as J. I. Packer would argue that these too are forbidden by the Second Commandment. Any human representation of the Lord Christ is bound to be hopelessly inadequate. Any such representation will invariably focus on one characteristic or another — for example, giving an impression of his human weakness while failing to convey his glory. Generations of children have grown up with a weak and distorted view of Jesus as a meek and effeminate shepherd, due to well-meaning but sentimental pictures in story Bibles. God is jealous of his glory. We tread on holy ground when we try to communicate what he is like. This command prohibits our poor and feeble artistic representations which fall so far short of his infinite majesty.

Even more challenging, this command not only prohibits images of God made by human hands, but it forbids idols made by human minds: 'I like to think of God as a benevolent grandfather'; 'My God would never send people to hell'; 'I like to think of God as Mother.' So much of what goes under the name of Christian teaching sets aside the plain truth of the Word of God and looks instead to human preference. We cannot pick and choose what qualities of God we like. We have to worship him in submission to his Word, which reveals all we need to know about him.

There is a strong warning in verse 5. People in Israel lived in extended families. If the patriarch had false ideas of the Lord, then all his family, even down through the generations, would be affected. But there is also a warm promise in verse 6. We are to love the one true God, and worship him as he has directed. The promise is that his steadfast love will then remain with us.

Prayer: Almighty God, I worship you for your glory, for your majesty, for your infinite power and love. Forgive me for my inadequate worship. Forgive me when I think of you with too small a vision. Help me to realize what an awesome privilege it is to come into the presence of the Most High God.

Text for the day: *God is spirit, and those who worship him must worship in spirit and truth* (John 4:24).

'You shall not take the name of the LORD your God in vain'

Names in the Bible are far more than mere identification labels. They indicate a person's character. To know someone's name is to understand something about him or her.

The name of the Lord is holy. It is not to be used carelessly or irreverently. Throughout the ages the name of God has been used as a blasphemy. That is offensive. But sometimes believers thought-lessly play with the name of God in a way that is wrong too.

Jesus accused the religious elite of his day of taking God's name in vain in their prayers. To come to worship without wholehearted love and sincerity is taking God's name in vain. To sing hymns and say 'Amen' to prayers while our thoughts are far away from him is to take his name in vain.

The priests in Malachi 1:6-8 were breaking this commandment, without uttering verbal profanity, by serving half-heartedly and carelessly. The worshippers likewise were 'profaning' the Lord's name (Mal. 1:12) when they couldn't be bothered to give the best to the Lord. If we call ourselves Christians, but there is no living reality to our testimony, we are taking the name of the Lord in vain.

Pagan religions make much of knowing the names of deities or spirits, and then using those names in incantations. The idea is that the power can be manipulated by use of its name. This command forbids any attempt at such manipulation. When we come to God in prayer, it is not mechanical use of the phrase 'in Jesus' name' that will force his hand to do what we want. Rather, we come in humility to the Creator and Lord of the universe, accepting that he has the sovereign right to do as he pleases. Prayer draws us closer into relationship with 'our Father' — the most intimate name of all, and one that we use with reverence, with wonder and with love.

Positively, this commandment reminds us that we should lift up and honour the name of God. The first petition of the Lord's Prayer is: 'Hallowed be your name' (Matt. 6:9).

Yes, LORD, walking in the way of your laws,
*   we wait for you;*
your name and renown
*   are the desire of our hearts...*
O LORD, our God, other lords besides you have ruled over us,
*   but your name alone do we honour*

                                        (Isa. 26:8,13, NIV).

Are the name and renown of the Lord the desire of my heart today? Can I sing the following words with sincerity?

Oh, for a thousand tongues to sing
my great Redeemer's praise,
the glories of my God and King,
the triumphs of his grace!

My gracious Master and my God,
assist me to proclaim,
and spread through all the earth abroad
the honours of your name

                                        (Charles Wesley).

Prayer: Take opportunity to pray for the great nation of China, with the largest population on earth (nearly 1.3 billion in 2000). There are 500 million children and young people under the age of eighteen, and at the date of writing it is illegal to teach them about any religion. Pray that it would soon be possible openly to teach and honour the name of God among these needy young people.

Text for the day: *Your name alone do we honour* (Isa. 26:13, NIV).

'Remember the Sabbath day, to keep it holy'

The 'Sabbath' principle goes back to the creation, when God set a cycle of six days of labour and one day of rest. This pattern is for all people everywhere, whether Israel of old, or Christians today:

> *And on the seventh day God finished his work that he had done, and he rested on the seventh day from all his work that he had done. So God blessed the seventh day and made it holy, because on it God rested from all his work that he had done in creation* (Gen. 2:2-3).

Within the Old Testament, the Sabbath also served a specific function within the Mosaic covenant. God used the Sabbath as a special sign of the covenant between himself and Israel (Exod. 31:12-17). Observance of the Sabbath became one of the 'boundary markers' (along with circumcision and observing the food laws) which marked the Jewish people out as distinct and different from other nations. With the coming of Christ and the new covenant, the Sabbath principle was transformed. The specific civil and ceremonial applications of the Sabbath were abolished. Paul argued against the observance of special Sabbath days as Jewish feast days which marked a person out as a Jew, and confirmed their membership of the Jewish covenant community (Gal. 4:9-11; Col. 2:16).

Jesus could have abolished the Sabbath when he was on earth. Instead he redefined it. He rescued it from the intricacies of Pharisaic legislation and removed its significance as a ceremonial law of Judaism. He pronounced himself to be Lord of the Sabbath. So, in the New Testament, we find the believers gathering on the first day of the week (Acts 20:7; cf. 1 Cor. 16:2), which is called 'The Lord's day' (Rev. 1:10).

Obedience to the abiding principle of the Fourth Commandment honours God and protects us. We are to honour God with the first of our time and the best of our time. In a materialistic society, all the pressure is for us to fill up our 'spare' time with pursuits which suit 'me'. If we fill every day with 'me'-orientated activity we dishonour God. The first day of the week should be devoted to worship of our Maker. We are to pray about how we use the Lord's Day. Prayer, reflection, corporate worship, hospitality, visitation of the lonely or needy — there is no shortage of things we can do to honour our God on his day. It should be a day of celebration when we remember the resurrection of our Lord from the dead. It should be a day of teaching when we learn more of our God from his Word. It should be a day of fellowship when we enjoy spending time with his people. It should be a day of mercy when we seek to do good to others.

A cycle of work and rest also protects us. As humans we may have a tendency either to laziness or to overwork. We are to be diligent and work, but we are not to make an idol of our work. Having to stop on the Lord's Day, and reflect on who it is all for anyway, protects us from being controlled by our work. William Wilberforce (1759-1833) was a hugely effective evangelical leader, who led the campaign against the abolition of slavery. He testified: 'Blessed be to God for the day of rest and religious occupation wherein earthly things assume their true size. Ambition is stunted.'

One day in seven of rest also points forward to the eternal 'rest' from painful toil in a sinful and fallen world. If we refuse this provision from the Lord, does it indicate that we are so addicted to the activities of this life that we do not really look forward to future glory?

Prayer: Almighty God, I worship you for the wonderful provision of the Lord's Day. Forgive me for the many times when I have failed to use this day for your glory. Please help me to honour you by keeping it special.

Text for the day:
If you ... call the Sabbath a delight...
if you honour it, not going your own ways
or seeking your own pleasure, or talking idly;
then you shall take delight in the LORD
(Isa. 58:13-14).

'Honour your father and your mother'

God's design for all of humanity includes his design for the family. The relationships between parents and children (the Fifth Commandment) and husband and wife (the Seventh Commandment) are fundamental to the stability of society. Many today say that the family is just a 'lifestyle choice'. It doesn't matter, they say, whether a child is brought up by a man, a woman, two men or two women, as long as they are 'caring adults'. But all the evidence points to the fact that God's design is best. Statistics show that the children at least risk of abuse are those living with their own biological mother and father who themselves are in a stable marriage.

God is our Father, and the parent-child relationship is designed to be a reflection of the relationship between him and his people. In one sense, God is the Father of all, as the giver and sustainer of life. But primarily the Bible refers to God as the Father of his redeemed people. God as Father cares for and provides for his children; he loves them and disciplines them. His people respond with love, obedience, submission and honour. This command reflects something deep about the character of God himself. When we are called on to love and respect our human parents, it reflects the way we are to love and respect God. Our submission to them is part of our submission to him.

Our parents are sinners, so there are limits to our obedience. Jesus is Lord, not our parents. If they command us to sin, 'We must obey God rather than men.' If they forbid us to follow Christ, we have to be willing to put him first. In such cases we have to take comfort with the psalmist: 'Though my father and mother forsake me, the LORD will receive me' (Ps. 27:10, NIV). But those are extreme cases. Generally, we are to respect our parents, and uphold parental authority in society.

For today there is a massive challenge to parental authority (cf. 2 Tim. 3:2). Yes, in a sinful world, authority is sometimes abused, and there need to be safeguards to protect children from abuse. But to dismantle the whole legitimacy of parental authority brings in a new risk of abuse. Children are told today that they have 'rights', and that their parents have no right to tell them what to do. Every home is said to be a 'democracy' where everyone has an equal say. But children and teenagers need boundaries. In a permissive society, they are protected from abuse and exploitation when their parents set firm limits. This command is telling children and young people to respect the rules set by their parents while they are living in the parental home. It is telling parents, both father and mother, that they have a responsibility for the protection and moral well-being of their children.

This command reminds us that we cannot live just as we please: God has placed us under authority. The home is where we are to learn the principle of submission. Then in later life we are better prepared to live as good citizens and employees under the other authorities ordained by God. That is why there is a promise attached to this command: '... that your days may be long in the land that the LORD your God is giving you.' A stable, happy, peaceful society depends on the members of that society learning to obey authority.

We are reminded that we have responsibilities to honour our parents throughout our lives. As children we are to obey them. As adults, we are to respect them and value their advice. As they grow elderly, we will need to make sure they are well looked after and provided for. Jesus was scathing about those who neglected the care of their own parents, under the pretext of engaging in ministry. Maybe we need to repent of our neglect of our parents, of our failure to love them and honour them.

Prayer: If your parents are still living, pray for wisdom in honouring them and grace in loving them. If not, pray for the Lord's help in submitting in a Christlike way to other authorities in your life.

Text for the day: *Honour your father and your mother* (Exod. 20:12).

'You shall not murder'

This is probably the most universally accepted of the Ten Commandments. 'You shall not murder' — who would argue with that? Yet there is enormous confusion about what this command actually means. The Authorized / King James translation, 'Thou shalt not kill,' is misleading. The people of Israel were commanded to engage in warfare, which necessarily involves killing. God's law called for the death penalty, which necessarily involves killing. On the other hand, in today's society abortion is routinely performed and there are increasing calls for euthanasia to be legalized. People evidently don't think that these things count as killing. And there are many who demand the end to the death penalty, as they argue that it runs counter to the sanctity of human life.

The Bible makes the application of this commandment very clear. The verb translated 'to murder' really means 'to assassinate' — in other words this command forbids a private individual taking the life of another. Every human being has been made in the image of God. This is why, in Genesis 9, murder is forbidden. This applies to humans of every age, race, class and capability.

Many today argue that the value of human life must be measured in terms of personal capacity (intelligence, communication, enjoyment of life). If, for example, an unborn child will not 'enjoy' such things, it is said that abortion is justified. In the case of the very elderly or chronically sick, some say that there is a case for euthanasia. But Genesis 9 shows that every individual is to be respected as made in God's image, whatever their capabilities. Others argue that the value of life can be measured in terms of contribution to the community. An able and well individual can contribute much; a badly disabled person is seen as a 'drain' on community resources. Society may judge that such people are not 'worth' keeping alive. Again, the clear teaching of Scripture is that the value of human life is to do with the image of God in each human. It is wrong to assess the value of life in crassly economic terms.

Far from the sanctity of life forbidding the death penalty, the argument in Genesis 9 is that every human life is so sacred that the deliberate taking of human life *must* be punished with the death penalty.

Unborn human life is sacred too. When there was the accidental taking of the life of an unborn child, it was taken very seriously, and a penalty had to be paid (Exod. 21:22-23). Biologically, from the moment of conception there is a genetically complete individual. Certainly it is dependent, but so is a newborn baby. Where there is an individual human being, there is the image of God. We are to grieve at the wanton destruction of human life that goes on in our society every day.

Positively, we are to respect all human beings as made in the image of God. Do we despise others because of their class or race or lack of education? We are to repent of this sin. We are never to look down on others because of their appearance or abilities. Jesus gave a radical interpretation of this command, saying that all anger is a transgression. If we hate any human being, we break this command. Rather, we are to love. Just as God loves the unlovely, so we are to have compassion for others, even those we find most difficult.

Prayer: Almighty God, please give me the eyes of the Lord Jesus, to look with compassion and love on all people. I pray that you would forgive me when I have responded with anger and hatred to others, even those nearest and dearest to me. Please give me that supernatural power to love that can only come from being united with Christ and filled with the Spirit. I pray that my life today would increasingly be characterized by the fruit of the Spirit, which is love.

Text for the day: *Now the works of the flesh are evident: ... enmity, strife, jealousy, fits of anger... But the fruit of the Spirit is love ...* (Gal. 5:19-22).

'You shall not commit adultery'

Along with the Fifth Commandment (to honour parents) this command against adultery confirms that the family is God's building block for society. And, like the Fifth Commandment, this too is based on the character of God. Marriage was created to provide an illustration for the faithful self-giving love of Christ for his bride the church. In the eternal purpose of God, Christ's love came first, and marriage was to be a signpost to that greater reality. Thus the marriage covenant is used throughout Scripture as a picture of the covenant between God and his people. When we are unfaithful to God it is compared with spiritual adultery.

In our permissive society we are all too often desensitized to sin. We need to go back to Scripture, to understand that fidelity is at the heart of 'covenant love'. God designed the marriage bond to be between one man and one woman, for life. The sexual union of husband and wife is designed to be utterly exclusive. No one else is to participate. It is designed by God to confirm the marriage bond. Adultery is the breaking of that bond.

The breaking of the marriage bond was regarded with such horror that it carried the death penalty in the Old Testament. In the New Testament, we are told that adulterers will not enter heaven (Rev. 21:8). Certainly there is full forgiveness in Christ whenever a sinner repents. But we are warned in the strongest terms through-out Scripture that we are to flee temptation. Giving way to lust can destroy lives. The book of Proverbs compares playing with sexual temptation to playing with fire. The godly young man Joseph fled rather than risk succumbing to the advances of his employer's wife (Gen. 39:12). Jesus tells us that we are in danger of hell itself if we fall into lust, and it is preferable to cut off one's own hand or tear out an eye (Matt. 5:27-30). He confirms that it is not only actual sexual infidelity that constitutes adultery. Desiring anyone other than one's spouse, looking with lust at another woman — all such things are adultery.

Paul warns that if we fall into sexual immorality, we sin against our own bodies, but also against the Lord (1 Cor. 6:18-20). God's design is for the husband and wife to enjoy their sexual relationship

(Song of Songs; 1 Cor. 7:3-5). Sexual activity of any kind outside of marriage is forbidden (the biblical term for this is 'fornication'). Single believers are to abstain from sexual relationships. Their devotion is to be focused exclusively on the Lord (1 Cor. 7:32,34).

This law shows us our sin, but does not give us the power to live a holy life. It is only in union with Christ and by the power of the Spirit that we can resist temptation. We are to pray daily that we may be given power to flee from situations where we are liable to be tempted. We may need to abstain from fiction or films that feed romantic fantasies, or avoid pictures that stir up lust. As with all temptation, the most effective antidote is to have our minds and hearts filled with the love of God. We need that hourly sense that we live in the presence of the Lord and we fear to grieve him. As Joseph said, 'How then can I do this great wickedness and sin against God?' (Gen. 39:9).

Boundless grace with you is found,
grace to cover all my sin:
let the healing streams abound;
make and keep me clean within.
Living Fountain, now impart
all your life and purity;
spring for ever in my heart,
rise to all eternity!

(Charles Wesley).

Prayer: Almighty God, I pray that you would guard my heart and mind. May your Holy Spirit convict me of anything that displeases you.

Text for the day: *You are not your own, for you were bought with a price. So glorify God in your body (1 Cor. 6:19-20).*

'You shall not steal'

This command affirms the right to private property. When God led Israel into the promised land he did not give it to the whole nation and command that they work in co-operatives, pooling all their resources for the common good. He allocated the land tribe by tribe, clan by clan, family by family. As each family brought their first fruits to the Lord, there was the understanding that he had granted that land and that prosperity to them (Deut. 26:10-11). The idea was that hard work should lead to prosperity, and that the family should benefit from that prosperity. If an individual's property was destroyed through the negligence or accident of another, there was the principle of restoration (Exod. 22:5-6,14-15). If an individual deliberately stole from another, the thief had to repay double. If he could not do that, he might be sold into slavery (22:3). There was punishment for theft, not just re-education or deterrence. If a robbery was attempted at night, the property owner could kill in self-defence if necessary (22:2-3).

The direct application of this is that we are to renounce all dishonesty. We are not to take the property of others; we are to avoid the theft of unpaid bills, unreturned borrowed items, underpaid fares on public transport, taxes wrongly withheld, or overcharging on items we sell. We are not to steal time from our employer, or cheat those we do business with. If we have any-thing to repent of in this area, we are not only to voice our contrition, but actually make practical restitution, as Zacchaeus did (Luke 19:8-9).

This commandment protects private property, but the law also had safeguards against the unbridled accumulation of property. God is the ultimate owner and Lord of all. 'The earth is the LORD's and the fullness thereof' (Ps. 24:1). God grants strength to work and acquire wealth: 'Beware lest you say in your heart, "My power and the might of my hand have gained me this wealth"' (Deut. 8:17). Many laws encouraged open-handed generosity to those less fortunate. Farmers were to leave ample gleanings of grain and grapes (Lev. 19:9-10). The prosperous were to lend freely to the poor (Deut. 15:7-8).

We may claim to have 'private' property, but we are only stewards. It has been entrusted to us by the Lord. He holds us responsible for how we use it. We are to give freely of our 'first fruits' to the Lord, at least tithing our income, and giving more if we can. We are to look after the needs of our families: 'If anyone does not provide for his relatives, and especially for members of his household, he has denied the faith and is worse than an unbeliever' (1 Tim. 5:8). We are to be generous in relieving the needs of those poorer than ourselves: 'Your abundance at the present time should supply their need' (2 Cor. 8:14).

When Paul commands believers not to steal, he contrasts ungodly taking with godly giving: 'Let the thief no longer steal, but rather let him labour, doing honest work with his own hands, so that he may have something to share with anyone in need' (Eph. 4:28). Conversion means a change of heart. Instead of selfishly wanting to take, we now feel compassion and want to give. The Lord has given us all we have. We now want to let him use it all for his glory and for the good of others:

Take my silver and my gold,
not a mite would I withhold;
take my intellect and use
every power as thou shalt choose

(Frances Ridley Havergal).

Prayer: Lord, please search my heart. Remind me if I have made promises I have not kept, borrowed goods I have not returned, or ever stolen anything. Please replace the selfish desire to take with a Christlike desire to give. Show me today how I can relieve the needs of others.

Text for the day: *The King will say ... 'Come, you who are blessed by my Father... For I was hungry and you gave me food, I was thirsty and you gave me drink... [As] you did it to one of the least of these my brothers, you did it to me'* (Matt. 25:34-40).

'You shall not bear false witness against your neighbour'

The primary application of this commandment was within the legal system. Because God is a God of truth and justice, justice was to be administered fairly and impartially. Even the best judicial system collapses if the evidence presented to the judge is fraudulent, or if relevant evidence is withheld (Lev. 5:1). Silence can be sinful too: we can deceive by what we don't say as well as by what we say.

But the principle of this command extends beyond the law court. 'Lying lips are an abomination to the LORD, but those who act faithfully are his delight' (Prov. 12:22). God is the God of absolute truth, and the devil is the father of lies (John 8:44). Our sinful nature constantly pushes us towards untruthfulness. We may deceive ourselves about our own goodness, shift the blame to others, or (worst of all), think evil thoughts of God. The devil perpetually stokes the fires of deceit, and we need the continual help of the Holy Spirit to convict us of the need for absolute truthfulness.

This commandment reminds us of the potentially devastating effects of our words. We can destroy another person's reputation in a few sentences: 'You shall not go around as a slanderer among your people' (Lev. 19:16). We can discourage others, and tear them down. We can dishonour God. We need to pray with the psalmist:

> *Put false ways far from me,*
> *and graciously teach me your law!*
> *I have chosen the way of faithfulness;*
> *I set your rules before me*
>
>   (Ps. 119:29-30).

Frances Ridley Havergal, author of the lovely hymn, 'Take my life, and let it be, consecrated Lord to thee,' once wrote to a young friend, urging her to take seriously the words of Jesus when he said, 'Whatsoever ye would that men should do to you, do ye even so to them' (Matt. 7:12, AV):

> *Now, be true to yourself, and to Him, as to these His own words. Would you like anyone to retell, and dwell upon, little incidents which made you appear weak, tiresome, capricious, foolish? Yet ... everything which we say of another which we would not like them to say of us (unless said with some right and pure object which Jesus Himself would approve), is transgression of this distinct command of our dear Lord's, and therefore sin, — sin which needs nothing less than His blood to cleanse, sin in which we indulge at our peril and to the certain detriment of our spiritual life.*

This is radical! But how we need this reminder! Jesus also teaches that 'On the day of judgement people will give account for every careless word they speak' (Matt. 12:36). Pray each day that all your words may be absolutely truthful and absolutely kind.

Prayer: Father God, I worship you that you are the God of perfect truth. I worship you that Jesus is the truth. I worship you that the Holy Spirit of truth convicts me with regard to truth. Please shine your light in my heart to show me where I make excuses for dishonesty. Please help me to be truthful in all my thoughts and words today.

Text for the day: *Do not lie to one another, seeing that you have put off the old self with its practices* (Col. 3:9).

'You shall not covet'

Human beings always seem to want more. Animals are content, broadly speaking, with food, shelter and a mate. We yearn for more. We were created to be lords of creation, with the job of subduing the earth. Civilizations are built because of that quest. Most of all, we were created to worship and enjoy God. Hence the 'God-shaped' hole inside each one of us. We try to fill that hole with more and more things, new experiences and fresh achievements. But, as Augustine found, 'Our hearts are restless until they find their rest in thee.'

The sin of covetousness is so serious because it insults God. It is looking for satisfaction in the wrong place. We are to be satisfied with God alone. To covet, says Paul, is to commit idolatry (Col. 3:5; Eph. 5:5).

What is my heart set on today? Where do most of my thoughts turn when my mind is in 'neutral gear'? Am I always thinking about the things of this world — my own possessions, my circumstances, my desires? Or am I delighting in the Lord? Certainly God gives us all good things to enjoy. Certainly we are to work hard to use our gifts in this world. But our motivation is to be for his glory, not our own.

Christian contentment is the capacity to be satisfied with God. Nothing can separate us from his love (Rom. 8:38-39). We possess everything if we have God himself (2 Cor. 6:10). The writer to the Hebrews points to the sources of contentment — the character and faithfulness of God:

Keep your life free from love of money, and be content with what you have, for he has said, 'I will never leave you nor forsake you.' So we can confidently say,

'The Lord is my helper,
I will not fear;
what can man do to me?'

(Heb. 13:5-6).

We are also to be satisfied with God's provision for us. Perhaps we are always dreaming of 'better' things: a bigger house, a better car, more possessions, holidays, a different job, more fulfilling relationships. But our present circumstances have not happened by chance. God's agenda for me today is not to increase my standard of living. His agenda is that I should become more Christlike. And even the difficulties of my circumstances may be used to that end. We are to trust him as the great provider. We commit our needs to him, and if the answer is 'No' or 'Not yet' we dishonour him by fretting and coveting.

Western economies are built on stimulating people to desire more and more. This can be a deadly trap. The love of money is a source of all kinds of evil. We are to be counter-cultural, loving God more than things. We are to set the example of a simple lifestyle. We are to use our wealth to help others as well as to provide for ourselves. The church in the Western world will never have any credibility as long as our materialistic lifestyles are indistinguishable from those around us.

Prayer: Lord, please help me today to find my greatest joy in you. Thank you for all the wonderful provisions and gifts you give me, but may they all point to you, the great Giver, and may I be satisfied in you alone. Forgive me when I make an idol of the gifts you give me.

Text for the day: *Keep your life free from love of money, and be content with what you have, for he has said, 'I will never leave you nor forsake you'* (Heb. 13:5).

'You shall not oppress a sojourner'

These few verses give a flavour of the social and civil rules that regulated every detail of the Israelites' lives. They are listed in Exodus 22 – 23, and then at greater length in Deuteronomy. Some of the rules functioned as 'boundary markers', separating the people of Israel from the surrounding peoples. Others governed their relations with each other. The Lord dealt with his people within the historical context of the time. He did not lift them out of it; rather he gave principles of justice that would transform the existing structures. Here are just a few of those principles, with one or two examples for each one:

• *The dignity of each person* (as made in the image of God): 'You shall not murder' (Exod. 20:13). 'You are to have the same law for the alien and the native-born' (Lev. 24:22, NIV).

• *The disabled, the powerless and the alien were not to be exploited:* 'You shall not curse the deaf or put a stumbling block before the blind' (Lev. 19:14; cf. Exod. 22:21-22).

• *No one, rich or poor, was to be the victim of false accusation or slander.* All were to be granted a fair trial. All were equally to be subject to the rule of law: 'You shall not pervert the justice due to your poor in his lawsuit. Keep far from a false charge, and do not kill the innocent and righteous… And you shall take no bribe' (Exod. 23:6-8).

• *Punishments were not to be excessive:* 'But if there is serious injury, you are to take life for life, eye for eye, tooth for tooth…' (Exod. 21:23, NIV). This was designed to prevent feuds from escalating; it was a general principle that the penalty was to fit the crime, not exceed it. An actual eye or tooth was not literally required; there is no evidence that such a penalty was ever carried out.

• *Everyone's property was to be respected:* 'You shall not steal' (Exod. 20:15; cf. 21:33-36).

• *All were to share in the plenty of the land:* 'The seventh year you shall let it [the land] rest and lie fallow, that the poor of your people may eat; and what they leave the beasts of the field may eat' (Exod. 23:11; cf. Deut. 14:28-29, where every third year the tithes were distributed to the poor).

• *All were to offer first fruits to the Lord*, including their time (the Sabbath principle): 'Remember the Sabbath day, to keep it holy' (Exod. 20:8, cf. 22:29-30).

• *Women, uniquely at that time, were protected from exploitation.* If a female concubine did not please her master and he took another wife, he was not to 'diminish her food, her clothing, or her marital rights. And if he does not do these three things for her, she shall go out [free] for nothing' (Exod. 21:10-11).

• *Animals were not to be gratuitously ill-treated:* 'If you see the donkey of one who hates you lying down under its burden, you shall refrain from leaving him with it; you shall rescue it with him' (Exod. 23:5).

• *Nature was to be respected:* 'When you besiege a city ... you shall not destroy its trees... Are the trees of the field human, that they should be besieged by you?' (Deut. 20:19).

The overriding principle is that the Lord sees every detail of life, and every detail of life is to conform to his character of love, justice and mercy.

Prayer: Lord, may every detail of my life today please you. May I deal with everyone fairly and kindly. May I not discriminate in my thoughts or deeds against those whom society despises.

Text for the day:
  ... what does the LORD require of you
  but to do justice, and to love kindness,
    and to walk humbly with your God?

                                        (Micah 6:8).

'They beheld God, and ate and drank'

This chapter is the high point of the Exodus account. God had rescued his people. Their sins were symbolically cleansed by blood-sacrifice so that they could enjoy fellowship with him. Now he summoned their representatives into his presence. They saw his glory and enjoyed a covenant meal in his presence. Moses, their mediator, spent forty days with God, receiving instructions about the tabernacle (the place where God would meet with his people as they continued their journey).

In Exodus 19 and 20 the people were terrified by the dramatic and awesome appearance of God in thunder, lightning, smoke and the loud trumpet blast. All these things typified the 'otherness' of God, his holiness and his hatred of sin. How different the scene here! The people had agreed to keep the covenant (24:3), sacrifices for sin had been offered (24:5) and the people had been sprinkled with sacrificial blood (24:6). Their representatives approached God without fear (24:11). His wrath had been appeased. The glory of God's presence here was not manifest in smoke and darkness. Instead they were dazzled by the loveliness of the sapphire pavement beneath his throne. The atmosphere was peaceful, even joyful: 'They beheld God, and ate and drank' (24:11).

Fellowship with God himself is what we were created for. Looking backwards, this scene of table fellowship evokes memories of the fellowship with God enjoyed by Adam and Eve before they rebelled. Looking forwards, it points to the fellowship meal taken by the Lord Jesus with his disciples the night before he died as the final sacrifice for sin:

> Now as they were eating, Jesus took bread, and after blessing it he broke it and gave it to the disciples, and said, 'Take, eat; this is my body.' And he took a cup, and when he had given thanks he gave it to them, saying, 'Drink of it, all of you, for this is my blood of the covenant, which is poured out for many for the forgiveness of sins' (Matt. 26:26-28).

Looking still further ahead, it anticipates the final consummation: the wedding supper of the Lamb when Christ returns. At the Last Supper Jesus himself said, 'I tell you I will not drink again of this fruit of the vine until that day when I drink it new with you in my Father's kingdom' (Matt. 26:29).

At the Lord's Supper we commemorate the once-for-all sacrifice by which Christ bore the punishment for our sins: 'For by a single offering he has perfected for all time those who are being sanctified' (Heb. 10:14). As we pray, we enter into the immediate presence of God because of the work of Jesus, our mediator.

Today our fellowship with God is 'by faith, not by sight'. We meet with him by faith, by reading his Word and having it illuminated to us by his Spirit. We long for the day when 'we shall see him' and 'we shall be like him', when, like the seventy Israelite elders, we shall sit in his immediate presence and eat and drink. 'Come, Lord Jesus!' (Rev. 22:20).

Prayer: Praise God for his gift of the Lord Jesus Christ, the final sacrifice to take away sin for ever. Praise God that because of the work of Christ we can enjoy fellowship with him today. Praise God that we can look forward in certain anticipation of the marriage supper of the Lamb when Christ returns.

Text for the day: *Blessed are those who are invited to the marriage supper of the Lamb* (Rev. 19:9).

A tabernacle was set up

The construction of the tabernacle and its various furnishings constitutes the largest single topic in the Bible. The detailed instructions given to Moses were recorded (Exod. 25 – 31), beginning with the sacred ark, which rested in the Holy of Holies, and then working outwards. Firstly, the table and lampstand for the Holy of Holies are described; then the construction of the tabernacle itself, with a thick curtain separating the Most Holy Place from the Holy Place; then the altar, the courtyard and the priestly garments.

The tabernacle was not a place for public gatherings, but the place where, symbolically, God dwelt. Daily sacrifices reminded the people of God's holiness and their own sinfulness, and that a price for sin had to be paid if he was to remain among them. The details underlined the fact that God could not be approached any way they wanted. He had to be worshipped in the way he prescribed. All of the details were repeated a second time. A precise report of the construction was given, to show that God's instructions were followed exactly. The second time, instead of working from the inside out, the descriptions begin with the outer court and work inwards (Exod. 35 – 39).

The sheer expanse of curtains required for the construction is very striking. These curtains symbolized the holiness of God. People could not just wander into his presence. When the high priest approached the tabernacle, he went through the entrance curtain into the outer court. Facing him stood the bronze altar for burnt offerings and the basin for washing. He would go through another curtain into the Holy Place, where the lamps were perpetually burning on the lampstand, and where bread was always displayed on the table. The altar of incense stood in front of the inner curtain, which separated off the Most Holy Place, in which stood the ark of the covenant. The high priest could only enter this most sacred place once a year.

The symbolism was carried over into the temple built in Jerusalem, and continued when the temple was rebuilt at the time of Herod. A huge, heavy, thirty-foot-high curtain screened off the Most Holy Place from all but the high priest. No one else could enter. It was this enormous curtain that was ripped in two from top to bottom at the moment of Christ's death: 'Jesus cried out again with a loud voice, and yielded up his spirit. And behold, the curtain of the temple was torn in two, from top to bottom' (Matt. 27:50-51).

This was a supernatural event. The curtain was torn from the top. God himself ripped apart the barrier into his presence, thus inviting us to enter his presence by means of the blood of Christ. Never again would he demand that we go through a human priest, or offer an animal sacrifice, or stay on the other side of a curtain.

> *The temple curtain is torn down,*
> *the living way to heaven is seen;*
> *through Christ, the middle wall has gone*
> *and all who will may enter in.*
> *The ancient shadows are fulfilled,*
> *the law's harsh sentence is applied,*
> *the sinless Lamb of God is killed,*
> *the covenant is ratified*
>
> (Charles Wesley).

All of the symbolism of the tabernacle and temple pointed forward to Christ. Once he had come, there was no need for the visual aids, no need for the symbols. They are obsolete. The tabernacle represented God himself dwelling with his people. 'And the Word became flesh and dwelt [or made his tent/tabernacle] among us, and we have seen his glory' (John 1:14).

Prayer: Praise God that we have free entry into his presence by the blood of Christ. Praise God that by his Holy Spirit he dwells with us now, and that one day our faith will be sight and we shall dwell with him for ever.

Text for the day: *The curtain of the temple was torn in two, from top to bottom* (Matt. 27:51).

Rebellion in the camp

The two lengthy descriptions of the tabernacle, and instructions on how to worship God, are divided by this tragic account of rebellion. There is huge irony in the fact that, while Moses was in the presence of God receiving precise details of the correct way to worship, the people were at the bottom of the mountain doing the exact opposite. While Moses was receiving instructions as to how to consecrate Aaron as high priest, Aaron was making an idol.

Moses spent forty days (nearly six weeks) with the Lord on the mountain. Down in the camp, impatience boiled over. The people wanted to move on, but they knew they needed divine help on the way. Retaining the mentality of Egypt, they thought an idol would help. But God repudiated such tarnished worship:

> They have turned aside quickly out of the way that I commanded them. They have made for themselves a golden calf and have worshipped it and sacrificed to it and said, 'These are your gods, O Israel, who brought you up out of the land of Egypt!' (32:8).

The people not only engaged in idolatry, but in immorality. The statement that they 'rose up to play' (32:6) implies a pagan orgy. Paul takes this incident as a terrible object lesson, a warning:

> Do not be idolaters as some of them were... Now these things happened to them as an example, but they were written down for our instruction, on whom the end of the ages has come. Therefore let anyone who thinks that he stands take heed lest he fall. No temptation has overtaken you that is not common to man. God is faithful, and he will not let you be tempted beyond your ability (1 Cor. 10:7,11-13).

In contrast to the folly of the Israelites, we see the faithfulness of Moses. When God threatened to destroy them, and promised Moses a people of his own (Exod. 32:10), Moses did not grasp the opportunity of personal preferment. Rather, he interceded in the strongest possible terms for the nation (32:11-13). He appealed to God on the basis of what God had already done for them and argued that the Lord's glory would be diminished if other nations heard that his people had been destroyed. He begged for mercy, and he reminded the Lord of his covenant promises to Abraham, Isaac and Jacob: 'You swore by your own self' (32:13, cf. Gen. 22:16). As the psalmist later said:

> *They made a calf in Horeb*
>   *and worshipped a metal image...*
> *They forgot God, their Saviour...*
> *Therefore he said he would destroy them —*
>   *had not Moses, his chosen one,*
> *stood in the breach before him,*
>   *to turn away his wrath from destroying them*
>   (Ps. 106:19,21,23).

Moses forgot his own welfare. He wanted the glory of God and the good of his people. He stood in the breach and interceded for the nation. He foreshadowed our great Intercessor. Jesus Christ prays for his people and stood in the breach, turning God's wrath away from us.

Prayer: Praise God that the Lord Jesus has stood in the breach for us and that he intercedes for us.

Text for the day: *He bore the sin of many, and makes intercession for the transgressors* (Isa. 53:12).

The covenant broken

Imagine that your only son has found the woman of his dreams, and this is the wedding day. He stands at the front of the church, waiting eagerly for the arrival of his bride. The moment comes. She begins the procession down the aisle on her father's arm. Suddenly she catches sight of a man who used to be her lover. She turns away from her groom into the arms of the other man. Such shameless behaviour is almost unimaginable and yet it hardly begins to capture the effrontery of God's people in this account. The Lord had done everything possible for them. He brought them out of Egypt 'on eagles' wings'. He defeated their enemies. He provided them with guidance and protection, both day and night, and gave them daily food. Above all, he invited them into covenant relationship with himself. Their sins would be covered if they kept the covenant and obeyed the requirements of the sacrificial system. The people accepted this covenant willingly: 'All that the LORD has spoken we will do' (Exod. 19:8; 24:3).

The presence of the Lord with his people would be symbolized by the centrality of the tabernacle at the heart of their camp. Moses returned into the immediate presence of God to receive detailed instructions about the construction of the tabernacle and about the sacrifices that would take place there. But as week followed week, the Israelites grew restive. By the fifth week impatience boiled over into anger. In the absence of Moses, Aaron was the target of the people's wrath. Where was Moses? Why had they been stuck at the foot of the mountain for so long? Why could they not just move on towards their destination? A short while before, Aaron, his sons and seventy elders had been given a vision of God's glory (24:9-11). Where were they now? Even if some remained faithful to the Lord, at the moment of crisis the mob prevailed. Aaron failed to display either courage or leadership. The worst elements took control and the camp degenerated into idolatry, anarchy and immorality.

When Moses first heard of the people's sin, his immediate instinct was to intercede for them. But when he saw the degradation to which they had stooped, he realized that their rebellion was so deep that only the most dramatic action would startle them into a realization of what they had done. They had shattered the covenant, so Moses shattered the tables of the covenant. This was no mere loss of temper. Moses burned with righteous anger, even as the Lord himself did (32:10).

Even then, Aaron continued to make excuses for himself and the people continued to run riot. Moses acted decisively. The breaking up and crushing of the idol demonstrated the absurdity of Aaron's claim that 'These are your gods, O Israel, who brought you up out of the land of Egypt!' (32:4). As the rebellion continued, the Levites rallied to Moses' cry: 'Who is on the LORD's side?' Without partiality they went through the camp, killing those rebel leaders who would not submit.

This decisive action was taken in order to save the whole nation from apostasy. It gave a brief preview of what will happen at the final judgement against the enemies of God. If we baulk at this, what of the dreadful Last Day when God's enemies will finally be destroyed? The Levites who rallied to the Lord's side were honoured. God's name was more important to them than family loyalty. Is this the case for us today? As Jesus said, 'Anyone who loves his father or mother more than me is not worthy of me; anyone who loves his son or daughter more than me is not worthy of me' (Matt. 10:37, NIV).

Moses' call to execute the ringleaders was not based on any personal pique — a point proved by his selfless intercession in verse 32. He literally offered his life for the life of his people. He appealed to the Lord to blot his name out of the book of life if only the nation could be saved. This offer foreshadowed the great work of substitution carried out for us by the Lord Jesus himself. Moses was not great enough to act as substitute for the people. Jesus was.

Prayer: Give thanks to the Father for the wonderful work of our Lord Jesus as our mediator and as our substitute.

Text for the day: *I am the good shepherd. The good shepherd lays down his life for the sheep* (John 10:11).

'Please show me your glory'

If your presence will not go with me, do not bring us up from here... Please show me your glory (Exod. 33:15,18).

Moses had interceded for the people and offered to be punished in their place. The Lord relented. He would send an angel with them. They could enter the promised land and enjoy its prosperity, but he himself would not go with them. The people realized that this was 'disastrous' news (33:4). Moses renewed his urgent intercession: 'Is it not in your going with us ... that we are distinct, I and your people, from every other people on the face of the earth?' (33:16). If the Lord was not with them, they did not dare leave that place.

This is to be our attitude today, and every day. We dare not go out into the day without the Lord's presence and blessing. Unless he is with us, all we do will be a waste of time; unless he is with us, we are vulnerable to the attacks of the Evil One. We long to experience his presence and his love. If we know his presence with us, then, like Moses, we are not content, but we want to know him better; we want to see more of his glory.

As soon as the Lord had answered Moses' plea, and agreed to go with them, Moses responded with another request: 'Please show me your glory.' He had been privileged thus far in being granted intimate communion with God. God had communicated the covenant to him. He and the seventy elders had seen something of the glory of God already on the mountain (24:9-10). But anyone who has begun to know anything of the beauty of the Lord hungers to know more of his inexhaustible radiance, holiness, goodness and love.

The Lord agreed to show Moses his goodness and proclaim his name, but he cautioned that this revelation would be partial and transient. Any greater vision of his glory would kill Moses: 'Man shall not see me and live' (33:20). When Moses ascended the mountain again, the Lord proclaimed his name, encapsulating his character (34:5), and passed before him, proclaiming his gracious covenant dealings with his people (34:6-7).

When the Lord caused his glory to pass before Moses, there is no rapturous account of Moses' mystical feelings, no description of an exciting vision. It is very different from some highly-blown 'religious' experiences which focus on the internal and subjective state of the person concerned. The essence of Moses' 'religious experience' is teaching about the character of God. God is merciful, gracious, slow to anger, abounding in love, one who forgives, but whose forgiveness is compatible with justice. Moses does not record his own feelings at the reception of God's revelation, only the fact that he worshipped. All the focus is on God.

We were created for fellowship with God. In Christ, he has revealed his glory, 'full of grace and truth' (John 1:14-18). Having experienced something of the Lord Jesus, our heart-cry should daily be: 'Show me your glory.' Do you want to know Christ more closely? Pray today that he would show you his glory. Under the old covenant, Moses was privileged to converse with the Lord face to face. After doing so his face shone with the Lord's glory. Under the new covenant, we all enter the Lord's presence by the blood of Christ. We remain in his presence through the Holy Spirit, who remains in us and is with us. Drawing near to God by faith, with unveiled faces, we can then reflect something of the Lord's glory.

Prayer: Pray that your life today would reflect something of the radiance of the beauty of the Lord. Meditate and pray through these verses:

> But when one turns to the Lord, the veil is removed. Now the Lord is the Spirit, and where the Spirit of the Lord is, there is freedom. And we all, with unveiled face, beholding the glory of the Lord, are being transformed into the same image from one degree of glory to another. For this comes from the Lord who is the Spirit (2 Cor. 3:16-18).

Text for the day: We all, with unveiled face, beholding the glory of the Lord, are being transformed into the same image from one degree of glory to another (2 Cor. 3:18).

The glory of the LORD filled the tabernacle

God had pardoned the people's betrayal of the covenant and committed himself to continue with them on their journey to the promised land. The tabernacle in the middle of their camp would be the visible reminder of his presence with them. Joy and gratitude at the Lord's longsuffering grace overflowed in the generous material and physical contributions to the building of this tabernacle. Moses did not say that anyone 'had to' give or to work: he appealed to those who were willing. The response was so overwhelming that he had to command the people to stop giving (Exod. 36:6). The emphasis is on willing, voluntary, enthusiastic giving: 'They came, everyone whose heart stirred him, and everyone whose spirit moved him... So they came, both men and women. All who were of a willing heart ...' (35:21-22; cf. 35:29). Both men and women also gave of their time and practical skills. There is emphasis, on the one hand, on the highly specialized crafts of a few and, on the other, on the more general gifts of the many. All worked together harmoniously.

The people were not only generous in giving of their time, energy and material possessions, they were also obedient to the Lord's directions for the construction of the tabernacle. We may find it tedious to read all the details twice over. But the repetition serves to emphasize the exact conformity to what God said. The first time we hear God's instructions; the second time we learn that this is exactly what was done. The point is further emphasized by the repetition of the phrase, 'as the LORD had commanded Moses', which recurs like a refrain throughout chapters 39 and 40. Moses did not add to, or subtract from, or modify any of his instructions. God's requirements were carried out to the letter.

God was pleased with the freely given gifts of the people, as well as the exact obedience to his directions. As soon as the tabernacle was completed, he filled it with his glory. Previously his presence with the people had been signified by the pillar of cloud by day and the pillar of fire by night. Now the cloud and the light were focused on the tabernacle, the cloud still serving as a guide (40:36-37).

We no longer see God's glory in the form of cloud and fire. The visible tabernacle was simply a signpost pointing forward to the greater reality of God's dwelling among us in the person of the Lord Jesus Christ. The glory of God, previously seen in the physical tabernacle, is now seen in Christ: 'And the Word became flesh and dwelt [literally 'tabernacled'] among us, and we have seen his glory, glory as of the only Son from the Father, full of grace and truth' (John 1:14).

Now that Christ has ascended, he has sent his Spirit, who 'tabernacles' within his people:

> *And I will ask the Father, and he will give you another Helper, to be with you for ever, even the Spirit of truth... You know him, for he dwells with you and will be in you* (John 14:16-17).

Jesus himself brought God's presence to us, and now by his Spirit he 'tabernacles' in his people. But the final consummation of God dwelling with his people will come in the new heavens and the new earth:

> *Behold, the dwelling place of God is with man. He will dwell with them, and they will be his people, and God himself will be with them as their God. He will wipe away every tear from their eyes* (Rev. 21:3-4).

Prayer: Almighty God, I worship you for the Lord Jesus, who dwelt among us and revealed your glory. I worship you for the Holy Spirit, who abides with us for ever. I pray that today I would reflect something of your glory to those around, and thus bring glory to you.

Text for the day: *He will give you another Helper, to be with you for ever, even the Spirit of truth... You know him, for he dwells with you and will be in you* (John 14:16-17).

The burnt offering

For many today this chapter makes gruesome reading. Such animal sacrifices are redundant now that Christ has come as the final, once-for all sacrifice for sin. It is tempting to skip over Leviticus, with its long descriptions of the sacrificial system.

But each of the different sacrifices in Leviticus points forward to an aspect of Christ's final work. They tell us something of the character of God, and how we are to worship him. We see that although the Israelites lived in the presence of God (signified by the cloud and fire on the tabernacle) yet God was a holy God. If there was wickedness in his presence, his wrath could break out. They had seen that after the incident of the golden calf. How could they survive in the presence of such a holy God? The answer was the sacrificial system. There was a constant shedding of blood, a constant ascent of smoke from the altar. All of the regulations in Leviticus served as a daily reminder to the people of their intrinsic uncleanness before a holy God, but also showed that he had provided a way for them to enter his presence and live at peace with him.

First, there was the whole burnt offering. Fire is associated with the presence of God, as in the case of the burning bush, or at Mount Sinai at the giving of the law. A burnt offering of a lamb was offered at the tabernacle by the priests every morning and every evening for the sins of the nation (Exod. 29:39-42). Each Sabbath, two lambs were offered in the morning and two lambs in the evening (Num. 28:9-10). Extra lambs were offered on special feast days (Num. 28 – 29). The process was continual. If you were an Israelite living in the camp, you would always smell the burning carcasses. Each night as the darkness fell there would be the continuing glow of the fire on the altar. The smoke never ceased to rise. There could be no more powerful symbol of God's unwavering intolerance of sin and evil. The smouldering fire speaking of the wrath of God was never extinguished. As long as God lives, so his wrath burns against wickedness. Both Old and New Testaments speak of the never-ending punishment with which this holy God consumes his enemies (Isa. 66:24; Matt. 13:42).

Such extreme language may well shock us. But we are rarely shocked enough at the wickedness of our own hearts, or at the evil of the world around us. The blazing purity of God must break out against evil. The Levitical burnt offerings provided a lightning conductor for the wrath of God. The whole animal went up in smoke. If the offering were not made, the people would have to bear God's wrath themselves (2 Chr. 29:7-8). It is clear from this passage that the whole burnt offering was not just an object lesson for the worshippers. It changed the attitude of God: it was 'an aroma pleasing to the LORD' (Lev. 1:9, NIV; Eph. 5:2). Supremely, in the cross of Christ God's righteous anger against sin was turned away, or 'propitiated'. A just and holy God must judge every sin, either on the cross of Christ, or in hell itself.

As well as the regular, communal burnt offerings, an individual could voluntarily bring a burnt offering at any time. The most prosperous could bring a bull, or a male from the flocks could be brought; the very poor could bring a male dove or pigeon. The person would bring the offering freely (there was no compulsion) as an act of worship to God, as an expression of sensing need for atonement for sin, but, most of all, as a declaration of total consecration to God.

Prayer: Lord, please show me if I am withholding anything from you today. Show me if there is anything in my heart that I value above you. Show me if I am guilty of idolatry. Thank you that the Lord Jesus poured out his blood for me. Can I withhold anything from him?

He is the substance of which they were but the shadow. Jesus is the Lamb of the morning, slain from before the foundation of the world, and the Lamb of the evening, offered up in these last days for his people (C .H. Spurgeon).

Text for the day: *This is my blood of the covenant, which is poured out for many for the forgiveness of sins* (Matt. 26:28).

The grain offering

The burnt offering symbolized atonement for sin, as well as complete devotion and surrender to God. It was accompanied by an offering of grain. This could consist of heads of grain, or fine flour, or baked cakes or wafers. Salt (symbolizing permanence and stability) would be added, also oil and incense (symbolizing joy). A portion would be burned up on the altar; the rest would be for the priests. This was a practical way of supplying the priests with daily food. When the people were on the point of entering the land, the book of Numbers records Moses' summary and reminder of the daily offerings, and we learn that a drink offering of wine was always offered alongside the grain offering.

The point of the grain offering (and the accompanying drink offering) was that it was a declaration of obedience and faithfulness to the Lord their King. The people were paying a tribute from the result of their daily toil. They were acknowledging that all the fruit of their labours, the grain from the field and the wine from the vineyards, was only possible because of his goodness in giving them the land in the first place. It was a token of consecration to the Lord of all their possessions and all their labour.

What about our consecration? Do we freely acknowledge that all we have and all we are is only as a result of God's grace? Do we freely give back to him of that which is, after all, his own? Are we generous with our talents, our time, our possessions, our finance?

Most of all, this grain offering points forward to the perfect consecration of the Lord Jesus Christ. The writer to the Hebrews pointed out that the sacrificial system could never finally solve the sin problem. But when Jesus came, his perfect consecration and obedience led him to offer himself as the final and complete sacrifice.

Therefore, when Christ came into the world, he said:

Sacrifice and offering you did not desire,
but a body you prepared for me;
with burnt offerings and sin offerings

you were not pleased.
Then I said, 'Here I am — it is written about me in the scroll —
I have come to do your will, O God'
                    (Heb. 10:5-7, NIV, quoting Ps. 40:6-8).

Christ gave himself willingly and completely. Surely we should hold nothing back from him!

The grain offering followed on from the burnt offering. it was an expression of thankfulness for the Lord's willingness to forgive. So our response to the gift of salvation should be to give ourselves back to God as 'living sacrifices'.

Take my soul and body's powers;
take my memory, mind and will,
all my goods and all my hours,
all I know and all I feel,
all I think or speak or do;
take my heart — but make it new

                                    (Charles Wesley).

Prayer: Almighty God, thank you for the freely given sacrifice of the Lord Jesus. Thank you for his willing obedience to your will. May I freely give of myself to you today. Please help me to hold nothing back. You have given me all things. May I devote all I am and all I have to you.

Text for the day: *Present your bodies as a living sacrifice, holy and acceptable to God, which is your spiritual worship* (Rom. 12:1).

The peace offering

The sequence in which the offerings were to be made was as follows: first the sin offering (symbolizing the removal of sin, Lev. 4), then the burnt and cereal offerings (symbolizing total consecration to God, Lev. 1; 2). Once the worshipper's sins had been removed and his life consecrated, there was nothing to hinder fellowship with God: hence the peace offering (Lev. 3). This was for special occasions of joy and thanksgiving. A worshipper might bring a peace offering when making a vow, or as an expression of thanks in the light of God's goodness.

An animal was presented, slaughtered, the blood sprinkled and the fat and internal organs burned (Lev. 3:1-5, 6-11 and 12-16 repeat the procedure for different types of animal). Then a portion was eaten by the priests, and the rest enjoyed by the worshipper and his or her family and friends (7:11-15,32-34). Thus the offering was literally shared between God, the priest and the worshippers. The shared feast represented the joy of peace with God.

It is as if God is the host at the party and the joy and enjoyment of all the guests reflect praise back to him, the host. Whatever our cause for joy, the source of all our blessings is God. And our greatest cause for joy is peace with him, our Maker and Redeemer. Moses commanded the people that when they entered the promised land: 'You shall sacrifice peace offerings and shall eat there, and you shall rejoice before the LORD your God' (Deut. 27:7).

Joy and celebration marked the dedication of the temple. Solomon's peace offerings consisted of 22,000 cattle and 120,000 sheep and goats over a fourteen-day period. Vast numbers of worshippers joined in the feast (1 Kings 8:63-65; 2 Chr. 7:4-9). More private occasions were also marked by peace offerings. When the Philistines seized David in Gath, he pleaded with the Lord for deliverance, and vowed to render thank offerings to mark his gratitude (Ps. 56:12-13). Psalm 100 was often used when sacrificing the peace offering:

Enter his gates with thanksgiving,
*   and his courts with praise!*
Give thanks to him, bless his name!

(Ps. 100:4).

Do we, like the Israelites, understand that, whatever the celebration, our joy must find its focus in God? He is the source of all our blessings and benefits. That is why we give thanks before eating. He provided our food. But we should also place the Lord at the centre of all our celebrations, whether birthdays, weddings, births, graduations, or getting a new job.

The peace offering also pointed forward to the Lord's Supper — a meal together in the presence of the Lord. Christ has himself provided our sin and guilt offering to cleanse us from guilt; he was offered up wholly consecrated to God (as in the burnt and grain offerings). On the basis of that finished work, we are brought into fellowship with God and each other. At the Lord's Supper we can celebrate in his presence, and it is a foretaste of the greater celebration to come — the wedding supper of the Lamb.

Prayer: Use the words of the following song as a prayer:

I come with joy, a child of God,
forgiven, loved and free,
the life of Jesus to recall,
in love laid down for me.

As Christ breaks bread and bids us share,
each proud division ends.
The love that made us makes us one,
and strangers now are friends

(Brian Wren).

Text for the day: *Therefore, since we have been justified by faith, we have peace with God through our Lord Jesus Christ* (Rom. 5:1).

The sin offering

Burnt, cereal and fellowship offerings were voluntary. The sin offering was compulsory. It was required when someone committed an unintentional sin. If the high priest sinned, he was to bring a bull; if a leader sinned, he was to bring a male goat; if a member of the community sinned he or she was to bring a female goat or lamb. People who were very poor could bring a dove or pigeon, or even an offering of flour.

At first sight, the ritual looks similar to the burnt offering. The worshipper presented the animal to be offered and laid his hand on the animal's head. The animal was thus identified with the sin of the worshipper, and took his place. This was the principle of substitution. The animal was then killed. The important thing with the sin offering was what happened to the blood. It was sprinkled seven times before the Lord in front of the curtain; some of the blood was placed on the horns of the altar, and the rest was poured out at the base of the altar. The carcass was disposed of. This was the case for all the sin offerings, the only exception being for the very poor, who might only be able to afford some grain. In such cases (Lev. 5:11-12) the grain was placed on top of the offerings made to the Lord by fire, in close proximity with other blood offerings, because 'Without the shedding of blood there is no forgiveness of sins' (Heb. 9:22).

On the Day of Atonement, the priest sprinkled blood on the horns of the altar to 'cleanse it and consecrate it from the uncleannesses of the people of Israel' (Lev. 16:19). In other words, the sprinkling of blood cleansed from the contamination, or pollution, of sin. The burnt offering was the propitiation for sin (appeasing God's wrath). The sin offering was the wiping away of sin, washing away the stain.

We are not only guilty because of sin; we are dirty. We are contaminated by sin whether or not it is intentional. The sin offering was for sins committed inadvertently, sins of carelessness, or forgetfulness. This kind of sin is just part of being a fallen human being. The various regulations of the rest of Leviticus underline the fact that sinfulness is woven into the fabric of daily life. People could be 'unclean' as a result of everyday things like skin diseases, or a woman's monthly cycle, or childbirth, or sexual activity, or the mildew growing on the wall of a house in damp weather. There was nothing intrinsically wrong with any of these things. But they served as reminders, as visual aids, that in our fallen humanity we are unclean before God and we need perpetual cleansing.

We may sincerely think we are 'good enough' for God, by virtue of living reasonably decent lives. But when we enter the presence of the holy God, we realize that all our righteousness is as filthy rags. We need to be cleansed by blood. Why blood? To pay the penalty for sin there has to be death, and poured out blood is a sign that death has taken place. Today, we can have confidence that 'The blood of Jesus his Son cleanses us from all sin' (1 John 1:7). Christ's blood provides a cleansing which reaches right into our consciences and our hearts. We all know the sense of having a really bad day, of being so ashamed of our sins of thought and word and deed. How, we wonder, can God ever accept us again? How can we serve him again?

The answer is that the blood of Christ cleanses us so completely that we go confidently into the Holy of Holies — the presence of God himself.

That rich atoning blood,
which sprinkled round we see,
provides for those who come to God
an all-prevailing plea

(John Newton).

Prayer: Praise God for the blood of Christ, so freely shed for the forgiveness of our sins.

Text for the day: *The blood of Jesus his Son cleanses us from all sin* (1 John 1:7).

The guilt offering

While the burnt offering consumed God's wrath, and the sin offering washed away uncleanness, the guilt or 'reparation' offering paid the price for sin. The emphasis is on the price of the offering. When there had been a sin God must be compensated. Sin detracts from the glory of God; he is thereby denied the service and worship due to him. Compensation is needed.

Two reasons are given for offering this sacrifice.

Someone may have committed a sin with regard to money, a form of theft (Lev. 6:2). This might involve a direct offence against the Lord if the person swore falsely about the matter (6:3). When anyone had been guilty of cheating in relation to material things, there had to be restoration of the value, plus an additional 20%, and a guilt offering was to be made.

Or a person may have committed a sin relating to the 'holy things of the LORD' (5:15). This might have been a failure to present a tithe, or to fulfil a vow. The worshipper had to offer restitution, plus an additional 20%, and make a guilt offering.

We learn here that when we sin and there are injured parties, they must be compensated. The guilty party must make amends. It is the principle of personal responsibility. If we have caused loss or harm, we are to do something about it. The converted tax collector Zacchaeus understood this well: 'Half of my goods I give to the poor. And if I have defrauded anyone of anything, I restore it fourfold' (Luke 19:8). The willingness to make restitution is clear evidence of real repentance.

Thus the sacrificial system could not be degraded into a system of 'cheap grace'. The worshipper was not left under the impression that by bringing a sacrifice he was getting quick forgiveness and the right to go off and sin again. He had to change his ways. The gospel is not a system of 'cheap grace' either. Genuine repentance means turning away from sin. If we claim to be forgiven and yet stubbornly cling onto our favourite sins, we are guilty of spurning Christ, profaning his blood and outraging the Spirit of grace (Heb. 10:29).

When a worshipper had sinned against someone else, it was not enough to compensate the injured party. Sin is not just a horizontal affair between us and our neighbour. The Lord is offended too. There had to be an offering to him. If that was true when the sin was against another party, how much more true was it when the sin was directly against the Lord! We constantly fall short of God's requirements, like a dart failing to reach the target. 'All have sinned and fall short of the glory of God' (Rom. 3:23). But how can we possibly compensate the one who owns all things? The sacrifices were only signposts, pointing forward to the ultimate sacrifice of infinite value. When Jesus died, he cried, '*Tetelestai*', which literally means, 'Paid in full!' The price is paid.

Prayer: Praise God with the words of this song:

> *The price is paid:*
> *come let us enter in*
> *to all that Jesus died*
> *to make our own.*
> *For every sin*
> *more than enough he gave,*
> *and bought our freedom from each guilty stain.*
> *The price is paid, Alleluia —*
> *amazing grace,*
> *so strong and sure!*
> *And so with all my heart,*
> *my life in every part,*
> *I live to thank you for the price you paid!*

(Graham Kendrick).

Text for the day: *You were ransomed ... not with perishable things such as silver or gold, but with the precious blood of Christ* (1 Peter 1:18-19).

The priests

The priests were appointed by God: 'No one takes this honour for himself, but only when called by God, just as Aaron was' (Heb. 5:4). Their special clothes marked them out as different. The high priest, in particular, wore an elaborate robe, an embroidered sash, a cape, an 'ephod', which supported a breastplate including twelve jewels representing the twelve tribes, and a turban with a gold plate saying, 'Holy to the LORD.' The impact was regal, and the message plain: 'This is God's man. Respect and honour him.' This was not a democracy (rule of the people). It was a theocracy (rule of God). God was King of the people, and the priests were his representatives. They gave judgement on what was clean and unclean; they instructed the people; they made known God's will by using the 'Urim and Thummim' (a kind of dice) and they conveyed God's blessing to the people.

The priests also represented the people to God, bringing their offerings. When the high priest entered the Holy Place he carried the stones on his shoulders and the jewels on his breastplate representing the people (Exod. 28:9-12,15-21).

The ordination ceremony included washing with water (symbolizing cleanliness) and anointing with oil (symbolizing the Holy Spirit). The priests were to be righteous and holy, consecrated to the Lord's service. But as sinners themselves, they needed the cleansing provided by blood sacrifice. Hence the daubing of their ears, hands and feet with blood at their consecration service; hence the sacrifices for their own sins. As long as they complied exactly with what God commanded, they and the people would be accepted. The phrase, 'as the LORD commanded', echoes through Leviticus 8 and 9. Because of this obedience, the Lord came down in glory. The institution of the priesthood was acceptable and pleasing to him (9:23-24).

Tragically, while God was giving the regulations for the priesthood, Aaron was leading the people in sinful idolatry (Exod. 32). Almost as soon as the tabernacle was consecrated, Aaron's sons Nadab and Abihu failed to follow the Lord's commands, and were killed (Lev. 10:1-7). There could be no clearer way of saying that human priests are not good enough.

Similarly, the sinful failure of David (2 Sam. 11) and that of Moses himself (Num. 20:12; cf. Deut.34:10) demonstrates that even the greatest of human kings and prophets were not good enough either. Aaron, David and Moses each foreshadowed Christ, yet each were sinners.

We need a perfect priest, king and prophet. We need the Lord Jesus Christ.

Before the throne of God above
I have a strong, a perfect plea,
a great High Priest whose name is love,
who ever lives and pleads for me.
My name is written on his hands,
my name is hidden in his heart;
I know that while in heaven he stands
no power can force me to depart

(Charitie L. Bancroft).

Prayer: Lord Jesus, the priests needed to be anointed with blood on their heads, hands and feet, but I worship you for the blood that flowed from your head, hands and feet at the cross. Today, I pray that I would be wholly consecrated and cleansed into your service, by your blood.

Text for the day: *For there is one God, and there is one mediator between God and men, the man Christ Jesus* (1 Tim. 2:5).

The Day of Atonement

The Day of Atonement was the most sombre of the Jewish holy days. Other festivals involved feasting. This was a fast day (Lev. 23:29). It was the only day of the year on which the high priest was allowed to enter the Holy of Holies. He had to put aside his regal clothes and wear a simple linen garment (more like the clothes of a slave than a king). Sin offerings were made, and blood sprinkled on the mercy seat over the ark of the covenant. Smoke from burning incense concealed the mercy seat, protecting the high priest from full exposure to the holiness of God, 'so that he does not die' (16:13). Sin separates us from God. To come into his presence, unless in the way he prescribes, meant death (16:1-2).

The offering of a 'scapegoat' was unique to the Day of Atonement. Two goats were brought to the tabernacle, and lots were cast. One goat was for the Lord. It was killed, its blood sprinkled in the Most Holy Place and its body burned outside the camp. This sacrifice pointed forward to Christ's paying the price for our sins. The other goat was for 'Azazel' (one of the fallen angels in Jewish tradition). Aaron laid both hands on its head and confessed over it the sins of the nation. Then it was taken into the wilderness, out of the presence of the Lord, into the realm of evil, and handed over to Azazel. It carried with it the guilt of all the people. This annual ritual pointed forward to Christ's removing the guilt of our sins by bearing their curse.

Christ bore our curse, on the cursed tree (Deut. 21:23), in the cursed place. Some have associated the place of crucifixion with the Valley of Hinnom (Gehenna), outside Jerusalem. This was where children had been offered in the fire to the evil god Moloch (2 Chr. 28:3; 33:6). Gehenna (a Greek word translated as 'hell' in English Bibles) is a biblical symbol for final punishment. The scapegoat bore the sins of the people into the realm of the evil spirits, a symbol of hell. Christ carried our sins into hell itself.

No single sacrifice could convey the power and scope of Christ's work. But the scapegoat was a tremendously powerful picture of substitution. As the priest's hands rested on its head, so the sins of the people were laid upon it. And it was an equally powerful picture of the removal of the guilt of sin, far, far away from the presence of God, into the realm of evil.

Prayer: Thank you, Lord Jesus, for your willingness to bear the curse of my sin. Thank you that you suffered 'outside the camp' at the hands of Satan and his hosts, for me!

My faith would lay her hand
on that dear head of thine,
while like a penitent I stand,
and there confess my sin.

My soul looks back to see
the burden thou didst bear
when hanging on the cursed tree,
and knows her guilt was there

(Isaac Watts).

Text for the day: *Christ redeemed us from the curse of the law by becoming a curse for us — for it is written, 'Cursed is everyone who is hanged on a tree'* (Gal. 3:13).

'Feasts of the LORD'

For the people of Israel, the daily, monthly and annual cycles of life were to revolve around worship. In our materialistic and self-absorbed culture it is very different. Christmas and Easter are nominally Christian, but for most the focus is on family and friends, not God. Other celebrations, whether birthdays, weddings or graduations, revolve around the people concerned rather than God. Holidays in our culture are for relaxation, spending time with the family, chasing the sun or exploring different cultures.

The Israelites used holidays to focus on God. All work had to cease on the feast days, but these were not 'paid holidays'; there was financial cost involved, especially if the day fell at harvest time. The message was clear: worship took priority, and you had to stop work in order to worship. The weekly and annual cycle of feasts underlined the people's total dependence on God. The weekly Sabbath reminded them of creation. God had made them, and everything else. As he rested at the end of the creation week, so they were to have a weekly day of rest and worship. The same principle was extended to the land: every seventh year was a sabbath year, in which the fields were to lie fallow. Every fiftieth year was to be a jubilee year, in which debts were cancelled and slaves were freed. All this was a check to greed and self-reliance. The people depended on the Lord for prosperity, and if they honoured and obeyed him, then he would grant prosperity. If they ignored him, and neglected these feasts, he would not prosper them. As Jesus taught, 'Seek first the kingdom of God ... and all these things will be added to you [as well]' (Matt. 6:33).

The annual Passover commemorated the Lord's deliverance of his people from Egypt. Then there were the 'pilgrimage festivals' three times a year, when all the adult males were required to gather together. The first of these was the Feast of Unleavened Bread, following straight on from the Passover. This helped the Israelites to remember how the Lord brought them out of Egypt in haste, carrying dough with them to bake as they went.

The First Fruits festival acknowledged that the Lord was the provider of all the fruits of the land. A sheaf of the first of the barley harvest was presented as a 'wave offering' before the Lord. Similarly, the Festival of Weeks (the second annual pilgrimage festival, also called Pentecost or Harvest) included offerings of the first of the wheat harvest. The people expressed their joy and gratitude for the Lord's bounty. This Festival of Weeks was so called because it took place seven weeks after the Feast of Unleavened Bread. Likewise, the third great annual pilgrimage feast, the Festival of Booths (also called Tabernacles or Ingathering) was a whole week of celebration to give thanks for the harvest, a week in which the people lived in booths to remember the time when they were camping on their way to the promised land, and to celebrate, in contrast, the joys of living in Canaan.

The other sacred days noted in this chapter were the Feast of Trumpets, when Israel was presented before the Lord to seek his favour; the Day of Atonement, a day of sacrifices to atone for the sins of the priests and the people, and to purify the Holy Place; and a final Sacred Assembly to mark the closing of the annual cycle of feasts. Two feasts were added later: Purim, to mark deliverance at the time of Esther; and Hanukkah (or Festival of Lights), to remind the people of deliverance in the Maccabean period (165-4 BC).

The whole rhythm of life inculcated gratitude and dependence on God. Regular rest meant that the Lord, rather than work, was the priority. We no longer celebrate the Old Testament festivals, but we have even greater cause for perpetual gratitude and worship.

Prayer: Pray about the way you use the Lord's Day. Is it a day of resting from labour and of wholehearted praise? Pray about taking time *each* day for devotion and worship. Pray about your use of time on holidays and about the way you plan family celebrations. Give thanks for the Lord's Supper — our opportunity to look back in gratitude for all that the Lord has done for us in salvation.

Text for the day: *Do this in remembrance of me* (Luke 22:19; 1 Cor. 11:24).

Obedience and blessing

The book of Numbers opens with the Israelites still at Mount
Sinai, thirteen months after the Exodus! It had taken a year to
teach them how they were to live in relationship with a holy
God. The law had been given. The sacrificial system and code of
holiness had been instituted. The tabernacle and all the necessary
furnishings had been built and put in place, exactly as commanded. Now more than two million people were formed into
an organized and disciplined army. They were ready, in the Lord's
name, to advance into the promised land. There is a great sense
of expectancy. The people are ready!

God told Moses to count the men of fighting age, and the
census was carried out (hence the English title of the book,
'Numbers'). God told Moses exactly how to order the different
tribes when they camped and when they marched, and these
instructions were put into effect. The Levites were counted
separately from the rest, as their special sacrificial duties precluded
them from fighting. They also served as substitutes for the firstborn of all the other tribes of Israel. The tabernacle was dedicated
and, to celebrate the occasion, each tribal leader brought magnificent gifts on twelve successive days. Various regulations concerning purity and worship were given and were obeyed. The Passover was celebrated as the Lord required.

The Lord's presence was signalled by the supernatural cloud
resting on the tabernacle, looking like a cloud by day and a fire
by night. God told the people when to move and when to halt
by means of this cloud, and they obeyed (Num. 10:33-36). The
people were ready to advance on the land of Canaan, and
provided with exact instructions about when to move and when
to halt in obedience to the sound of silver trumpets.

The complex regulations, the detailed instructions, the exact
obedience were only means to an end. The great end in view was
that the people were to live in peace with God. This is beautifully
expressed in the blessing which the high priest was to pronounce
over the people:

The LORD bless you and keep you,
the LORD make his face to shine upon you and be gracious to
    you;
the LORD lift up his countenance upon you and give you peace
                                       (6:24-26).

By blessing the people in this way, the priest 'put [God's] name upon' the people (6:27). They were in covenant with him and he loved them. They were now to establish his kingdom in the promised land. God himself would lead this disciplined army into battle, and fight for them.

The first ten chapters of this book thus set the stage for the conquest of Canaan. But then it all went horribly wrong. The rest of the book is a dismal record of failure of faith, on behalf of the people, and even on behalf of Aaron and Moses. Instead of being in the promised land within a few weeks or months, the people were condemned to wander in the wilderness for forty years (the commonly used Hebrew title for the book is 'In the Wilderness').

The book of Numbers is a powerful warning against complacency. We may have started well, but perseverance is all-important. Don't rest on your past experiences of the Lord. Are you obeying him today?

Prayer: Almighty God, thank you for bringing me into relationship with yourself through the perfect work of Christ. I pray that you would empower me to live in obedience to you today.

Prone to wander, Lord, I feel it,
prone to leave the God I love!
Take my heart, Oh, take and seal it,
seal it from your courts above!

                                       (Robert Robinson).

Text for the day: *Therefore let anyone who thinks that he stands take heed lest he fall* (1 Cor. 10:12).

'Arise, O LORD, and let your enemies be scattered'

When the people set out from Sinai, ready to advance on the promised land, the ark of the covenant always went first. The Lord was going in advance, leading his army. This was no ordinary invasion. God had called out a people to be set apart for him. They were to live in the promised land as his representatives on earth. They were to live for his glory in such a way that they would be a light for the other nations.

The establishment of God's kingdom would involve a battle against evil. While God's covenant people were multiplying in Egypt, the inhabitants of Canaan had lapsed further and further into moral depravity and decay. The time had come for judgement, and the armies of Yahweh were to be instruments for that judgement. The advance of the ark, with the people following, was the advance of God's forces against evil. Hence Moses' prayer each time the ark set out: 'Arise, O LORD, and let your enemies be scattered, and let those who hate you flee before you' (Num. 10:35).

When David brought the ark of the covenant to Jerusalem, this also signalled the establishment of the righteous kingdom of God. Moses' prayer was quoted in Psalm 68 (v. 1), which marked the arrival of the ark in Jerusalem. This psalm also pointed forward to the much wider extent of the establishment of the kingdom of God on earth. It celebrates the universal power of Yahweh, the one who rides on the clouds (vv. 4 (NIV),33). It exalts in his mercy and compassion: he is the one who pities the widow and orphan (v. 5). His kingdom is established by power (v. 2), but it is maintained with joy and with justice (vv.3,5). The psalm looks back to the initial establishment of God's kingdom in the promised land, by reminding the people of the momentous journey from Sinai to Canaan (vv. 7-10). It also looks forward to the universal kingdom to be established by a King greater than David (v. 31).

The triumphant entry of the ark into Jerusalem demonstrated God's power and kingship. It was as if God were ascending to the throne in Jerusalem, which was just an earthly symbol of his heavenly throne. Paul uses Psalm 68 (v. 18) to illustrate the ultimate triumph of God — not this time the ark moving from Sinai to Canaan, nor the ark being placed in Jerusalem, but Christ ascending to heavenly glory (Eph. 4:8). The earlier conquests were just signposts pointing towards Christ's great and final conquest over all powers of evil. The atrocities and cruelties carried out by the inhabitants of Canaan were temporarily stopped by the first conquest but, sadly, God's people never did live out their vocation as people 'holy to the LORD'. They failed as the servant of the Lord, the 'firstborn son' of God. But Christ triumphed in this role. The incarnation, the cross, the resurrection, the ascension — all were part of his final victory over evil, his establishment of God's kingdom on earth.

Moses' prayer, glorious as it was, was like the prelude to a great orchestral piece, introducing something greater and more beautiful. Psalm 68, beautiful as it is, remains obscure until the light of the gospel is shone backwards onto it. The whole of the Old Testament points forward to Christ.

We are living in exciting days. We are seeing the triumph of the gospel in previously unreached nations and people groups. Moses and David led literal armies, but the gospel of Christ does not now advance by physical force. We work for, pray for, and rejoice in, the extension of the kingdom of Christ by the power of the Word and the Spirit. Ultimately we look forward to his return in glory. Moses' prayer for the foes of God to flee (Num. 10:35) and David's vision of foreign princes bowing before God (Ps. 68:29,31) will then literally be fulfilled, when at the name of Jesus every knee will bow (Phil. 2:10).

Prayer: Thank you, Lord, that we are living in days when Moses' prayer is being fulfilled by the spread of the gospel.

Text for the day: *Arise, O LORD, and let your enemies be scattered, and let those who hate you flee before you* (Num. 10:35).

'Graves of Craving'

The first ten chapters of Numbers emphasize obedience. The Lord instructed the people. They did just as he commanded. Everything changes in this chapter. Just three days into the journey from Sinai towards the promised land, the people begin grumbling (11:1).

Verbal complaints are only the outward expression of what is in our hearts. Looking back on the wilderness experience, Moses reminded the people that the Lord had consistently provided for their every need, providing food, and even ensuring that their clothes did not wear out (Deut. 8:3-5). Rather than giving thanks, the people grumbled. Paul draws the direct lesson that we are not to 'grumble, as some of them did and were destroyed by the Destroyer. Now these things happened to them as an example, but they were written down for our instruction' (1 Cor. 10:10-11). We are to guard our hearts. An ungrateful spirit is offensive to the Lord.

The Lord was aware of the people's grumbling before Moses knew anything about it (Num. 11:1), and he acted swiftly in judgement. Moses again interceded for the people, and the Lord heard and answered his prayers (11:2-3). One would have thought that the terrifying judgement of fire from heaven would have been sufficient warning, but no, the people then turned to open grumbling about the food provided by God. Memory can be very selective! Thinking back to Egypt, they forgot the slave labour, the beatings, the efforts to kill all the baby boys and the groaning that had gone up to heaven. They only remembered the food. This mutiny was too much for Moses. His patience gave out and he too complained against the Lord — blaming God for giving him such a recalcitrant people to lead (11:11-15).

The Lord did not blame or judge Moses for this complaint. He provided other men to help Moses in the task of leading the people. It was a different matter with the people. God provided meat to satisfy their cravings, but an over-abundance of meat would be a fitting judgement for greed. The people gorged themselves. While they were still eating, God struck many of them with a plague. The dead were buried, and Moses called the place 'Graves of Craving' (11:34, footnote).

If our hearts crave after things that the Lord has not yet provided, there is only one thing to do: pray. If the people had prayed humbly for meat, the Lord would have provided. But they did not pray; they complained, they lusted and when the Lord gave them what they wanted they overindulged, so that the meat led to revulsion rather than pleasure. If we crave and grasp and take pleasures for ourselves, there will be no long-term pleasure or enjoyment. The very provision of the thing we have lusted after may turn out to be a terrible judgement.

> What you should feel and say when you meet something you would like: 'Lord, if this is your will, let it happen like this. Lord, if you see that this will help me and do me good, then grant that I may use it to the honour of your name. But if you know that it will harm me and not advance my soul's salvation, then take the desire away.' You cannot find complete satisfaction in any temporal gift, because you were not created to find your delight in them. Even if you possessed all the good things God has created, you could not feel happy and glad; all your gladness and happiness rests in the God who created those things (The Imitation of Christ).

Prayer: Lord, forgive me for the times when I am discontented, when I crave things you have not provided and when I am ungrateful for those things you have provided. Help me to trust you to provide all my needs.

Text for the day: We must not ... grumble, as some of them did and were destroyed by the Destroyer (1 Cor. 10:9-10).

Miriam's pride and fall

Miriam and Aaron, the elder sister and brother of Moses, had been called and used as leaders of God's people. They now failed miserably. As a young girl, Miriam had been used to save Moses' life. After the crossing of the Red Sea, she had led the people in joyful praise and singing. She was gifted as a prophetess. As an elderly woman, she had years of experience and much maturity. But now she took the lead in turning Aaron against Moses.

Moses' marriage triggered huge family tensions. (We don't know for sure whether the 'Cushite' wife was Zipporah, or a second wife.) Miriam's objection to Moses' wife's race was probably patriotic and religious. Miriam was first and foremost a Jewess. Fiercely loyal to her race, she may have resented an 'outsider' having more influence over Moses than she had. Whatever her grievance, pride and ambition lay behind her complaint. She put her own reputation ahead of that of Moses. She was not cultivating meekness and humility, in contrast to Moses, the meekest man on earth (Num. 12:3).

Aaron was drawn into the dispute, although the subsequent judgement shows that Miriam was the instigator. We don't know whether the complaints of his siblings actually reached Moses' ears. But the Lord heard. As the one who had commissioned Moses, he regarded the complaints as rebellion against himself. God summoned the three of them into his presence, and vindicated Moses. When he had spoken, and the cloud symbolizing his presence had departed, Miriam was left with leprosy.

Bishop Hall quaintly observed that 'Her foul tongue was justly punished with a foul face.' Moses, whose face shone when he had spoken with the Lord, was vindicated; his sister, who had stirred up trouble in the family against him, was humiliated. Moses needed a veil to conceal his glory; Miriam needed a veil to conceal her shame. Aaron was spared — perhaps because he had not instigated this rebellion, perhaps because he would then be ritually unclean and unable to preside over the sacrifices. But he humbly confessed the sins of himself and Miriam and pleaded for mercy for her. In turn, Moses appealed to the Lord for healing for his sister.

If we speak ill of others, even in the privacy of our own homes, we must remember that the Lord hears. If we speak rebelliously of the authorities God has placed over us in our lives, the Lord is angry. He not only hears the words of our lips; he discerns the thoughts of our hearts. We are to cultivate a humble and submissive spirit. Enjoying being well thought of by others can be addictive and spiritually destructive.

A gentle and quiet spirit is very precious in God's sight. This is the way that we are to make ourselves truly beautiful (1 Peter 3:4). God gave Miriam great gifts, but she failed in this regard. The danger for those with outstanding gifts is the danger of spiritual pride. Pray today for a gentle and quiet spirit.

Let holy charity
mine outward vesture be,
and lowliness become my inner clothing;
true lowliness of heart,
which takes the humbler part,
and o'er its own shortcomings weeps with loathing
                    (Bianco da Siena, trans. R. F. Littledale).

Prayer: O Lord, free me of the addiction of seeking a reputation for myself. Free me from the desire to be well thought of by others. Grant me that humility that delights to see others advance ahead of myself. Grant me above all a burning desire for your glory.

Text for the day: *Your beauty ... should be that of your inner self, the unfading beauty of a gentle and quiet spirit, which is of great worth in God's sight* (1 Peter 3:3-4, NIV).

Doubt, fear and unbelief

The Lord had guided the people through the 'great and terrifying wilderness' (Deut. 1:19), and to the very border of the promised land. In this dramatic and emotional speech, delivered forty years later, as the next generation once more stood ready to enter the land, Moses looked back at that first disastrous attempt to enter. (Moses' account is a summary of the events recorded in Numbers 13 and 14.)

Moses stressed that the Lord had gone ahead and had prepared the land, so that all that was needed was for the people to take possession: 'See, the LORD your God has set the land before you' (1:21). There was no need for fear or discouragement. All that was needed was obedience. The land would be theirs.

Instead of obeying, the people hesitated. Ten of the spies looked at the land from a sheerly human point of view. It was a prosperous and attractive land, but it would be too difficult to conquer. Caleb and Joshua alone urged the people to believe in the promise of God. He would go ahead of the people. 'Yet in spite of this word you did not believe the LORD your God, who went before you in the way to seek you out a place to pitch your tents' (1:32-33).

As a punishment for this wilful unbelief, the Lord condemned that entire generation to wander in the wilderness for forty years until they died, with the exception of Joshua and Caleb. 'In the Wilderness' (the opening word of the book in Hebrew, cf. Deut. 1:1) is the commonly used Hebrew title for the book of Numbers, which provides a summary of these forty years. Numbers begins with a census, the 'numbering' of the people before the first, abortive entry into the land, and ends with another 'numbering' of the new generation forty years later before the second, successful entry.

This instance of Israel's unbelief stood as a terrible warning of what happens when we resist the grace of God. The people refused to live by faith; they wanted to live by sight. The writer of the letter to the Hebrews uses this incident as an object lesson to warn of the danger of unbelief (Heb. 3:7-19, quoting Ps. 95:7-11).

'They were unable to enter because of unbelief' (Heb. 3:19). The writer pleads with the young Christians not to turn back from their faith in Christ, and not to risk forfeiting their hope of eternal rest.

For us today, the temptation to slip back from living by faith is just as strong. We naturally want to 'see' what is ahead; we find it so hard to trust God for the future. But this account warns us that doubt, fear and unbelief are an insult to the Lord. If the Israelites were judged for belittling God's provision of manna and the pillar of cloud and fire, we shall be judged even more severely if we belittle God's amazing provision of his own Son.

> *When Satan appears*
> *and hinders our path*
> *and fills us with fears,*
> *we triumph by faith;*
> *he cannot take from us,*
> *though often has tried,*
> *this heart-cheering promise:*
> *'The Lord will provide'*

(John Newton).

Prayer: Lord, I believe; help my unbelief! Help me to walk by faith and not by sight today, trusting in your promises and confident in your Word.

Text for the day: *We walk by faith, not by sight* (2 Cor. 5:7).

Rebellion again

This chapter is a sobering reminder of the way that sin spreads and multiplies. Resentment against leaders is a universal human failing. Here, a few individuals cherished jealousy, they shared their complaints with others and the infection spread as quickly as a contagious disease. Just four ringleaders are mentioned in verse 1, but more than 14,700 were judged for rebellion by the end of the chapter (Num. 16:49).

Initially, Korah attacked the exclusivity of the priesthood. Why should Aaron be a priest, and not him? Anyway, hadn't God said that all the Israelites were holy? (cf. 15:40). This was a classic case of misquoting God's Word. Yes, all the Israelites were separated from the other nations for God, but God had clearly also revealed that the priests were set aside for special duties. 'Why then do you exalt yourselves above the assembly of the LORD?' demanded the malcontents (16:3). Far from Moses and Aaron putting themselves forward for leadership, God himself had chosen them. But it is all too easy to misrepresent the motives of leaders, to accuse them of self-aggrandizement. In fact, by attacking God's chosen leaders, these men were attacking the Lord himself (16:11).

When Moses summoned Dathan and Abiram, the accusations escalated (16:12-14). The rebels now maintained that Moses wanted to kill the people. Instead of seeing that the continued wanderings in the wilderness were entirely the fault of the rebellious people, they had the audacity to put the blame on Moses. Not surprisingly, he was incensed (16:15). But God himself intervened, coming in glory (16:19), judging the main ringleaders with swift and devastating ruin.

At Sinai, God had revealed himself in earthquake and fire. Now the main ringleaders and their families were destroyed by an earthquake and the 250 who had followed them were consumed by fire (16:31-35). One would have expected the watching multitudes to be utterly subdued by such a dramatic display of divine and supernatural power. Astonishingly, they were so hardened that they turned on Moses and Aaron (16:41) and accused them of having killed the rebels! Once again, the Lord

came down in glory and in further judgement. Scores, then
hundreds, then thousands began to drop down with a terrible
plague.

It would have been understandable for Moses and Aaron to
welcome the Lord's vindication. Instead, they showed the heart of
true leadership. Moses instantly delegated Aaron to make atonement for the people's sin. Aaron obeyed, and 'stood between the
dead and the living' (16:48) until the plague was halted. What a
marvellous foreshadowing of the mighty work of our great High
Priest, who made atonement for our sins and who rescued us
from the death we deserved!

How do we respond? We need to watch our hearts. It is so easy
to cherish resentful and envious thoughts. We can feed our own
sinful self-righteousness by grumbling about the faults and failings of
our leaders. Let us be warned by this chapter that the complaints of
a few can wreak havoc in the life of a whole community.

Love is kind and suffers long,
love is meek and thinks no wrong,
love than death itself more strong;
therefore give us love

(Christopher Wordsworth).

Prayer: Lord, please help me to guard my heart and guard my
tongue. Do not let me be the source of dissension and destruction
among your people.

Text for the day: *Obey your leaders and submit to them, for*
they are keeping watch over your souls, as those who will have to
give an account (Heb. 13:17).

God vindicates his leaders

The judgements brought on the rebels in chapter 16 were a negative sign vindicating Moses and Aaron. In this chapter God gives a positive sign, and one full of beautiful symbolism. Overnight, a dry stick burst into life, with leaves, blossoms and almonds. A process which naturally would take place over several months happened all at once. Only God could do this! The almond tree, in Hebrew, was called 'the watcher', or 'the awake one', because it was the first to bear blossom after the winter. God's ordained priesthood was there to watch over the people and to be fruitful, even as the almond branch was.

The Lord intended this sign to silence the grumbling of the people. Complaints against his chosen leaders were, by implication, complaints against himself (Num. 17:5,10). The immediate effect was profound. The people were awestruck (17:12). They realized their peril before a powerful and holy God. As never before, they appreciated the role of the priests in standing between them and God.

The blossoming staff was to be kept as a continual reminder of the legitimacy of the Aaronic priesthood. It would be placed alongside the stone tablets on which the Ten Commandments were recorded and the jar of manna. These visual aids would help the people to remember the Lord's authority over their lives (the law), his daily and merciful material provision (the manna) and his provision of forgiveness through the priestly ministry (the blossoming staff). How soon we forget the grace and mercy of God! Today, instead of the tablets of the law, the manna and the staff we have the visual aids of baptism and the Lord's Supper — powerful symbols to remind us of the finished saving work of Christ. Do we take these for granted? Do we become forgetful of God's grace? Or do these visual signs move us to love and worship the triune God who has provided such a great salvation for us?

This miraculous sign was followed by a series of regulations for the generous support of the priesthood. Firstly, the Levites were to submit to their role in supporting and assisting Aaron and his family (18:2-6). Secondly, the people as a whole were to contribute cheerfully to the material support of the priesthood (18:8-32). The priests would not be able to minister effectively if they were anxious about how to provide for their families, or if they failed to receive backup in terms of the physical labour necessary to organize the tabernacle (18:4). The New Testament confirms the principle that those who engage in full-time ministry on behalf of God's people should be generously supported (1 Cor. 9:3-10), and that those engaged in the ministry of the Word and prayer should receive necessary administrative backup so that they are not distracted from their main task (Acts 6:1-7).

What is my attitude towards the leaders in my church? Do I cheerfully support their work? Do I regularly pray for them? Are they generously provided for? Are those who are called to preach and teach given adequate administrative help? Is there any way in which I could help them?

Prayer: Almighty God, thank you for your mighty power. You made a dry staff produce blossom, leaves and fruit in a single night, doing the work of months in a matter of hours. Thank you that this is true in the spiritual realm also. I pray that you would bring days of great fruitfulness in my life, in my church and in the church worldwide.

Text for the day: *The staff of Aaron for the house of Levi had sprouted and put forth buds and produced blossoms, and it bore ripe almonds* (Num. 17:8).

'Do not harden your hearts, as at Meribah'

When the people of Israel went through hard times in the wilderness, it was a test of loyalty. Would they remain faithful to God and loyal to his appointed leaders? The first time they encountered a critical lack of water was soon after the Exodus. Despite the wonderful deliverance from Pharaoh and the miraculous crossing of the Red Sea, the people grumbled and quarrelled with Moses. 'Why do you put the LORD to the test?' he asked (Exod. 17:2, NIV). The Lord then told Moses to strike the rock at Horeb with his staff, and water gushed out for the people to drink. That place (Rephidim in southern Sinai) was then named Massah ('testing') and Meribah ('quarrelling').

Forty years later, the next generation repeated the sin of their parents. Now, at Kadesh near Canaan, there was no water. Instead of praying, they quarrelled with Moses, even repeating the same absurd accusations: Moses and Aaron had brought the people into the desert to kill them (Num. 20:4-5; cf. Exod. 17:3). They ignored the fact that for forty long years they had lacked nothing (Deut. 2:7). Once again, the name Meribah, or 'quarrelling', is given to this place to remind the people of their failure (Num. 20:13).

How do we respond in times of severe trial? With submission? With gratitude to the Lord for past mercies and trust that he will again help in the future? Or with bitter complaints and criticisms that our leaders are not doing enough to help? The failure of the people of Israel became a dire warning to future generations; it stands as a sober warning to us today:

Today, if you hear his voice,
    do not harden your hearts, as at Meribah,
    as on the day at Massah in the wilderness,
when your fathers put me to the test
    and put me to the proof, though they had seen my work.
(Ps. 95:7-9).

Numbers 20 contains an even more sombre message. Moses himself, the chosen leader, the meekest man on earth, failed at this point. The pent-up frustration of forty years burst out. He failed in self-control, obedience and trust. He failed God, himself and his people. God told him to speak to the rock (20:8). Instead, in a rage, he struck it twice. His angry words, '... must we bring you water out of this rock?' (20:10, NIV), detracted from God's gracious and mighty provision. Aaron joined his brother in the angry outburst against the people.

Who would have thought it? Moses had, thus far, been exemplary in obedience. Everything the Lord had commanded, he had done; all that the Lord had commanded him to speak, he had spoken. But now he failed to believe in God. He failed to uphold the Lord's honour. He indulged in selfish passion. There could be no clearer illustration of the fact that we battle against sin until the moment we die. Those who hold out hopes of sinless perfection in this life offer a delusion. We must guard our hearts and our minds constantly; we must be alert for the devil's schemes. Our flesh will continually cry out to be indulged, and our natural self will not want to give God honour. This also illustrates the fact that leaders are the special target of satanic attack, and need to be upheld in prayer.

God always keeps his word. He had said that those who disbelieved him would not enter the promised land. Miriam — one of those swayed by the faithless spies — had already died (20:1). Aaron would be next (20:28). And Moses himself, though there was still significant work for him to do, would die without entering the land.

Prayer: Lord, protect me from complacency. Help me today to depend on your grace for the strength to obey you and honour you.

Take time to intercede for the leaders in your church, that they would be protected from satanic attack, from temptation and sin.

Text for the day: *Today, if you hear his voice, do not harden your hearts* (Ps. 95:7).

'As Moses lifted up the serpent in the wilderness'

A significant military victory (Num. 21:1-3) is followed by a terrible spiritual defeat (21:4-5).

Almost forty years earlier, after the Lord had condemned the people of Israel to wander in the wilderness for forty years, some of them disobeyed God's orders and attacked the Canaanites. The result was ignominious defeat (14:44-45). Now, at exactly the same place, a Canaanite king attacked the Israelites and took prisoners. God's people had learned their lesson. This time they prayed, recognizing their dependence on the Lord, and vowed that if he helped them they would destroy the Canaanite towns. (The Hebrew word for 'destroy' conveys the idea of devoting something totally to the Lord.) God did help his people, and they won a great victory at Hormah.

One would imagine that they would have been full of gratitude and humility. If so, it was short-lived, because the victory was followed by a long and heartbreakingly discouraging journey south, in the wrong direction, back to the tip of the Red Sea. This was because the King of Edom had refused Moses' request for the people to travel through his land (20:14-21). Edom (descended from Esau), was a brother nation to Israel. God had forbidden Moses to fight against it (Deut. 2:4-6). The King of Edom's arrogant refusal to accommodate Moses' diplomatic and reasonable request necessitated a discouraging and lengthy detour. The people rebelled again. They may have resented Moses' reluctance to engage Edom in open battle; at any rate they could not bear to be trekking south in the opposite direction to the promised land.

Their resentment and impatience erupted into their most bitter attack yet on God, on the food he had provided and on the leaders he had appointed (21:5). The people's contempt for God's provision was nothing short of blasphemous. God responded with swift judgement. The camp was infested with poisonous snakes. Multitudes were bitten and died.

The effect was dramatic. Hours after slandering Moses, the people came and pleaded with him: 'We sinned when we spoke against the Lord and against you' (21:7, NIV). They knew that they needed mercy from God. They realized that they needed an intercessor.

Once again, Moses prayed for the rebellious people. The Lord's provision for their healing was unexpected. Moses was to make a bronze snake and lift it up on a pole. Whoever looked at it would be healed.

If God had simply caused the snakes to leave the camp, or healed the people without visible means, the doubters could have put the healing down to purely natural causes. This way, each individual exerted a choice. Would they look up at the bronze snake? If so, they lived; if not, they died. Healing came from the Lord alone. It was offered indiscriminately to people who were guilty of unbelief, rebellion, cynicism and blasphemous criticism of his provision. Truly, this was 'amazing grace'!

It was a fitting symbol of the most amazing grace of all: 'And as Moses lifted up the serpent in the wilderness, so must the Son of Man be lifted up, that whoever believes in him may have eternal life' (John 3:14-15). The offer is open to all. It requires 'only a look' of faith.

There was a tragic postscript to this incident. The bronze serpent was preserved. Eventually some of the Israelites began to worship it as an idol, and King Hezekiah had to destroy it (2 Kings 18:4). Thus, encapsulated in this short account, we have a terrifying picture of the sinfulness of the human heart: a great victory followed by total ingratitude; a gracious provision followed eventually by perversion of the means of that provision into idolatry.

Prayer: Lord, preserve my heart from sinful ingratitude; preserve me from making idols of any of the means of grace you provide. Help me to worship you alone and depend only on Christ's work for my salvation.

Text for the day: *As Moses lifted up the serpent ... so must the Son of Man be lifted up, that whoever believes in him may have eternal life* (John 3:14-15).

The defeat of Sihon and Og

Psalm 136 is a glorious liturgy of praise to God, which is often used for congregational reading because of its 'call and response' structure. When we read this wonderful psalm in unison we need to appreciate the significance of the defeat of Sihon and Og, for otherwise verses 17-23 make little sense:

> [Give thanks] to him who ... killed mighty kings,
>   for his steadfast love endures for ever;
> Sihon, king of the Amorites,
>   for his steadfast love endures for ever;
> and Og, king of Bashan,
>   for his steadfast love endures for ever...
>
> (Ps. 136:17-20).

Who were these kings? The King of the Amorites controlled territory east of the Dead Sea (from the River Arnon, about halfway up the sea, to the River Jabbok, about twenty-four miles north). The King of Bashan ruled the territory north of that, right up to Mount Hermon. These victories gave the Israelites a significant strip of land east of the Dead Sea and the Jordan, right up beyond what later came to be called the Sea of Galilee. This would be the base from which they would launch their attack on the Canaanites across the Jordan. When Moses looked back on these events (Deut. 2:26 – 3:11) he explained that these victories were utterly miraculous. The Lord gave these territories into the hands of his people.

For their part, the people were careful to obey God's instructions exactly. They did not intrude on any of the land belonging to the Ammonites (God had promised it to Lot's descendants). The cities they destroyed were devoted to the Lord (put under the 'ban'). In Bashan, this involved the destruction of sixty cities fortified with high walls, gates and bars, as well as numerous unfortified villages. The King of Bashan himself was evidently of legendary size: Moses records that his iron bed measured thirteen foot by six foot (4 metres by 1.80 metres, Deut. 3:11).

When God promised Abraham to give his descendants a land, he had said that they would come back and receive it 'in the fourth generation, for the iniquity of the Amorites is not yet complete' (Gen. 15:16). The 'iniquity' referred to included gross inhumanity such as child sacrifice. Moses offered to travel through the land peaceably. It was only when met with total hostility that he engaged in battle (Num. 21:21-24).

As promised, the Lord gave the Amorites over to defeat at the hands of his people. The remarkable nature of the victory is underlined in Deuteronomy by the repeated emphasis on God's action (Deut. 2:17,24,31,33,36) and in Numbers by the quotation from an ancient Amorite 'taunt poem' in which they had mocked the neighbouring Moabites for their failure to defeat them (Num. 21:27-30). The Moabites, under their god Chemosh, had failed to defeat the Amorites, but the Israelites, under their God, succeeded.

These great victories went down in Israelite history as standing alongside the Exodus events in illustrating the Lord's commitment to his people. God's power was unleashed on his people's behalf, enabling them to fight against enemies that seemed, to human eyes, to be invulnerable. Forty years earlier, fortified cities and massive warriors had terrified the ten spies and caused the entire nation to rebel against Moses, refusing to go forward. Now, a new generation, trusting in the Lord, advanced against high walls and fearsome warriors, and prevailed.

Prayer: Thank you, Lord, that you fulfil all your promises. Thank you that nothing is impossible for you, and that I do not have to fear any enemies, however terrifying, if you are with me. Thank you that the military victories over Sihon and Og were just foretastes of the final victory over Satan and all his evil forces which we shall see at the Last Day.

Text for the day: *Christ ... sat down at the right hand of God, waiting from that time until his enemies should be made a footstool for his feet* (Heb. 10:12-13).

'His precious and very great promises'

In these remarkable chapters, a pagan king employed a pagan magician to place a curse on God's people as they encamped ready to invade Canaan. Far from cursing them, the magician found himself impelled to bless them. Inspired supernaturally by the Spirit of God, he reiterated the promises given centuries before to Abraham.

The narrative is packed with dramatic suspense, irony and humorous episodes. Ironically, the Moabites were paralysed with fear when they heard of Israel's victories against Sihon and Og, not realizing that God had specifically told his people not to harm Moab (Deut. 2:9). Balak, the Moabite king, resorted to alliance with the Midianites (nomadic warriors), and together they decided to pay the expenses of the best-known professional seer of the time to come all the way from Mesopotamia. Balaam, attracted by the large sums offered, wanted to oblige, but for the first time in his career found himself up against the terrifying and irresistible power of the one true God. The Israelites would always laugh in later years when they heard of the frantic efforts made by the king to get the prophet to say something different. Financial inducements, elaborate sacrifices, threats, different views of the encamped Israelites — all were unavailing. Even against his own covetous instincts, the pagan seer was impelled to speak the words God gave him to speak. Most memorably, the spiritual obtuseness of this so-called seer was highlighted by the fact that his own donkey could see the presence of a supernatural being before he could! His 'dumb' animal also spoke a word from God. The Lord thus demonstrates in an unforgettable way that he will use the most humble instruments to further his purposes.

Even more significantly, this account was a powerful and memorable lesson to God's people, who were about to enter a land riddled with pagan worship and sorcery. Here one of the most powerful pagan sorcerers was, against his will, used as a mouthpiece of the one true God. And through this ungodly magician, God delivered a searing rebuke to the other nations and a glorious encouragement to his own people.

King Balak offered a massive reward if Balaam would disable the Israelites by means of a curse. Instead, Balaam uttered seven oracles. Each one was a blessing that would be a huge encouragement to the Israelites as they faced the terrifying challenge of crossing the Jordan and invading Canaan.

The first oracle (Num. 23:7-10) echoed God's promise to Abraham: 'Whoever curses you, I will curse.' Here, Balaam admitted: 'How can I curse whom God has not cursed?' (23:8). God had said that Abraham's descendants would be more numerous than dust. Balaam now asked, 'Who can count the dust of Jacob?' (23:10). He also acknowledged that God's people were utterly secure, a chosen people (23:9).

The message today is clear. God keeps his promises. He has chosen a people for himself, and he is committed to keeping us secure. All of Satan's power is unavailing against his will. God's people had nothing to fear then, and nor do we.

My life I yield to your decree,
and bow to your control
in peaceful calm, for from your arm
no power can snatch my soul:
no earthly omens can appal
the one who heeds God's heavenly call
                    (Columba, *Irish Church Hymnal*).

Prayer: Father God, I worship you that you are more powerful than any pagan magician. I worship you that you have given all authority in heaven and on earth to your Son, King Jesus. Thank you that I can rely absolutely on all your promises, and that today I have nothing to fear.

Text for the day: *How can I curse whom God has not cursed?* (Num. 23:8).

'The LORD their God is with them ... the shout of a king is among them'

Balak was desperate for Balaam to deliver an effective curse. Instead Balaam came out with a devastating rebuke, both to Balak (Num. 23:18-19) and also by implication to himself. Balaam had travelled all the way from Mesopotamia, no doubt in hopes that he would profit from this assignment. Already on the journey he had encountered the reality of the power of the one true God. Now, when he attempted to prophesy, he was given words by God that he could not tamper with. Always before, Balaam had been 'in charge', able to produce the oracles that would suit his employers, able to manipulate situations to his advantage. Similarly, Balak assumed that the right amount of money and the services of a professional magician would be enough to swing things in his favour in the future. In total contrast to this conniving we see the truthfulness, the faithfulness and the sovereignty of God. God had promised blessing to his people. He would bless them:

> God is not man, that he should lie,
>   or a son of man, that he should change his mind.
> Has he said, and will he not do it?
>   Or has he spoken, and will he not fulfil it?

(23:19).

This word comes to us today with the same power. God is totally reliable. We can trust his promises. He will not alter them, and he has the power to carry them through.

The second glorious truth in this oracle is the reality of the presence of God with his people: 'The LORD their God is with them' (23:21). If we have God with us, what can men do to us? The presence of God with his people is a theme running through the whole of Scripture.

Thirdly, the Lord is with us as our King: 'The shout of a king is among them' (23:21). We have a King who is King of kings and

Lord of lords, sovereign over all earthly rulers, to whom every knee will one day bow.

Fourthly, the presence of God the King with his people meant that they were safe: 'There is no enchantment against Jacob, no divination against Israel' (23:23). They were about to enter a land riddled with magic and superstition, but they did not have to fear. God is more powerful than all evil spirits; he is supreme over all demons and all occult forces. With such a God as their captain, these forces would be invincible (23:24).

> The child of God need fear no ill,
> his chosen dread no foe;
> we leave our fate with you, and wait
> your bidding when to go:
> for not from chance our comfort springs—
> you are our trust, O King of kings!
> (Columba, *Irish Church Hymnal*).

Prayer: Thank you, Almighty God, that you have appointed the Lord Jesus Christ to be King of kings and Lord of lords, and that he will reign for ever and ever. Thank you that your people need fear no earthly or demonic powers. I pray for those in situations of dire persecution, that they would be given grace to believe that standing over and behind their persecutors is the King of kings, who will bring their tormentors to account at the Last Day.

Text for the day: *Hallelujah! For the Lord our God the Almighty reigns* (Rev. 19:6).

'A star shall come out of Jacob'

Things were getting worse for Balak. Instead of cursing the massed Israelites, Balaam had blessed them. Now, in the third oracle (Num. 24:3-9), he gave a glowing picture of their prosperity in the promised land, beautifully describing God's generous provision for his people. They would enjoy peace and prosperity, fertile productive soil and abundant water. Just as God had brought them out of Egypt (24:8), so he would continue to guarantee success against their enemies (24:8-9). On hearing this, Balak was beside himself with anger and frustration (24:10-11). All he wanted now was for Balaam to get out of his sight, and stop delivering such terrifying prophecies.

But Balaam was by now under the control of one mightier than Balak. He had to speak, whether he wanted to or not. Balak had to listen, whether he wanted to or not. Balaam's final prophecy would be a warning of 'what this people will do to your people in the latter days' (24:14). Carried along by the Holy Spirit, the seer was inspired to look far into the future:

I see him, but not now;
   I behold him, but not near:
a star shall come out of Jacob,
   and a sceptre shall rise out of Israel

(24:17).

The Israelites were focused on the immediate challenge of conquering the inhabitants of Canaan. This oracle pointed far beyond that. The nation would enjoy a secure future and their hope rested on a leader whom God would provide, who would decisively conquer their enemies. Initially this promise seemed to be fulfilled in David, the godly king who led God's people in many victories over the surrounding nations (as predicted in 24:20-24), and under whom Israel's territories were extended. But God's people soon began looking beyond their human, flawed and fallible kings to the Messiah whom God would send to deliver them in a mighty and supernatural way. The victories over specific people groups portrayed in this message became symbolic of the greater victories over all his foes won by Christ on the cross. These victories were merely a small foreshadowing of that great day when every knee will bow to the King of kings and Lord of lords (Phil. 2:10). The message then, and the message for us today, is that, however menacing and powerful the earthly nations are, God is sovereign over them all.

Balaam's prophecy that 'A star shall come out of Jacob' was initially fulfilled with the first coming of Christ. But we look ahead with the eyes of faith to the return of Christ, when all nations will bow before him. The final words of the Bible pick up on this imagery: 'I, Jesus, have sent my angel to testify ... about these things... I am the root and the descendant of David, the bright morning star... Surely I am coming soon' (Rev. 22:16,20).

Prayer: Thank you, Father God, for the certain hope of the return of the Lord Jesus. Thank you that all rulers will bow before him. Thank you that your people need not fear any power on earth. Thank you that Christ is indeed the bright morning star.

On nations near and far
thick darkness gathers yet:
arise, O Morning Star,
arise and never set!

(Lewis Hensley).

Text for the day: *I am ... the bright morning star... Surely I am coming soon* (Rev. 22:16,20).

'Israel yoked himself to Baal of Peor'

Balak had been unable to purchase a curse which would disable the Israelites. His plan had backfired when the magician he had hired became the mouthpiece of God's blessing. Tragically, just as God's magnificent revelation at Sinai was followed immediately by the worship of the golden calf, so God's revelation of blessing through Balaam was followed by another national apostasy. Balaam had been unable to deliver a curse on the people. Now he came up with an alternative plan. Why depend on magic when the Israelite men could almost certainly be seduced by the attractions of food and sex?

Balaam suggested to Balak that the Israelite men be invited to the feasts which accompanied the worship of Baal Peor (Num. 31:16). Thus, 'Israel yoked himself to the Baal of Peor' (25:3). The whole nation was implicated in this spiritual adultery. Once again, as the people of God were on the very brink of entering the land, Satan seemed to have triumphed. God had revealed himself at Sinai as a 'jealous' God. He had given himself unreservedly to love his people and he expected their total allegiance. This blatant idolatry kindled his wrath. Moses was instructed to act decisively. The ringleaders had to be executed to avert God's anger.

The majority of the people then came to their senses and wept bitterly. At this moment of national repentance, Zimri, the son of a leading Simeonite family, brought a daughter of a Moabite chief into his tent. It was an act of blatant defiance, at once declaring contempt for God's law and rejection of Moses' leadership. It was also an appalling example to the younger generation of Israelites. The people were about to enter a land full of shrines involving cult prostitution. Were they going to succumb to such temptation from the very start?

God's honour was on the line. Who would stand up to defend it? Zimri had no respect whatsoever for God. Phinehas, Aaron's grandson, was utterly committed to God. When Phinehas saw Zimri take Cozbi into his tent he acted instinctively to protect God's honour, as rapidly and violently as would a father who saw his child in mortal danger. He burst into the tent and killed the couple.

He was right to do so. God's glory had been tarnished. As a result, God had already broken out in wrath against the people, and a plague had begun to rage through the camp. Phinehas' action stopped it. His name would go down in Israelite history as a role model in zeal for God's glory.

What do we learn from this? Phinehas 'made atonement for the people of Israel' (25:13) by plunging a spear into the bodies of two sinners. We need never emulate such physical violence, for atonement for sin has been accomplished once and for all when the perfect man, consumed by zeal for the Father, was pierced for our iniquities.

But how we need more of the zeal displayed by Phinehas! Our day is characterized by gross sexual immorality, reckless pursuit of ever-increasing material wealth and comfort, and worship of anything but the one true God. We need godly people consumed with zeal for the Lord who will commit themselves to taking a stand against the gross evils that pervade our society. Within the church, how many of us have fallen prey to materialism, which is idolatry? Balaam's stratagem is a warning that false teachers can seduce God's people by persuading them to indulge in greed and impurity (Rev. 2:14, cf. 1 Cor. 10:8). When this happens, we need courageous church leaders to practise biblical church discipline, even if it is unpopular to do so. Open adultery is tolerated among members in some churches. Too many Christians in the twenty-first century seem to think that toleration is the supreme virtue. It is not; zeal for God's glory is.

Prayer: Forgive me, Father, when my zeal for your glory is only lukewarm! Please fill me with your Holy Spirit and give me a passion for your glory above all things.

Text for the day: *Your name and renown are the desire of our hearts* (Isa. 26:8, NIV).

The second census

Thirty-nine years had passed since the Lord had ordered a census to be taken of the fighting men after the Exodus. The total count of men twenty years or older at that time had been 603,550. Every one of them had since died, except Moses, Joshua and Caleb. Yet despite the plagues sent on the people as punishment for wickedness, and losses in fighting, the number of men had very nearly been replaced. The total number was now 601,730. God had kept his promise to Abraham to multiply his seed.

The purpose of the census was twofold. Firstly, Israel was being prepared and organized for battle. Secondly, the ultimate purpose of God was for them to enter the land; it was his land and they were to be stewards of it on his behalf. Land was to be divided fairly and proportionately, with the larger tribes having more land than smaller ones. It would be distributed by lot, which acknowledged the Lord's right to determine how it should be shared out.

As the tribes were listed, there were reminders along the way of just how faithless many had been. The first verse of Numbers 26 recalls the fact that 24,000 potential warriors had fallen to plague, following the apostasy at Baal-Peor (25:9). Dathan and Abiram had rebelled against Moses' leadership and had been swallowed up by the earth (26:9-10). Nadab and Abihu had disobeyed God's instructions regarding worship and had been consumed by fire (26:61; cf. Lev. 10:1-3). Despite the repeated sin and rebellion of the people, of which these were just dramatic examples, God had not given up on them. He had kept his word. Although over 600,000 had died in the wilderness, God had overruled that nearly the same number were ready to enter the land. As John Calvin commented, '[People] must be blind four times over who do not behold in this bright mirror God's wonderful providence ... and his steadfastness in keeping his promises.'

Today we too are engaged in fierce warfare. Our battle is not against flesh and blood, but against spiritual forces which are set upon destroying our faith. The writer to the Hebrews is brutally realistic about how believers can be seduced into apostasy. He points to the generation of Israelites who doubted God's power and goodness, and lost the opportunity to enter the land because of unbelief. He pleads with his readers not to fall into the same trap: 'Let us therefore strive to enter that rest, so that no one may fall by the same sort of disobedience' (Heb. 4:11).

How we need this warning today! The majority of people around us have no belief in the Bible, no respect for God and no comprehension that there is a coming judgement. The devil whispers to us that the majority must be right. Why bother to keep going with such an outdated faith? But we are to resist the devil, and he will flee from us. We are to meditate on the Word of God, which is mightier than any human sword. We are to plead with God to strengthen our faith, our love and our hope in him.

> We win no battles through our might,
> we fall at once, dejected;
> the righteous one will lead the fight,
> by God himself directed.
> You ask, 'Who can this be?'
> Christ Jesus, it is he,
> eternal King and Lord,
> God's true and living Word,
> no one can stand against him
> (Martin Luther, translated by Stephen Orchard).

Prayer: Lord, thank you that although I am faithless, you are faithful. I pray that you would help me to engage in the spiritual battle today depending on your power and grace and relying on your resources. I pray that you would protect me from the attacks of the Evil One. I pray that I would not grow weary in doing good, but would have confidence that you will bring me into your eternal rest.

Text for the day: *Let us therefore strive to enter that rest, so that no one may fall by the same sort of disobedience* (Heb. 4:11).

Five women of faith and courage

Mahlah, Noah, Hoglah, Milcah and Tirzah were sisters whose father had died and who had no brothers. They knew that when the land was conquered and apportioned out, their father's line would effectively cease to exist, unless they were given the right to inherit land. They took their case to Moses, to find out what the Lord's will would be concerning this matter.

They showed, firstly, absolute confidence that the people of God were going to enter and conquer the land. John Calvin comments: 'They had not yet entered the land, nor were their enemies conquered,' but they made their request 'as if the tranquil possession of their rights were to be accorded to them that very day'. Secondly, they showed willingness to submit their case to Moses, as God's leader, and wait patiently to see what God's will would be. Thirdly, they showed great family loyalty. They honoured the memory of their father, and their case was brought not to demand their individual rights, but to preserve their family inheritance. Fourthly, they showed that they recognized the importance of obeying God. They were at pains to point out that their late father had played no part in the rebellions against God's leader.

When they had stated their case clearly to Moses, they waited patiently to see what was God's will with regard to this matter. In this event, the Lord honoured them and said that they should inherit their father's property. Their case became a test case for other families in the same situation, and further inheritance laws were laid out for families where there might be no surviving children at all.

The final chapter of Numbers gives a postscript to this request. The tribal leaders asked what would happen if the women married outside the tribe of Manasseh. Would the land go outside the tribe? The Lord said that they should marry within their own tribe. If they married outside the tribe, their rights to the land would be forfeit. The women agreed to this, and married within their tribe (Num. 36:10-12). Their willingness to submit to this ruling demonstrates that their original request was not selfish or individualistic: it was the cohesion of the family and tribe that was uppermost in their minds. In both accounts, the sisters demonstrate a submissive and obedient spirit. They wanted, above all, to know the mind and will of the Lord.

Where is my heart today? Am I concerned, above all, to know what the will of the Lord is? These five women did not have the written Word. They had to take their request to Moses, who had to go in turn to the Lord, and they had to await the outcome. We are privileged to have the Bible, which reveals the will of God, and in situations where we need to know in detail how to act we have immediate access to the Father, through the Son and guided by the Holy Spirit. But, with all these privileges and advantages, let us seek to be as faithful, submissive, patient and obedient as these sisters.

Prayer: O Lord, please give me a trusting and submissive spirit today.

Only your restless heart keep still
and wait in cheerful hope, content
in taking what his gracious will,
his all-discerning love, has sent;
for all our inmost needs are known
to him who chose us for his own
    (Georg C. Neumark, translated by Catherine Winkworth).

Text for the day: *The law of the LORD is perfect, reviving the soul* (Ps. 19:7).

'Go in and take possession of the land'

The scene opens in Deuteronomy at the borders of Canaan. The people of Israel had reached this point forty years before. Previously, when they had been given the opportunity to enter the land, they had refused. The challenges had seemed too frightening. They had failed to trust the Lord.

They had been punished by having to wander in the wilderness for forty years. Moses now reminded them that this had been a totally unnecessary hardship. The journey from Horeb to Kadesh Barnea was only an eleven-day journey! (Deut. 1:2). Moses deliberately rehearsed this dismal record of failure and sin. The people needed to be warned not to turn back a second time. They needed to remember that previously, when they failed to trust God, he did not help them in war. They had suffered a humiliating defeat (1:42-45) and then endured four decades of having to live as nomads in the desert. Sin has consequences! Paul warned his New Testament readers to learn from such Old Testament examples. Certainly, when we repent, God offers full forgiveness in Christ Jesus and the penalty of our sins is wonderfully lifted. But if we wilfully rebel against God we sow seeds that bear bitter fruits.

Like the people of Israel, we need to learn from our past sins and failures. But this chapter also contains wonderful promises to encourage us. The New Testament also uses the picture of spiritual warfare. Our battle is not against Canaanites, walled cities or giant Anakim (1:28). We fight against satanic hosts, against our own sinful nature, against the temptations of the world and the flesh. As New Testament believers we are to go in and 'take possession of the land'. We are to claim victory over sin. We are to claim power in witnessing. We are to claim love and joy and peace in the Holy Spirit.

As we engage in this spiritual battle we, like the Israelites, are to remember that we are not alone. The battle is not ours, but God's. The Israelites had to go in to claim the land that God had already promised to give the patriarchs (1:8). They advanced with the assurance that God would fight for them (Deut. 1:30). We claim the victory that has already been won on the cross (Col. 2:15). And we do not fight alone. The Captain of our salvation fights with us and for us. He has decisively defeated Satan. The struggles of this present age are the 'mopping-up' operation.

Most comforting of all, we can know the presence of God as our loving Father. Moses assured the people of God's love and care using the language of the family: 'The LORD your God carried you, as a father carries his son, all the way you went until you reached this place' (1:31, NIV). God knows your struggles. He cares, as a concerned parent agonizes over each new struggle of a dearly loved child. When the going gets too rough, he will lift you up and carry you:

He will tend his flock like a shepherd;
  he will gather the lambs in his arms;
he will carry them in his bosom,
  and gently lead those that are with young

(Isa. 40:11).

With such wonderful assurances, let us be confident to 'go in and take possession of the land'. We do not go alone; we do not fight alone. We go in union with the Lord Jesus Christ, who has won the victory for us, with the loving care of our heavenly Father and in the power of the Holy Spirit.

Prayer: Forgive me, Lord, for my faithlessness and lack of trust in you. Help me to go in and possess the land today: grant me victory over sin, power in witness and joy in service.

Text for the day: *Go in and take possession of the land* (Deut. 1:8).

'When all your mercies...'

How do you respond when facing a challenge that seems impossible? When you wake up in the morning and simply can't face the day ahead? When you feel only weakness and fear spiritual defeat? The people of Israel, encamped on the borders of Canaan, felt deep apprehension as they thought of the battles to come. They were going to fight people who had a terrifying reputation for size and strength. They were going to be attacking walled cities. They were inexperienced in such siege warfare. There would doubtless be many casualties. They could focus on the human impossibility of the assignment, as their fathers had done forty years before. Or they could focus on the power and goodness of God, as demonstrated in his dealings with them in the past.

Moses eloquently reminded them of past mercies. God had cared for all their needs: 'These forty years the LORD your God has been with you. You have lacked nothing' (Deut. 2:7). God's constant care for his people is portrayed elsewhere in the Old Testament in parental terms: 'When Israel was a child, I loved him, and out of Egypt I called my son' (Hosea 11:1).

Even more intimately, God's loving care for them in the wilderness is described using marital imagery:

I remember the devotion of your youth,
    your love as a bride,
how you followed me in the wilderness,
    in a land not sown

                                                              (Jer. 2:2).

Moses reminded the people of the victories God had already won for them: 'The LORD our God gave all into our hands' (2:36). So, today, remember what the Lord has done for you. Look back at Calvary. Give thanks that God did not spare his only Son, but freely gave him up, for you. Look back through your life, and recall those answered prayers. Think of the way that the Lord has provided. And be encouraged to face the battles of today in his strength.

But what about unanswered prayers? Today you may feel discouraged if you have been faithfully praying for something, and God does not seem to hear. The Israelites may have felt perplexed when they arrived so near to the promised land, and the lands of Edom, Moab and the Ammonites looked so very tempting, but God said these were lands they were not to conquer — not Edom, not Moab, not the Ammonites (2:5,9,19). Israel may not have fully understood why, but God was concerned with the bigger picture. He is the God of the whole earth, not just the Israelites. Note how he used one pagan nation to bring judgement on another (2:21-22): the Ammonites as an instrument of judgement against the Zamzummim, the Edomites against the Horites, and the Caphtorim against the Avvim. He is a God of patience, delaying judgement as long as possible. He is also a God of justice, acting decisively when a nation had sinned so grossly that judgement was the only option left. We may not understand why some of our prayers seem unanswered. God sees the big picture. We can trust him.

We may well be repelled by the language of conquest (2:34), but the wrath of God against the pagan nations was expressed only after they had sinned so long and so comprehensively that his patience, as it were, had to come to an end. It was a foretaste of the Day of Judgement. God's mercy delays that day, as he wants all to come to repentance. But the time will come when the opportunity to repent is over.

Prayer: Lord, I worship you for all the mercies you have shown to me in the past. I praise you for Christ and his sacrifice; I thank you for your loving care for me throughout my life. Please help me to trust you for the future; help me to trust you for strength for the spiritual battle today. Please give me patience to trust you for my 'unanswered' prayers.

Text for the day: *The LORD your God has been with you. You have lacked nothing* (Deut. 2:7).

Godly leadership

God had equipped Moses to be a great leader, spiritually, militarily and administratively. Now he began the major task of allocating land to the tribes of Israel (Deut. 3:12-20). They had not yet crossed the Jordan into Canaan itself, but they had conquered the lands of Sihon and Og. Moses gave these territories to the tribes of Reuben and Gad and the half-tribe of Manasseh. But they were still required to go up with their brothers and complete the conquest of Canaan (3:18). They might have been tempted to settle down, but they were not allowed to forget the wider concerns of the whole nation. They were not allowed to make themselves comfortable while their brothers still faced the perils of war in conquering the promised land.

Whatever blessings God has given us, we are not to use them for our own personal advantage without considering the needs of the wider body of God's people. Paul explains the principle clearly: '... as a matter of fairness, your abundance at the present time should supply their need' (2 Cor. 8:13-14). Whether we have received spiritual gifts, financial resources, or anything else, we should see that God has entrusted us with them for the benefit of the whole body. The same applies to local churches. We need to maintain a vision for what God is doing in the church worldwide, and be willing to release our resources (prayer, finances, members) for the benefit of gospel work elsewhere.

This passage also highlights the great spiritual responsibilities of leadership, as we are reminded of God's judgement on Moses. When the Israelites were at Meribah, they had rebelled because there was no water. The Lord had told Moses to speak to the rock, and water would come out. Instead, Moses could not contain his anger against the Israelites. He struck the rock twice in anger. It looked more like a temper tantrum than a man of God performing a miracle. And God told Moses then that he would not enter the land.

Now that the land was so close, Moses begged the Lord that the verdict might be reversed. But it was not. Why?

We get a hint from Moses' own words: 'The LORD was angry with me because of you' (3:26). He was suffering judgement as an example to the Israelites. Consider the numerous times the Israelites grumbled. Certainly one whole generation was condemned to die in the wilderness, but the generation who entered were by no means sinless! Moses sinned once and the way was blocked. Because Moses was the leader of God's people, and because at that crucial time he did not show God to be holy among the people, he had to be judged. The judgement would teach the whole nation that the holiness of God cannot be compromised. As the New Testament teaches, those who teach must be judged more strictly.

But the Lord answered Moses' prayer in a different way. He was not allowed to enter the promised land, but he was called into heaven. And there Moses would see God's glory in a greater way than he ever imagined in this prayer.

God may say 'No' to many of our prayers, but he will always say 'Yes' to our request to see and know more of his glory, to go on in grace, to see the Holy Spirit's work advance and increase in our lives.

Prayer: Take time to pray for your church leaders, locally and nationally, and your political leaders.

Pray also for willingness (personally and in your local church), to release resources for the good of the worldwide church.

Text for the day: *Remember your leaders, those who spoke to you the word of God* (Heb. 13:7).

'If you love me, you will keep my commandments'

Moses had brought the people of Israel to the very borders of the promised land. He knew that he was not the one to lead them in. That task would fall to the younger, fitter, military leader, Joshua. But Moses could not leave the people without telling them what was on his heart. He longed for them to trust and obey the Lord, who had brought them so far. He wanted them to remember the goodness, patience and faithful provision of the Lord over the past forty years. He wanted them to be stirred up with gratitude for the covenant God had made with them. He wanted them to teach their children about the mighty deliverance God had afforded his people while they were in Egypt.

When Moses urged the people to obey the Lord, he did not use the cold legal language of obligation. He used the language of a covenantal relationship. The Lord loved his people, and had proved his love by acting on their behalf. In return, he expected loyalty and wholehearted obedience.

Obedience to God would signify the people's love for the one who had loved them first. Disobedience would break the relationship, as surely as infidelity breaks a marriage relationship. If the people disobeyed, they were not just 'breaking a law'; they were rejecting the Lawgiver himself. This principle continues in the New Testament: 'If you love me, you will keep my commandments' (John 14:15). Here in Deuteronomy, we also glimpse the missionary heart of God. When the people of Israel love and obey him, it will be a sign to the surrounding nations that he is a great and incomparable God. This principle too is developed in the New Testament: 'By this all people will know that you are my disciples, if you have love for one another' (John 13:35).

Because obedience is all about relationship with God, it then makes sense that the people practise obedience in the presence of God, i.e. in his land (Deut. 4:5,14). If they disobeyed, they would be expelled from his presence and banished from his land (4:27). This echoes the penalty suffered by Adam and Eve when they sinned against God. They were expelled from his presence and had to leave the Garden of Eden. It points to the final judgement, when impenitent sinners will be banished from God's presence and cast into hell.

But for the people then, as for all people now, there was hope, and the offer of renewed fellowship with God. Having sinned, even when they had been sent into exile, if they sought the Lord and obeyed him once again, then they would be restored to the land. They might despise and break the covenant, but God never would (4:29-31).

Are you enjoying fellowship with God today? To do so, we have to obey his commands (John 14:21-23). Sometimes we lose a sense of the enjoyment of God because we have grieved the Spirit. It may be because we have filled our lives so full of other things that we have simply let times of fellowship with God get pushed out. But the promise that Moses gave to the people of Israel still applies today: '... you will seek the LORD your God and you will find him, if you search after him with all your heart and with all your soul' (Deut. 4:29).

Prayer:
Search me, O God, and know my heart! ...
And see if there be any grievous way in me,
and lead me in the way everlasting!

(Ps. 139:23-24).

Text for the day: *You will find him, if you search after him with all your heart and with all your soul* (Deut. 4:29).

Remember what God has done for you

Ask from one end of heaven to the other, whether such a great thing as this has ever happened or was ever heard of (Deut. 4:32).

Nothing like this had happened in all of human history. No other God had rescued a people for himself, and cared for them with such tender care. Pagan deities had to be placated with endless offerings: they never delivered the goods. But Israel's God was a God who spoke (4:33), a God who loved (4:37) and a God who rescued (4:34,37-38). And they were never to forget it! They were to remember that it was pure grace that caused God to choose them, out of all the nations on earth. They were to remember that the miracles they had witnessed showed that there was only one God who actually acted, who intervened in human history. Other so-called 'gods' were powerless; they were created images, unable to intervene or influence events in any way at all: 'The LORD is God; there is no other besides him' (4:35).

The appeal comes to us today with the same force. Just as the Israelites were summoned to remember their rescue from slavery, so we are to remember our rescue from sin and death. How can we begin a new day without thanking the Lord Jesus that he gave his life for us? How can we find our minds and hearts taken up with other idols, relying on anything or anyone else to give us satisfaction and security, when we remember the price that has been paid? Not only when we celebrate the Lord's Supper, but every day, we are to remember the cross, and the 'amazing love' of our Lord. 'Ask from one end of heaven to the other.' Has any other God died to save a people for himself? Has 'such a great thing as this' ever happened, or ever been heard of — that the Creator of life himself should suffer death for me? Meditate on the blood of Jesus Christ poured out, and all else falls back into its proper place:

His lifeblood like a crimson robe,
clothes all his body on the tree;

then I am dead to all the globe,
and all the globe is dead to me.

Were the whole realm of nature mine,
that were an offering far too small;
love so amazing, so divine,
demands my soul, my life, my all!

(Isaac Watts).

Moses knew that, as the people entered the promised land, they would be faced with an array of competing religious practices. There would be many temptations to unfaithfulness. It would be so tempting to go along with some of the pagan practices, putting them alongside the worship of God. But they were to remember that the Lord alone is God, and that he alone had saved them.

Today we are faced with a dazzling array of competing claims on our time, our energy and our love. We are called to be single-minded. We are to focus on love for, and obedience to, the one true God. We fulfil all sorts of different responsibilities, but God is to be the sun around which all the other 'planets' revolve. Right here and now, to refocus your heart on God, you need go no further than the cross.

Prayer: Father God, Lord Jesus Christ, Holy Spirit, I worship you that you alone are God. I worship you that you have provided a way of salvation so extraordinary, so amazing, that nothing like it has been heard of 'from one end of heaven to the other'. Thank you for the cross. I pray that today my heart would be fixed on you, and dead to all temptations to idolize anyone or anything else.

Text for the day: *Ask from one end of heaven to the other, whether such a great thing as this has ever happened or was ever heard of* (Deut. 4:32).

The fear of the Lord

Oh that they had such a mind as this always, to fear me and to keep all my commandments...! (Deut. 5:29).

The giving of the law at Sinai was accompanied by thunder, lightning and smoke — dramatic symbols of the intense and unapproachable holiness of God. The people were terrified. They knew that they needed a mediator, and pleaded with Moses to speak on their behalf (5:27).

God did not challenge this reaction. It was a correct response to his holiness and glory. Indeed, he wanted them to continue fearing him: 'They are right in all that they have spoken. Oh that they had such a mind as this always, to fear me and to keep all my commandments...!' (5:28-29). To 'fear' God is, indeed the only sane and proper response to his blazing glory and holiness, his incomparable power. The psalmist summoned all nations to this proper response to God:

> *Let all the earth fear the LORD;*
> *let all the inhabitants of the world stand in awe of him!*
> *For he spoke, and it came to be;*
> *he commanded, and it stood firm*
>
> (Ps. 33:8-9).

The writer of Ecclesiastes concluded, after having tried everything that life has to offer: 'Fear God and keep his commandments, for this is the whole duty of man' (Eccles. 12:13).

To fear the Lord is to hate evil (Prov. 8:13). So Moses urged the people never to forget the powerful visual aids God had given their fathers and mothers, and never to forget the commands he had given them.

We also are to respond to God with awe and reverence. Everything in our culture militates against respect for anyone or anything. We live in the age of democracy, of first-name terms, of 'dressing down'. All too often a disrespect for authority in general spills over into church life. Our worship services have to be 'seeker-friendly' and we do not want to 'put anyone off' by anything as old-fashioned as talk of 'fearing God'. But the gospel only makes sense when we put the foundation in place. We are answerable to our Creator God, a holy God who is going to judge sin. If that truth is removed, the only thing left is sheer sentimentality.

Let us go into each day, having worshipped our holy God, acknowledging that we can only enter his holy presence through the work of our mediator, Jesus Christ.

Prayer: Holy Spirit, please convict me of my own sinfulness before a holy God. Forgive me for my irreverence, my casual attitude towards holy things. Please revive my sense of reverent fear towards God, Father, Son and Holy Spirit.

How wonderful, how beautiful,
the sight of thee must be,
thine endless wisdom, boundless power,
and awful purity!

Oh, how I fear thee, living God,
with deepest, tenderest fears,
and worship thee with trembling hope
and penitential tears!

Yet I may love thee, too, O Lord,
almighty as thou art;
for thou hast stooped to ask of me
the love of my poor heart

(F. W. Faber).

Text for the day: *Oh that they had such a mind as this always, to fear me and to keep all my commandments...!* (Deut. 5:29).

'Love the LORD your God with all your heart and ... soul and ... might'

God does not want mechanical obedience: he desires the love of our hearts. The heart stands for the control centre of our beings, including our minds, our emotions and our will. In our day, we associate 'love' with sentimentality, with our feelings, but here love is something that is commanded (Deut. 6:5). And Moses gives down-to-earth practical advice on how to make sure we love God. We are to deliberately focus our thoughts on him. We are to speak of the great things he has done for us. If we have children, we are to tell them daily of God's love, and of his gracious provision for us (6:7). If we allow our minds to be filled with other things, to the exclusion of God, then our love will grow cold. But if we discipline ourselves to remember his grace, our love will become more and more intense. We are not to wait until we 'feel' love for God. We are to use the spiritual disciplines — Bible reading, meditation, prayer, worship, fellowship with other believers — and if we do this, our love for God will increase in intensity and passion.

When the Israelites entered the promised land, it would be easy for them to grow complacent and slip into thinking that the peace and security and prosperity of the land had been given to them because of their own goodness. Rather, says Moses, they are continually to remember that they had started off as slaves in Egypt, and it was only God's goodness that had led to their rescue. Such remembrance should stir up love and gratitude. Similarly, whatever good things we have today, whatever pleasures we enjoy, we are to remind ourselves that these are all gifts of God. We do not deserve them; we do not have them because we are in any way more virtuous than the many millions who are not so fortunate. They are gifts of pure grace.

We are to love the Lord with all our soul. We are to love him from the depths of our being, and we are to love him exclusively. We are not to offer our allegiance or our worship to anyone or anything else (6:13). There is nothing and no one to compare with God. All the wealth and glory of this world is, after all, his creation. If you truly love God you would never sell him, by exchanging his love for merely worldly wealth or pleasure. As the old chorus puts it:

I'd rather have Jesus than silver or gold,
I'd rather be his than have riches untold...

We love him even in the darkest days; we devote ourselves to him alone. And we are to love him with all our might. We are to apply our best energies, our best gifts, our best time, our best efforts and the first part of all our money to serving him.

Take my life and let it be
consecrated, Lord, to thee;
take my moments and my days;
let them flow in ceaseless praise

(Frances Ridley Havergal).

It doesn't matter how loudly we *say* we love God. The test comes in practice. Where do we place our best energies? How do we spend our best time? Where does the first portion of our income go? Does God get the leftovers, or the best? Our obedience and devotion must spill over into every part of our lives. We may not literally have boxes containing copies of God's law tied to our foreheads and our front doors (6:8-9), but our obedience and devotion should be clear for all to see, and we are to acknowledge the presence of God in every activity and every project.

Prayer: Almighty God, Lord, forgive me for the times when my love is lukewarm. Remind me that spiritually I was a 'slave in Egypt', but that Christ paid the price for my release. Free me from self-love today, so that I may love you with all my heart, with all my soul and with all my might.

Text for the day: *Love the LORD your God with all your heart and with all your soul and with all your might* (Deut. 6:5).

'You are a people holy to the LORD your God'

Israel is described as 'a people holy to the LORD your God' (Deut. 7:6). We often think of 'holiness' as something we have to earn by our own efforts, but it is clear here that holiness is a state that has been granted by God, not because Israel is any better than any other nation, but because of grace. So when God looks for a way to say, 'I love you', he says, 'You are a people holy to the LORD your God.' This 'holiness' or state of being 'set apart', is something that he has done for them, not the other way round.

It is exactly the same for us. We are saved by pure grace. We are now called to live up to the holy calling that we have been granted by God's free grace. Our efforts to be holy are not what 'win' us God's love. Our obedience to God is an absolute obligation, one which flows from our relationship of love and gratitude for what he has already done for us in Christ.

The Israelites were to express their holy calling by repudiating allegiance to the gods of Canaan. They were not to compromise their exclusive relationship with God by political alliances or intermarriage. In the early years of the settlement this was expressed in the most extreme possible way — by the 'herem', or 'ban', commanded in verses 2 and 16. This was not going to be normal practice throughout Israel's history. Later on in Deuteronomy there are laws governing warfare which emphasize compassion and humanity. But the initial conquest of Canaan was a unique incident in salvation history. The sins of the Canaanites were so gross and corrupt that there was no alternative but to destroy them totally. The Israelites were also being taught a powerful lesson: the Canaanite practices were so seductive that the Israelites would only be safe if the temptations were removed altogether.

This is a powerful object lesson for us. We cannot risk negotiating with sin. When we start down the route of compromise, we are lost. It is not worth taking any risks with sinful thoughts, activities, or habits. Jesus uses the radical images of plucking out our eyes or chopping off our hands if we are in danger of sinning.

But we shall never overcome sin by sheer willpower. We need God's enabling. This is what Israel was promised. They looked with alarm at the prospect of invading Canaan. How could they possibly overcome the native inhabitants? Only with God's help (7:18-21). But they were to be patient. God was going to enable them to take control of the land 'little by little' (7:22). This is a comforting truth to remember today. We so often grow impatient. We want to see victory over our sins all at once. We want to see God's work advanced with mighty revivals. We want to see the kingdom established now! But God's normal way throughout the history of the church has been to advance his cause steadily, 'little by little'. His normal way in our lives is for us to use the spiritual disciplines commanded by his Word. Then, by his Spirit, he helps us to overcome our besetting sins 'little by little'.

Prayer: Give thanks for the work of God in your life, in your local church and in the church worldwide. Pray for the Lord to work today to bring about greater holiness in your own life, in your local church and in the church worldwide.

Text for the day: *But you are a chosen people, a royal priesthood, a holy nation, a people belonging to God* (1 Peter 2:9, NIV).

'Take care lest you forget the LORD'

Beware lest you say in your heart, 'My power and the might of my hand have gained me this wealth' (Deut. 8:17).

This chapter could well be entitled 'Coping with prosperity'. Moses looks ahead to the conquest and settlement of the promised land. God's promise to Abraham that a vast number of his descendants would possess the land was about to be fulfilled. The people would find that this land was fruitful and that they would enjoy plenty (8:7-10). But, once they were experiencing peace and wealth, would they still rely on God? The whole desert experience had been a lesson in trust. Each day the Lord had provided manna. Water had been supernaturally supplied from rocks. The blazing heat, the poisonous snakes, the opposition of enemy armies — all had forced the Israelites into radical dependence on God. The difficulties had been in order to 'humble you and test you, to do you good in the end' (8:16). Once the difficulties were removed, Moses warned the people to 'Take care lest you forget the LORD your God ... lest, when you have eaten and are full ... then your heart be lifted up, and you forget the LORD' (8:11,14).

We too need this warning. In the West we enjoy a standard of living undreamed of by the majority of people in the world, and far beyond that of the vast majority of people throughout history. The Scripture warns that wealth can so easily be attended by arrogance and complacency. So when other troubles arise, whether family conflicts, emotional turmoil, job insecurity, or health issues, these are to 'humble us and test us, to do us good in the end'. In these times of trouble we are forced back into that radical dependence on God. The whole point of this life is for us to be 'conformed to the likeness of his Son' (Rom. 8:29, NIV). Trials are the means our Father uses for this end.

Moses reminds the people of the intimate detail of God's care for his people throughout the wilderness experience: 'Your clothing did not wear out on you, and your foot did not swell these forty years' (8:4). And Jesus reminds us that our heavenly

Father fully knows all our needs for food and clothing. If he feeds the birds of the air and clothes the flowers of the field, we can trust him to care for us too.

Moses pleads with the people, urging them to ongoing obedience. In view of God's generosity, how can it be possible that they might take his blessings for granted and turn to other gods? We have seen even greater mercy in the breathtaking condescension of Christ, who for our sake became poor, and went so far as to give his life for us. How could we ever take this blessing for granted, become complacent and disobedient and value other things above our Saviour?

Let every blessing we enjoy today be a signpost to the love of God. Let us be grateful, obedient and worshipping people.

> We thank you, then, our Father,
> for all things bright and good,
> the seed-time and the harvest,
> our life, our health, our food:
> accept the gifts we offer
> for all your love imparts;
> and that which you most welcome —
> our humble, thankful hearts!
> 　　　　　　　(Jane Campbell, based on Matthias Claudius).

Prayer: O Lord, forgive me for ingratitude and complacency. Forgive me for disobedience and self-reliance. Help me today to lean only and wholly on you.

Text for the day: *Beware lest you say in your heart, 'My power and the might of my hand have gained me this wealth'* (Deut. 8:17).

'The LORD ... is not partial and takes no bribe'

The statement that 'The LORD ... is not partial and takes no bribe' (Deut. 10:17) does not mean that God treats all people with exactly equal physical or material blessings. Throughout the Bible it is acknowledged that there are rich and poor. There are those in authority, with power to command in the workplace, or leaders of nations, while others serve and follow. The circumstances of our lives might vary in all sorts of ways. Nor does God give everyone exactly the same spiritual blessings: he gave Israel unique and wonderful privileges (10:15). Today there are special blessings for the church, for those who know and trust the Lord Jesus Christ. God's spiritual blessings are not universal. Not everyone will be welcomed into heaven on the Last great Day. So this verse does not mean that God makes everyone the same. But it does mean that God treats every single individual with justice and compassion and dignity. Whether we are rich or poor, or Jew or Gentile, black or white, young or old, God does not show favouritism.

When God says that he is a God of impartiality, it means that his justice is not affected by the personal importance, power, or wealth of individuals. He shows no partiality and accepts no bribes. And that means that the life of a famine victim in Africa is worth just as much as a millionaire in Britain. A homeless drug addict is worth just as much as the wealthy businessman. God looks at every individual as a creature made in his own image and likeness, someone whom he loves and who is precious in his sight. Rich and poor are equally valuable before God. Before him we all stand on level ground. And so God commands us also to treat the needy with equal respect.

Teach us to serve our neighbour's need,
the homeless help, the hungry feed,
the poor protect, the weak defend,
and to the friendless prove a friend;
the wayward and the lost reclaim
for love of Christ and in his name

(Timothy Dudley-Smith).

In the New Testament, Peter explains that, with the coming of the Lord Jesus Christ, God's invitation to spiritual blessing does not apply only to Jews, but to the whole world. When Cornelius, a non-Jew, came to know God and received the Holy Spirit, Peter quoted these words from Deuteronomy (Acts 10:34-35). The God who does not show favouritism now opens up his invitation for all of us to come to know him, to be the recipients of his spiritual blessings. All are invited to come to God through Christ.

Prayer: Lord, forgive me for my foolish pride. Forgive me for thinking that the gifts and privileges you give me so freely make me any better than those who seem to have nothing. Grant me humility to realize that all I am and all I have is a gift of free grace.

Forbid it, Lord, that I should boast,
save in the cross of Christ my God;
the very things that charm me most,
I sacrifice them to his blood

(Isaac Watts).

Text for the day: *God does not show favouritism* (Acts 10:34, NIV).

The one place of worship

When you invite guests to dinner, you may check to see whether they have any allergies. You do not want to give them something that will make them ill. How much more, when we approach the living God, we should take care that we worship in the way that he prescribes! Today we are often told that we should worship in 'the way that we feel comfortable with'. Who has the right to tell us what to do? The answer, of course, is that God does.

While the inhabitants of Canaan did what they wanted as regarded religious practice, the people of God did not have that freedom. 'The place that the LORD your God will choose' is a phrase that recurs six times in Deuteronomy 12 (vv. 5,11,14,18,21,26). The tabernacle had travelled with the people while they were in the wilderness. Once they had settled in the land, God would choose a place (Jerusalem) where a permanent place of worship would be built. The sacrificial system would be centralized. If the people were able to offer sacrifices wherever they liked, their worship would degenerate very quickly. If they began to imitate the obnoxious religious practices of the previous inhabitants of the land, it would be very difficult to control. With a central place of worship, the practices of sacrifice could be overseen by the recognized priesthood, and worship would be more likely to remain free from syncretism (i.e. mixing with pagan practices).

The urgency of this was underlined when Moses outlined the Canaanite practices that were so repulsive to God. They offered their children as sacrifices; they practised witchcraft; they consulted the dead (18:9-12). It was because of this that God's patience had been exhausted, and he was using his own people to drive the Canaanites out of the land. But memories of the old ways would remain, and might prove a temptation to the Israelites. Hence the precaution of centralizing religious practice.

How does this apply today? When Jesus was asked about the place where God should be worshipped, he replied that true worshippers now do not have to go to Jerusalem. We must worship him 'in spirit and truth' (John 4:24). How do we approach the Father to worship him today? 'Jesus said to him

[Thomas], "I am the way, and the truth, and the life. No one comes to the Father except through me"' (John 14:6).

The principle of Deuteronomy 12 is unchanged. We are to worship God alone; our worship must be exclusive. We are to examine our lives for idolatry of all kinds. Anything or anyone that absorbs our hearts to the exclusion of the one true God is an idol. We are to worship God in the way that he prescribes. We come to him through Christ alone. The people of Israel could only come to God if the right sacrifices were offered in the right way at the right place. These sacrifices all pointed forward to the Lamb of God. We also can only come to God by means of the great and final sacrifice. We do not depend on our own good works to gain favour with him. Note also that the people of Israel had to come to God with joy. Acceptance with God was something to celebrate. Hence the emphasis on feasting, on plenty, on happiness and joy (12:12,18). God does not want cold, mechanical, ritualistic worship. He wants our hearts.

And when we think of the great price that the Lord Jesus willingly paid for our salvation, surely the only appropriate response is one of joy and celebration.

> *The joy, Oh the joy of this glorious thought!*
> *My sin, not in part but the whole,*
> *is nailed to his cross, and I bear it no more;*
> *praise the Lord, praise the Lord, O my soul!*
>
> (Horatio G. Spafford).

Prayer: Lord, I acknowledge you as my only God. Help me to tear down the idols that compete for my allegiance. I come to you through the finished sacrifice of Christ. I rejoice that he was willing to pay the price for me to be forgiven and restored to your service.

Text for the day: *Jesus said to him, 'I am the way, and the truth, and the life. No one comes to the Father except through me'* (John 14:6).

The Lord's release

We see here God's heart for the poor. If his laws were obeyed, then there should never be any abject need in Israelite society: 'There will be no poor among you' (Deut. 15:4). For example, when people enjoyed the regular feasts, they were to share with those who were needy (16:11-12). Every third year, the regular tithes were to be set aside for the use of the Levites and the poor (14:28-29). When the harvest took place, the harvesters were only allowed to go through the fields once; whatever was missed was to be left for the poor (Lev. 23:22). Every seven years, the fields, vineyards and olive orchards were to be left fallow, and whatever grew naturally was to be left for the needy to harvest (Exod. 23:11). If an Israelite lent anything to a fellow Israelite, he was not to charge any interest (Deut. 23:19-20). Every seven years, debts were to be suspended for that year: 'You shall grant a release' (15:1). If you lent to a poor person in the year leading up to the seventh (fallow) year, you might not get anything back. But you were still to give help without grudging it (15:9-10). If the Israelites obeyed all these instructions, and other laws for the protection of the vulnerable, and if they were fully obedient to all God's commands, God promised that he would bless them so abundantly that no one would ever be in need (15:4-6).

Moses was aware, however, that the people were going to fail. Given human sinfulness, manifested in greed and sloth, personal tragedy and individual misfortune, the note of realism is also struck: 'There will never cease to be poor in the land' (15:11). But the Lord demands that the poor be treated with mercy and generosity. The release from payment of debt every seventh year was to give a window of opportunity and hope for the poor. In the most extreme cases, the very poor might have been forced to sell themselves into service. But fellow Israelites were always to be treated with dignity, and they were to be released from service every seven years (Lev. 25:39-41). When they were released, generous provision was to be made for them (Deut. 15:14-15). They were to have a chance of a new start. But if the servant wanted to remain in service to his master, then a ceremony was provided whereby he or she could symbolically become part of the family. The doorpost was the symbol of the household, so being joined to it (15:17) was a powerful visual aid to demonstrate the permanent addition of a new member to the household.

Every forty-nine years a jubilee would be declared, and everyone in Israel would be able to repossess their own land, even if they had fallen into debt (Lev. 25:8-12). This special year provided a once-in-a-lifetime opportunity to start afresh. God wanted there always to be hope for the poor. He ordered society so that there were built-in safeguards against the rich growing richer and richer while the poor grew poorer and poorer.

Human greed means that there is always the temptation to become addicted to work, wanting to earn more and more. The Sabbath principle and the regular cycle of festivals meant that God's people had to stop, to worship, to remember what all that work was about and who, ultimately, it was for. The New Testament principle is that we are to work as unto the Lord, and to use the wealth we earn to provide for ourselves and our families, and then to help those in need. Jesus reminds us that it was the 'rich fool' who hoarded his wealth, with no thought of relieving the needs of others.

Prayer:
God of the poor, friend of the weak,
give us compassion we pray,
melt our cold hearts,
let tears fall like rain,
come change our love
from a spark to a flame

(Graham Kendrick).

Text for the day: *Blessed is he who is generous to the poor* (Prov. 14:21).

The righteous King

As Moses addressed the people, he knew that he was soon to die. Who then would lead them? Moses looked forward to the time when God himself would provide a king for his people. The people did not have the right to choose their own leader. Israel was not a 'democracy' (where the people rule); rather, Israel was a 'theocracy' (where God is the ultimate ruler). The people were to submit to God in the choice of a king (Deut. 17:15). When the king was appointed he was to be God's man, not chosen for human considerations, such as popularity, or appearance, or skill. He was to be committed to God's laws and accountable to God. He was to depend on the Lord for victory, not on great military resources, nor on great wealth, nor on foreign alliances (this is the significance of forbidding many wives).

Such a king would have to remain humble. As one who was dependent on God's help for victory, not self-sufficient, he could not become tyrannical. His leadership was not to be exercised for his own benefit, but for the good of his people. He was to rule according to the law of God (17:18-20), not his own ideas.

By the end of the time of the judges, the people of Israel had lost sight of the fact that they were dependent on God to give them victory in battle. They wanted a king to give them victory, looking to the surrounding nations for the kind of leader they should appoint. Their attitude offended the Lord, and he responded by giving them just what they wanted. Saul was, humanly speaking, a hero. He was good-looking, powerful, a great fighter. But of course it all went disastrously wrong. Then, when David came to the throne, he also failed to fulfil these high ideals, even though he was God's chosen leader, and his son Solomon failed even more catastrophically.

The kings of Israel never did live up to the ideal set out in these verses. Their failure set the scene for the coming of the great Messiah ('Christ' is a Greek translation of the Hebrew word 'Messiah' or 'Anointed One'). In Israel, the king sat on his throne to give judgements in the most difficult cases. But Jesus is entrusted with all judgement by God the Father. He is the great

King. Psalms 2 and 110 are just two of the Old Testament passages which point to the kingship of Christ: 'For he must reign until he has put all his enemies under his feet' (1 Cor. 15:25, quoting Ps. 110:1). Jesus is 'the ruler of kings on earth' (Rev. 1:5).

> *One Lord, one kingdom all secures:*
> *he reigns and life and death are yours;*
> *through earth and heaven one song shall ring:*
> *'The Lord omnipotent is King!'*
>
> (Josiah Conder).

Moses' vision for the King of Israel would ultimately be fulfilled in Christ. But these verses lay down some vitally important principles which are applicable to all leadership, including leadership in the Christian church. Leaders are to be 'God's people', not chosen for merely human reasons. They are to be godly. Humble prayer should precede appointments, recognizing that whoever is appointed for a task should ultimately also be God's choice (cf. Acts 13:2). Leaders are to be dependent on God, not looking to their own strength and capability to achieve anything. They are not to exercise 'absolute' power; they are always to be in submission to the Word of God. Leadership is not to be exercised for their own benefit, but the benefit of those they lead.

However large or small our own spheres of responsibility are, these principles apply to us too. Today we are on divine commission to serve wherever God has placed us. We are to be governed by God's will as revealed in his Word. We are to depend on him for success. We are to exercise all our responsibilities not for our own benefit, but for the benefit of others.

Prayer: Almighty God, I worship you that Jesus Christ is the King of kings and Lord of lords.

Text for the day: *As for me, I have set my King on Zion, my holy hill* (Ps. 2:6).

The promise of a Prophet

As the people of Israel stood on the verge of the promised land, Moses warned them in the strongest possible terms of the dangers of straying away from true worship. The inhabitants of Canaan worshipped other gods. Behind all such idolatry we see the ceaseless activity of God's enemy the devil. He is clever and creative and well able to trick God's people into moving away from pure worship — for example, by speaking through prophets who sound convincing and use miraculous signs to confirm their claims:

> If a prophet or a dreamer of dreams arises among you and gives you a sign or a wonder, and the sign or wonder that he tells you comes to pass, and if he says, 'Let us go after other gods,' which you have not known, 'and let us serve them', you shall not listen to the words of that prophet or that dreamer of dreams. For the LORD your God is testing you, to know whether you love the LORD your God with all your heart and with all your soul... But that prophet or that dreamer of dreams shall be put to death, because he has taught rebellion against the LORD your God (Deut. 13:1-3,5).

Supernatural power by itself is no proof of truth. Christ warned that false prophets would perform great signs and wonders 'so as to lead astray, if possible, even the elect' (Matt. 24:24; cf. Rev. 13:13-14). In the Old Testament, the people of God were identified with a nation. False teachers had to be excluded. The only way to exclude them from the nation was by capital punishment. God's people are not now identified with a nation, so capital punishment for this offence is obsolete. Rather, false teachers are to be excluded from the church, by means of church discipline.

Moses assured the people that God would not leave them without witness: 'I will raise up for them a prophet like you from among their brothers. And I will put my words in his mouth' (Deut. 18:18). Throughout the Old Testament, God provided a line of prophets, who summoned the people back to him. But all these prophets pointed forward to the great Prophet, the one who not only spoke for God, but was God. Christ is our great and final Prophet, Priest and King.

When the Jews sent people to question John the Baptist, they asked, 'Are you the Prophet?' (John 1:21). Of course he was 'a' prophet (Luke 1:76), but not 'the' prophet: hence his emphatic denial.

'Long ago, at many times and in many ways, God spoke to our fathers by the prophets, but in these last days he has spoken to us by his Son' (Heb. 1:1). After Christ, there are no more prophets. We are to refuse to listen to those who claim infallible revelation. The various sects and cults have typically been founded by a 'prophet' who has claimed a hotline to heaven, and who says that he or she has something to add to Scripture. Rather we place our confidence in Christ the Word and in the Word of God, which is sufficient and reliable (2 Tim. 3:16-17).

Our prophet, he explains
all we can know of God,
for only he eternal reigns,
the uncreated Word.
In ages long since gone,
God spoke in various ways,
but now has spoken by his Son —
obey him all your days!

(Andrew King).

Prayer: Almighty God, thank you that Christ came as the great and final Prophet, bringing the certain and true message of salvation. Help me to hear him and submit to him today, and through him to worship you.

Text for the day: *I will raise up for them a prophet like you from among their brothers. And I will put my words in his mouth, and he shall speak to them all that I command him* (Deut. 18:18).

Blessings and curses

Visual and dramatic aids were put in place to impress the solemnity of the covenant on the people. Deuteronomy 26:16-19 gives the heart of the agreement between the Lord and his people. They had to commit themselves to obeying his law with all their heart and with all their soul. The Lord committed himself to them: they were his treasured possession and he would set them high above the nations.

The visual aid took the form of the large stones set up at the entry to the promised land (27:2-3,8). Some suggest that it was this summary of the covenant (26:16-19) that was placed on the stones; others that it was the whole of the law (as contained in chapters 12-26) that was engraved. Perhaps it was the Ten Commandments. The people were to be perpetually reminded of the law of God which they had committed themselves to obey. Near the stones an altar was built for burnt offerings and peace offerings. A sinful people would constantly disobey, but God himself provided a way for them to enter his presence and live at peace with him. The burnt offerings, offered morning and evening, were a continual reminder of the wrath of God against sin. They also continually pointed forward to Christ's final sacrifice. The peace offering was shared between God, the priest and the worshippers, representing the joy of restored relationship with the gracious covenant Lord. It anticipated the Lord's Supper, the celebration of what Christ has done to bring peace between ourselves and God.

The dramatic aid was the ritual of the communal chanting of the curses for disobedience (27:11-26). Joshua 8:30-35 records how this was carried out. The tribes stood in two groups in the valley in front of the mountains; the solemn curses for breaking the law were announced by the Levites, and all the people said 'Amen'.

Deuteronomy 28 commences with the promise of blessing if the people loved and obeyed God. They would be protected and would prosper in family life, community life, farming and relations with other nations. Israel was being asked to be faithful to the Lord who had rescued them, kept them, provided for them, been patient with them, and had now brought them into a land 'flowing with milk and honey'. The Lord regarded Israel as a precious son, and wanted the people's joyful trust and allegiance.

But the breaking of such a relationship of grace would have appalling consequences. The curses give a glimpse of the horror of life without the presence of God. If the people wilfully abandoned God, then he would turn them over to the consequences. We glimpse the breakdown of a social order when God is rejected (28:30). If sexual morality breaks down, family life collapses. If theft and corruption flourish, then there is no individual security. If there are no constraints on the rich, the poor suffer. The devil always paints God's law as restrictive, as if it will destroy our enjoyment of life. In fact the opposite is true. Real happiness is only attainable within healthy boundaries. Romans 1 gives a searing picture of what life is like when people choose their own 'morality'. God turns them over to it — and to the consequences.

Chapter 28 actually gives us a glimpse of hell itself, the place where God is not. As we look at our hearts, we have to acknowledge the sin of trying to live life without God, and then we look at the fearful consequences. It also gives us a glimpse of the terrible curse which the Lord Jesus willingly bore for his people: 'Christ redeemed us from the curse of the law by becoming a curse for us' (Gal. 3:13).

> Saved from the legal curse I am;
> my Saviour hangs on yonder tree:
> see there the meek, expiring Lamb!
> 'Tis finished! He expires for me
>
>   (Charles Wesley).

Prayer: Almighty Father, I worship you that your Son has borne the curse that I deserve.

Text for the day: *Christ redeemed us from the curse of the law by becoming a curse for us* (Gal. 3:13).

'Choose life!'

This is the appeal at the climax of Moses' address. Having laid out in the starkest of terms the consequences of obedience and disobedience, he now pleads fervently with the people to trust God. He explains that the way of obedience is not difficult! It simply means staying in relationship with God. Note the emphasis on the heart (Deut. 30:17). Will the people respond to the Lord with love? (30:20). If so, then they have chosen life; but if they reject God they, in effect, choose death (30:15).

We have to make the same choice, but the choice for us is even clearer. Paul quotes Moses' exact words, but places them in the context of a call to respond to the gospel:

> *For Moses writes about the righteousness that is based on the law, that the person who does the commandments shall live by them. But the righteousness based on faith says, 'Do not say in your heart, "Who will ascend into heaven?"' (that is, to bring Christ down) or '"Who will descend into the abyss?"' (that is, to bring Christ up from the dead). But what does it say? 'The word is near you, in your mouth and in your heart' (that is, the word of faith that we proclaim); because, if you confess with your mouth that Jesus is Lord and believe in your heart that God raised him from the dead, you will be saved* (Rom. 10:5-9).

Those encamped on the border of Canaan could take God at his word and choose life, or reject the word of God and choose death. The Word has now been made flesh, and we have to choose. Do we accept and confess Jesus as Lord, and choose life? Or do we reject his claims, refuse his lordship, and choose death? The glorious thing is that to choose life is not difficult. We do not have to ascend to the heavens or descend into the depths. As Moses told the people, 'The word is very near you. It is in your mouth and in your heart, so that you can do it' (Deut. 30:14).

Renew your commitment today to confess with your mouth that 'Jesus is Lord' and believe in your heart that God raised him from the dead, and rejoice that by so doing you will be saved.

Who is on the Lord's side?
Who will serve the King?
Who will be his helpers
other lives to bring?
Who will leave the world's side?
Who will face the foe?
Who is on the Lord's side?
Who for him will go?

By thy call of mercy,
by thy grace divine,
we are on the Lord's side;
Saviour, we are thine

(Frances Ridley Havergal).

Prayer: Almighty God, I worship you that you raised the Lord Jesus from the dead. I worship you that you have declared him with power to be the Son of God. I pray that you would give me courage today to confess him as Lord.

Text for the day: *If you confess with your mouth that Jesus is Lord and believe in your heart that God raised him from the dead, you will be saved* (Rom. 10:9).

'I will never leave you'

For forty years Moses had led the people. Now he was to be taken from them. How would they be able to enter the land, with all the terrifying unknowns involved? The Lord assured them that he himself would be with them (Deut. 31:6). He would empower the leader he had prepared to take Moses' place.

Joshua was one of the two faithful spies who had brought a good report of the land forty years before. He had always been reliable, loyal and at Moses' right hand. Moses publicly commissioned Joshua (31:7) and assured him too that the Lord would never leave him or forsake him (31:8).

When Moses and Joshua went to the Tent of Meeting for Joshua's commissioning, the Lord appeared in the pillar of cloud, the visible symbol of his presence and blessing (31:15). He then repeated his assurance to Joshua that he would be empowered to lead the people into the land: 'Be strong and courageous, for you shall bring the people of Israel into the land that I swore to give them. I will be with you' (31:23).

'I will be with you.' This is the golden thread of promise running throughout the Bible. The Fall into sin brought a breach in the fellowship between God and his people. Immediately, God announced the plan of salvation, the gospel, the good news of reconciliation. The outworking of this wonderful plan would take centuries but, beginning with one family, God was calling an elect people to himself and, despite their own failures, he promised, 'I will be with you' (e.g. Gen. 26:3,24; 28:15; 31:3; Josh. 1:5; Jer. 1:8,19; 15:20).

Many years after the commissioning of Joshua, the disobedience predicted in this chapter led to humiliation, defeat and exile. But God spoke again to the demoralized exiles in Babylon:

> Fear not, for I am with you;
>   be not dismayed, for I am your God;
> I will strengthen you, I will help you,
>   I will uphold you with my righteous right hand
>
> (Isa. 41:10).

Supremely, the promise, 'I will be with you,' is fulfilled in Christ, Emmanuel, 'God with us' (Matt. 1:23). And, as he commanded his followers to go out and make disciples of all nations, he once again promised: 'And behold, I am with you always, to the end of the age' (Matt. 28:20).

Whatever your situation, remember God's word to you today: 'I will never leave you.'

Alone with none but you, my God,
I journey on my way:
what need I fear, when you are near,
O King of night and day?
More safe am I within your hand
than if a host did round me stand
                              (Columba, *Irish Church Hymnal*).

Text for the day: *I will never leave you nor forsake you* (Heb. 13:5).

Truth on fire in song

The message of Deuteronomy is now drawn together into a song. Singing conveys God's truth in a way that stirs our emotions and warms our hearts. Truth is set on fire in song. No wonder Paul exhorts believers to sing psalms and hymns and spiritual songs as we exhort each other (Col. 3:16). This song of Moses was to be memorized and repeated, to 'live unforgotten in the mouths of their offspring' (Deut. 31:21). We may wonder to what sort of tune this song would have been set. The greater part of it is very dark, calling, in our terms, for a minor key. Modern choruses select the more 'cheerful' verses (32:3-4) and lift them out of their grim context.

Yet this song can only be understood as a seamless whole. The golden theme is the faithfulness of God. The dark theme is the faithlessness of his people. The two strands are warp and woof: remove the one, and the other makes no sense. The staggering nature of the grace of God only sparkles in full glory when displayed against the background of his graceless people. If his people only sing of his goodness, they will forget the evil of their own hearts, their tendency to backslide, and they will fall away even more quickly. They must sing of God's mercy. They must also sing of their own sin.

Moses called on all creation to listen to this song of the covenant (32:1). He then called on the people to listen to the Word of God (32:2). Just as grass flourishes with regular rainfall, so we need to listen to God's voice each day. It may be tempting to replace study of Scripture with other Christian books. We may sometimes fill our devotional times with prayer. But there is no substitute for exposing ourselves daily to God's own infallible Word.

Moses then called the people to praise. We naturally praise those things or people we admire or love; but God is far above them all, as the one who created all. And the best way to stir ourselves to praise him passionately is to remember all the wonderful things he has done. So Moses reminded the people of God's tender and loving acts (32:10-14), as well as his mighty acts (32:8).

What is the natural reaction of the human heart to the goodness of God? In verse 15 we find out. Jeshurun (literally 'the upright one') is God's 'pet name' for Israel. But when God showers love on him, he takes it for granted, demands more and 'kicks against' God. What a picture of our own hearts! Plenty and prosperity should lead us to wholehearted praise of God the giver. All too often, we demand more. And so we need to sing of our own sin. We remember that without divine aid our inclination is to rebel. We need to remind ourselves that our righteous and upright God must judge sin, and that we are in terrible danger if we wilfully backslide.

The main part of this song is a solemn warning. The Old Testament is the outworking of this song. The people constantly rebelled against God. Their judgement was inevitable. But against this dark backdrop, the glory of the coming of a Saviour shone all the more brightly. Judgement is not the end of the story. God will show mercy for the glory of his own name (32:27). At the last day, God will finally bring about the judgement against evil conveyed in this Song. But he will also have a people for himself, redeemed by the blood of the Lamb. We shall sing the Song of Moses, rejoicing in God's uprightness and confessing our own sinfulness and rebellion. We shall also sing the Song of the Lamb, celebrating the only way in which that justice could be reconciled with our rebellion (Rev. 15:3).

Prayer: Almighty Father, I pray forgiveness for the times when I respond to your grace with complacency and rebellion. Keep my heart today. Help me not to sin against you, but rather to praise you. I worship you for the Lamb, for the price that was paid for me.

Text for the day: *And they sing the song of Moses, the servant of God, and the song of the Lamb* (Rev. 15:3).

'Yes, he loved his people'

In an egalitarian age, we are brought up to think that everyone should be treated the same. God does not. Moses gives a particular blessing to each tribe (just as Jacob on his deathbed blessed his sons one by one). Each is to be allotted a different territory. Each will have different responsibilities and face different challenges. So there is a distinctive blessing for each.

Some of the tribes were promised *prosperity* — notably Joseph (Deut. 33:13-17). Consult a map to see that the tribes of Ephraim and Manasseh (Joseph's sons) occupied by far the greatest part of Israel: the great central swathe of land, including some of the most fertile regions. Asher (33:24), Zebulun and Issachar (33:18-19) and Naphtali (33:23) were also promised much. Who would not want material blessings? But there was the danger that physical prosperity would lead to complacency. Moses had warned in his song that Jeshurun would grow fat and kick (32:15). The northern tribes (including all those mentioned above) were the first to be exiled because of unfaithfulness. The book of Proverbs contains the prayer, 'Give me neither poverty nor riches' (Prov. 30:8), a recognition of the danger of wealth. Only one man has received the gift of prosperity and used it with perfect wisdom. The Son, the true Israel, was rich, but was willing to become poor for us. That is the model for us.

Then there is the blessing of *ministry*. The tribe of Levi was privileged to act as priests, offering sacrifices, interceding for the people and teaching them. Those who minister on behalf of the Lord need to show unflinching faithfulness. They must not be swayed by personal favouritism. The Levites are commended for their part in ending the idolatry of the golden calf. They carried out God's judgement, even on their own relatives (33:9). How we need to pray for our leaders, that they would serve God without fear or favour! Sadly, the Levites did not continue faithful (e.g. Hosea 4:6-7). But Christ, our final and great High Priest, was perfectly faithful.

Then there are blessings of *strength*. Judah's role was to go ahead of the other tribes (Num. 2:9). Thus it was appropriate that the blessing should evoke the Lord's protection and help against enemies (33:7). Gad (33:20) and Dan (33:22) were also promised strength. But would these tribes always use their strength wisely? Would they remember that it is only through the Lord that they would prevail? Sadly not. There is only one mighty Warrior, the one who came to destroy the devil and all his works (Isa. 63:1-5).

Reuben was simply promised protection (33:6). Simeon is not even mentioned; their territory formed an enclave within that of Judah (Josh. 19:1-9). Maybe we feel that we do not possess any dramatic gifts. But the greatest blessing of all is relationship with God. As the psalmist said, 'I would rather be a doorkeeper in the house of my God than dwell in the tents of wickedness' (Ps. 84:10). The most valuable blessings in this chapter are not prosperity or ministry or strength. The intimacy of relationship with the Lord enjoyed by Benjamin (33:12) is what we should desire more than anything else. (The reference to the Lord's 'dwelling between the shoulders' of Benjamin may refer to the fact that the temple was sited on the hill of Jerusalem in their territory.) In Christ, we are promised that intimacy with God. The Lord Jesus is the one on whom the blessing of God rests without any limit. If we are united with Christ we enjoy every single spiritual blessing: 'Blessed be the God and Father of our Lord Jesus Christ, who has blessed us in Christ with every spiritual blessing in the heavenly places' (Eph. 1:3).

In Christ, we can enjoy the glorious security that is pictured in Deuteronomy 33:26-29. The great God rides through the heavens to rescue his people (33:26); the tender God catches his people in his arms (33:27). No wonder the chapter ends with the exclamation of verse 29: 'Happy are you, O Israel!'

Prayer: Give thanks for the Lord Jesus Christ, on whom God's blessing rests without limit. Give thanks that in union with him, we are promised every spiritual blessing.

Text for the day: *The eternal God is your dwelling place, and underneath are the everlasting arms* (Deut. 33:27).

Moses was faithful in all God's house

We feel uncomfortable about speaking ill of the dead. Whatever someone's flaws, they tend to be covered up once the person is in the grave. The Scripture is more realistic. Moses was the greatest prophet and leader Israel had known (Deut. 34:10). He had led Israel for many years, persevering with them despite continual opposition and many frustrations. He knew the Lord face to face. Yet the account of his death reminds us of his sin. He had lost his temper and dishonoured the Lord in the sight of all the people. For that reason, he was not allowed to enter the promised land.

At first sight this seems harsh. The Israelites who did enter the promised land were doubtless worse sinners than Moses. But great privilege leads to great responsibility. Moses, as leader, was expected to uphold the honour of God. His failure is a sombre warning that a long life of serving God should never lead to complacency. Great leaders can sin greatly. The temptations of old age can be as severe as the temptations of youth. Solomon began well and sinned greatly as an older man. So did Hezekiah. We need God to keep us right to the end.

It also seems harsh that Moses was allowed to see the beauty of the promised land, but not to enter. Was this rubbing salt into the wound? No. The viewing of the land was a demonstration to Moses that he had achieved the task the Lord had laid before him. In that culture, the viewing of a property was tantamount to taking possession of it. Moses was laying claim to the vistas before him on behalf of his people.

Moses died a sinner, but this chapter leaves no doubt about his greatness. The writer to the Hebrews notes that his characteristic was faithfulness. His had been a thankless task. The people had been ungrateful and rebellious. At the end of his life, Moses was told that they would turn back to idolatry. He could have despaired. What had the decades of faithful leadership all been for, if the people were going to revert so quickly to idolatry? But he served, not for the sake of 'success', but because he was obedient to God. The Bible commends his faithfulness, not his 'success' measured in crass human terms. And actually, the people's failure was the whole point! The Old Testament story was a visual aid in the failure of Israel and the need for the true 'servant of God' to save his people from their sins. Moses, like Joshua after him, pointed forward to Christ.

Moses died without entering the land. But he gained something far better. He entered that eternal rest of which the earthly land of Canaan was only ever a temporary picture. He is 'for ever with the Lord'. And that is where we also long to be.

> 'For ever with the Lord!'
> Amen, so let it be!
> Life from the dead is in that word,
> 'tis immortality.
> Here in the body pent,
> absent from him I roam,
> yet nightly pitch my moving tent
> a day's march nearer home
>
> (James Montgomery).

Prayer: Lord, thank you for the example of Moses. Help me to know today that I am called to obedience. I pray that you would help me to be faithful to you, whatever the seeming discouragements. I pray that I would be watchful against sin. Protect me from complacency. And help me to be inspired by the knowledge that I too will be 'for ever with the Lord'.

Text for the day: *Moses was faithful in all God's house* (Heb. 3:5).

Acknowledgements

In preparing these devotional readings, I have been greatly helped by listening to the systematic expository ministry of my husband Bill, who has preached through Genesis, Exodus, Leviticus, Numbers and Deuteronomy in recent years.

I am also very grateful to Anne Williamson for her careful editing of the manuscript.

The following extracts are all used by permission of the copyright holders:

Stanzas from the following:
    'Beneath the cross of Jesus' (E. C. Clephane)
    'Alone with none but you, my God' (attributed to Columba)
    'When peace like a river' (H. G. Spafford)
taken from *PRAISE*, © copyright Praise Trust, P. O. Box 359, Darlington, DL3 8YD

Stanza 3, 'Teach us to serve our neighbour's need' from 'O God, whose all-sustaining hand', © copyright Timothy Dudley-Smith

Stanzas 1 and 2 from 'The heroes of Scripture', © copyright John Tindall

Stanza 1 from 'Trouble may break with the dawn', © copyright Malcolm MacGregor

Stanza 2 from 'Jesus, eternal God' (Andrew King), © copyright Haywards Heath Evangelical Free Church

Stanza 2 from 'Our God stands like a fortress rock' (Martin Luther, trans. Stephen Orchard), © copyright Stephen Orchard

'In Eden — sad indeed that day' (William Williams, trans. R. M. Jones), © copyright R. M. Jones